The Political Writings

JOHN DEWEY

The Political Writings

Edited, with Introduction, by
Debra Morris and Ian Shapiro

Hackett Publishing Company, Inc.
Indianapolis/Cambridge

99   2   3   4   5   6   7

Cover design by Listenberger Design & Associates
Text design by Dan Kirklin

For further information, please address
Hackett Publishing Company, Inc.
P.O. Box 44937
Indianapolis, Indiana 46244-0937

Library of Congress Cataloging-in-Publication Data

Dewey, John, 1859–1952
    The political writings/John Dewey; edited, with introduction, by Debra
Morris and Ian Shapiro.
        p.   cm.
        ISBN 0-87220-191-0 (cloth: alk. paper)   ISBN 0-87220-190-2
(paper: alk. paper)
        1. State, The.   2. Political science.   3. Democracy.   I. Morris,
Debra, 1960–   .   II. Shapiro, Ian.   III. Title.
JC251.D467   1993
320 ' .092—dc20   93-8944
                                                                CIP

The paper used in this publication meets the minimum requirements of
American National Standard for Information Sciences—Permanence of
Paper for Printed Library Materials, ANSI Z39.48–1984.

Contents

Note on Sources and Editions

All selections of Dewey's writings are taken from *The Early Works of John Dewey, 1882–1898, The Middle Works of John Dewey, 1899–1924,* and *The Later Works of John Dewey, 1925–1953,* edited by Jo Ann Boydston (Carbondale, Illinois: Southern Illinois University Press).

Waldo Frank's "Our Guilt in Fascism" originally appeared in *The New Republic* (May 6, 1940), pp. 603–8. Reinhold Niebuhr's "The Pathos of Liberalism" was published in *The Nation* (September 11, 1935), Vol. 141, No. 3662, pp. 303–4, and is reprinted with the permission of The Nation Company, Inc., and Randolph Bourne's "Conscience and Intelligence in War" was published in *The Dial* (September 13, 1917), pp. 193–95.

Most selections have been edited for length and pertinence to an anthology on Dewey's political writings. Cuts made in the body of the text have been indicated by ellipses. In several instances, cuts have been made at the beginning of selections. Such cuts are indicated by the absence of initial paragraph indention.

Editors' Introduction

After languishing for decades in relative obscurity, John Dewey's writings about politics and society have come to enjoy considerable attention since the 1970s. Historians, philosophers, and political theorists have turned to these works for political inspiration as well as for political analysis. Major studies of the significance of Dewey's political ideas, for his time and for ours, have appeared in print, and they have become standard fare in courses on democratic theory, modern American history, and contemporary political ideas.[1]

Intellectual revivals of this kind are rooted as much in the circumstances that give rise to them as in the ideas that are rejuvenated. Part of the explanation for the Dewey renaissance is doubtless to be sought in the exhaustion of the liberal and socialist worldviews that have dominated American political argument for much of the twentieth century. The collapse of communism and concomitant triumph of liberal-democratic ideas in the East has accompanied, ironically perhaps, a loss of confidence in many of those same ideas in the West. Intractable urban and ethnic problems, the persistence of poverty amid plenty, and a variety of perceived cultural failures are all frequently laid at the door of dynamics inherent in liberal-democratic capitalism. In such circumstances it cannot be surprising that many in the West detect an ideological void, or that Dewey is one of the principal figures to whom American public intellectuals turn in hopes of filling it.

1. The most important historical studies are James Kloppenberg, *Uncertain Victory: Social Democracy and Progressivism in European and American Thought, 1870–1920* (New York: Oxford University Press, 1986) and Robert Westbrook, *John Dewey and American Democracy* (Ithaca: Cornell University Press, 1991). The philosopher who has paid most attention to Dewey's politics is Richard Rorty, especially in *Consequences of Pragmatism* (Minneapolis: University of Minnesota Press, 1982), pp. 61–71, 160–75 and *Contingency, Irony, and Solidarity* (New York: Cambridge University Press, 1989). The principal political theorists are Timothy Kaufman-Osborn, "John Dewey and the Science of Community," *The Journal of Politics*, 46:1, pp. 1142–65 and "Pragmatism, Policy Science and the State," *American Journal of Political Science*, 29:4, pp. 827–49; and Alfonso Damico, *Individual and Community: The Social and Political Thought of John Dewey* (Gainesville: University of Florida Press, 1978).

IN SEARCH OF "THE REAL JOHN DEWEY"

Although many agree that Dewey's political writings offer the possibility of a revivified third way through the contemporary political landscape, there is little agreement as to what this third way signifies. Louis Menand sees Dewey as a liberal "who believed that the liberalism of his own day was founded on error." Christopher Lasch regards him as a naive believer in progress if not an apologist for corporate capitalism. James Kloppenberg claims him as the intellectual giant behind the American progressive movement, whose political influence reached even across the Atlantic. Richard Rorty co-opts him for the postmodernist cause. Alfonso Damico portrays him as a participatory communitarian, and Robert Westbrook sees him as an under-appreciated radical democrat. Rejecting these and other characterizations, Alan Ryan insists that he was a rather muddled thinker, whose almost frantic desire to avoid all dualisms led him to collapse everything into everything else, and whose democratic theory lacked innovative edge as a result.[2]

Dewey's politics have always elicited divergent reactions, as the present volume illustrates.[3] This should not surprise us. Writers who avoid absolutist commitments, as Dewey did on principle, are often attacked and defended from all sides of the ideological spectrum. That Dewey's ideas do not fit neatly into preconceived categories is a source of their continuing interest as well as controversy. He prized autonomy and individuality but resisted the standard conception of "negative liberty" that is supposed to follow inexorably from them; he took socialist ideas seriously but had no time for Marx; he believed in science and technological advances as engines of human progress, but much of his writing bristles with skepticism toward arguments from authority. Some of this is explained by Dewey's longevity. He received his Ph.D. from Johns Hopkins

---

2. Louis Menand, "The Real John Dewey," *New York Review of Books* (June 25, 1992), pp. 50–55; Christopher Lasch, *The True and Only Heaven* (New York: Norton, 1991) [contrast his earlier judgment in *New Radicalism in America, 1889-1963* (New York: Alfred Knopf, 1966)]; Kloppenberg, *Uncertain Victory*; Damico, *Individuality and Community*; Rorty, *Contingency, Irony and Solidarity*; Westbrook, *John Dewey and American Democracy*; and Alan Ryan, "The Legacy of John Dewey," *Dissent* (Spring 1992), pp. 273–78.

3. Consider, for example, the debate spawned by Reinhold Niebuhr's attack on Dewey's faith in social science as the solution to social problems in *Moral Man and Immoral Society* (New York: Charles Scribner's Sons, 1960), pp. xiii–xxv, 35–38. These issues are taken up in Damico, *Individuality and Community*, pp. 32–121, and Ian Shapiro, *Political Criticism* (Berkeley: University of California Press, 1990), pp. 283–98.

in 1884 and was still producing substantial philosophical works half a century later (*Experience and Nature* was published in 1925, *Art as Experience* in 1934). He was in his late fifties at the time of the Russian revolution, yet he was still an actively engaged intellectual at the time of the Second World War. At his death in 1952 he was ninety-two years old.

Dewey certainly changed his views on many subjects over his long life, but longevity alone does not explain his iconoclastic and unpredictable political allegiances. The antidogmatic character of his experimental method inevitably put Dewey at odds with architectonic political ideologies; party lines by their nature were offensive to him. It cannot, therefore, be surprising that most people would find in Dewey an ally on some issues, but not on others.

Another reason for the revival of interest in Dewey is that he was a public intellectual, one of the last of what seems to be a dying breed. "Better it is," he insisted, "for philosophy to err in active participation in the living struggles and issues of its own age and times than to maintain an immune monastic impeccability."[4] Throughout his life he combined abundant academic theorizing with popular essays, contributing regularly to magazines such as *The New Republic, The Atlantic Monthly, The Dial, The Nation,* and many others, his ideas on the momentous political issues of his day: war, religion, educational and social reform, the League of Nations and the New Deal, and freedom of speech (which he defended vigorously throughout his life). Dewey did more than merely talk about practical problems; he became practically involved. It was not enough for him to theorize about educational reform, for example: in 1896 he opened the Laboratory School, where he tested his ideas on learning as engaged "directed living," spelled out three years later in *The School and Society.* From the vantage point of the late twentieth century, when most of philosophy has become a highly technical specialty-subject with little obvious relevance to the social and political problems of our world, Dewey's sustained philosophical engagement with the social and political issues of his day stands as an attractive beacon. Dewey represents, perhaps, what social philosophy can hope to become.

Two caveats, however, should inform any reading of Dewey's political writings. First, much as he aspired to a frank, "no-nonsense" analysis of narrowly political affairs, his political writings are suffused with philosophical, even metaphysical, concerns. He was more political than almost any writer today—if general renown is taken as the measure—but certainly no less theoretically inclined, or technically astute. As one critic

---

4. John Dewey, *Characters and Events: Popular Essays in Social and Political Philosophy,* ed. Joseph Ratner (New York: Henry Holt, 1929).

has observed, however unpretentious Dewey's public style, and however broadly humane his political impulses, his egalitarianism is as much a function of the rather unlikely combination of Hegel, Darwin, and functional psychology as American political history. Pragmatism itself is a comprehensive attack upon idealism of all kinds. Thus Dewey's varied denunciations of philosophical and psychological "mentalism" mirror his attacks on political "individualism": he regards both as meaningless concepts that lead to misleading antagonisms between mind and world on the one hand, and individual and society on the other.[5] It is necessary therefore, even in a work focused on Dewey's political writings, to give voice to his concerns on different academic terrains, including the psychological, logical, and the epistemological.

The second caveat is this: the reader seeking answers in Dewey's writings will find few, indeed. If she is accustomed to institutional analysis, to pondering how systems of "rights" and "votes" can be engineered to best reconcile Americans' conflicting interests, then much in Dewey's political theory will disappoint, if not bewilder. As one such disappointed reviewer remarks, if "Dewey's obsession with grounding democracy in the culture and the psyche of modern Americans *is* a sort of answer to the question of how to institutionalize democracy, . . . it is an answer that takes an unfamiliar view of institutions."[6] Dewey offers not a program, but rather a political morality—an ethic of self-government and self-realization through collective life.[7] Much of its appeal as political morality derives from the fact that it is offered by someone who eschews every kind of moralizing, who rather exalts modern scientific method for fostering a dispassionate and selfless regard for the truth and a supremely respectful attitude toward one's fellows.

DEMOCRACY: TWO THEMES

To use a phrase that fell on hard times more than once in Dewey's day, his political writings embody "free-thinking" at its best: however much one might be provoked to disagree with them, they are bold and original. Two themes, in particular, are today as provocative as they ever were. The first concerns democracy's scope: although institutions aimed at fair

5. Menand, pp. 50 and 52.

6. Ryan, p. 278.

7. Westbrook's *John Dewey and American Democracy* is particularly good for conveying the diffuse moral character and significance of Dewey's thought. See also Stephen Rockefeller, *John Dewey: Religious Faith and Democratic Humanism* (New York, NY: Columbia University Press, 1991).

representation and distributive justice are an important part of it, democracy encompasses far more than "process." When Dewey claims that democracy is "organized intelligence," it is his understanding of intelligence that is radical; it challenges every settled conception of politics, and distinguishes thereby the ideal of democracy from the more or less fortuitous institutionalization of "political democracy."

In Dewey's mind, political democracy does not differ much from political liberalism: they evolved together, each reflecting the tenets of individualism, equality, and the possibility, in principle, of distinguishing public from private interests and delineating the confines of legitimate state authority. Still, Dewey is often viewed as indifferent to (if not profoundly critical of) some of the major achievements of Western liberalism, in particular its stress upon individual liberty. He blames liberalism for the truncated development of democracy and its unique properties ("fraternity," for instance), and regards "the individual" as abstraction and ideology at variance with the facts of our everyday interdependence. *Liberalism and Social Action*, for example, is deeply critical of liberal philosophy and psychology for being too atomistic, and for denying the corporatist forces and institutions increasingly shaping American material and social life. Yet there can be no doubt that Dewey believes the book to contribute positively to the liberal cause, to a "renascent" liberalism in fact. He argues that liberalism's original and justly enduring values such as autonomy and self-realization are best served now, as the book's title suggests, by organization and "social action": thinking, working, and pursuing our social and political ideals together.[8]

Although published several years before *Liberalism and Social Action*, *The Public and Its Problems* is at least as emphatic regarding "the public": this, for Dewey, is an entity as real and present as "the individual," with acute interests of its own, and possessing resources of intelligence, deliberation, and control for realizing those interests. Nevertheless it is remarkable in a book which asserts a single criterion for judging among particular states—that being "the degree of organization of the public which is attained"—that Dewey proffers mainly traditional liberal means to this end. The solution to "*the* problem of the public," as he defines it, is refinement of the intelligence brought to bear on collective problems. He proposes that there be considerable "freedom of social inquiry and of distribution of its conclusions." This can mean two things; Dewey certainly means both. First, for inquiry to be genuinely social and socially useful, the public has to be consulted. Its desires and needs are the raw material—the basic facts of the matter—with which we have to work.

8. See the excerpt from *Liberalism and Social Action* in Part V of this volume.

Second, if it is to be consulted, the public has to be educated. This depends upon a free press, uninhibited debate, and a flourishing of the humane as well as the natural sciences, for "free social inquiry is indissolubly wedded to the art of full and moving communication" as much as to the facts discovered.[9] The reader may respond that this all sounds remarkably like the liberal individualism defended in John Stuart Mill's *On Liberty*. (Indeed, Mill figures prominently in *Liberalism and Social Action*—along with the bourgeois economists, utilitarians, English "organic idealists," and romanticists—for his positive contributions to liberal-democratic theory.) How does Dewey's solution to "the problem of the public" differ from Mill's?

The answer lies in the much-disputed weight Dewey accords expertise in his conception of democracy as the organization, indeed the very embodiment, of "intelligence." It seems that improving public discussion, debate, and persuasion "depends essentially upon freeing and perfecting the processes of inquiry."[10] Although Dewey would be the last to push a bright-line distinction between public debate and expert inquiry, there is clearly some difference between the two. He evidently places considerable faith in "social engineering," but he conceives of it more as the experimentation necessary to inquiry than as advocating a society based on experts' blueprints. We must have social engineering in order to have social science—not the reverse. Dewey admits, at least at times, that the desirability of social planning is debatable, but he does insist that "if we want something to which the name 'social science' may be given, there is only one way to go about it, namely, by entering [into] . . . social planning and control. . . . [W]e shall begin to attain a measure of at least intellectual order and understanding[,] . . . the surest possible promise of advancement to practical order."[11]

No doubt there is ample reason, here and elsewhere, for Dewey's reputation as a kind of "technocrat"; he is an emphatic champion of controlled and corroborated experimentation for its contributions to material and social progress, even more for its proving the possibility of a new and more humane "morale" among equals.[12] His faith in the capacity of scientific method to improve and inspire our investigations in other arenas often seems limitless: even human values, long considered "subjective" and thereby immune to disinterested inquiry, are fair game.

9. *The Public and Its Problems* (1927), reprinted in *The Later Works, 1925–1953,* Vol. 2 (1925–1927), pp. 256, 339–40, and 345–50.

10. *Ibid.,* p. 365.

11. "Social Science and Social Control" (1931), reprinted in *The Later Works, 1925–1953,* Vol. 6 (1931–1932), pp. 67–68.

12. See the excerpt from *Freedom and Culture* in Part II of this volume.

Because values have their cause as well as consequence in human behavior, they too are "capable of rectification and development by use of the resources provided by knowledge of physical relations." There are no unchanging values, or "ends-in-themselves" whose nature only philosophy can penetrate. On the contrary, science has taught us that "valuations are constant phenomena of human behavior," "pivots" for redirecting our conduct. At the very least, Dewey's understanding of science and scientific progress is exceedingly optimistic: "The generalized ideal and standard of economy-efficiency which operates in every advanced art and technology," he suggests, "is equivalent . . . to the conception of means that are constituents of ends attained and of ends that are usable as means to further ends."[13] This impatience to extend the principle of control to virtually every domain of social life invited charges of anti-intellectualism (indeed, of openness to fascism) in Dewey's own day—and it continues to raise legitimate concerns in our own that Dewey is politically naive, elitist, or both.

The historical Dewey was more ambivalent about technocratic expertise than these critiques suggest. Consider the publication of *Theory of Valuation* and *Freedom and Culture*, both in 1939. In the former, dedicated primarily to problems of method, Dewey is confident, as his praise of "efficiency" and "control," above, would suggest. In the latter he is no less emphatic regarding the potential of science to energize and inform democratic culture, but he is more willing than ever to acknowledge the component of faith in normative political theory. Just because we can no longer count on a teleology of human nature, human virtue, or human good to justify democratic over other arrangements, "[w]e have to see," says Dewey, "that democracy means the belief that humanistic culture *should* prevail; . . . [it] requires a positive and courageous constructive awakening to the significance of faith in human nature. . . ."[14]

Thus, however much Dewey trumpets scientific method, he remains, to the reader eager for answers, strangely speculative. It is easy to believe, upon reading Dewey's more popular writings on such things as technology, education, and political and economic reform, that he thinks political philosophy can be more than merely "sincere": it can tell us what to do, too. But as one of his last public statements proves, he never abandons his earliest conception of philosophy as a vehicle for clarifying a society's dominant interest, for speaking "the authentic idiom of an enduring and dominating corporate experience." In other words, philoso-

13. *Theory of Valuation* (1939), reprinted in *The Later Works, 1925–1953*, Vol. 13 (1938–1939), pp. 241, 242–50, and 235.

14. See *Freedom and Culture*—especially "Democracy and Human Nature"—in Part VII of this volume, pp. 225–26.

phy expresses not "truth," but as its etymology suggests, "wisdom"—"a sense for the better kind of life to be led." "Meaning," Dewey contends, "is wider in scope as well as more precious in value than is truth, and philosophy is occupied with meaning rather than with truth."[15]

It is in "Philosophy and Civilization" that Dewey calls for "speculative audacity" and "more faith in ideas." It would not matter, he says, if American philosophy were "materialistic"—as its critics have long lamented—so long as it were sufficiently "bold." No doubt this understanding of philosophy is responsible for Dewey's occasional flights of rhetoric regarding democracy; at a deeper level it is responsible for a second, more elaborate understanding of democracy, one for which Dewey remains justly famous: the view of democracy as a way of being in the world, a way of experiencing the world *whatever* the domain. If, as the previous section suggests, there is a genuine tension in Dewey between science and democracy—if, that is, he fails to confront, much less solve, the problem of expertise, experimentation, and control in a society dedicated to cultivating "personality" on an immense scale—then perhaps it is because the problem is not, after all, decisive in his mind. Dewey would be the first to insist that we must always strive to improve public debate and persuasion and strengthen the bases of public accountability: the whole point of his educational progressivism is just that, to equip citizens to participate in all manner of experimentation, questioning, and inquiry. Still, his political agenda is bigger than even that, and so too his vision of democracy.

There is reason to suspect that some core notion of "experience" (or, as he sometimes puts it, "intelligent action") is what holds together Dewey's corpus; indeed, "experience" is a ubiquitous term throughout his writing. He tends, says one reviewer, to "dissolve every subject into an amorphous stew," to "blu[r]," says another, "the aesthetic experience, the religious experience, the educational experience, the work experience, and the political experience: they all . . . turn into versions of the same thing, . . ."[16] No doubt "experience" is a profoundly important metaphor in Dewey's estimation, a way of representing the genuine harmony possible to supposed antagonists such as mind and world, knowing and doing, stability and change, individual and society. Yet he believes harmony to be more than metaphorical; there are actual forms of life which redeem at one and the same time a community's rich heritage and its members' distinct lives and personalities.

15. See "Philosophy and Civilization" as well as "Philosophy and Democracy" in Part II of this volume, pp. 32–37 and 38–47.
16. See Ryan, p. 275, and Menand, p. 54.

Science is one such form, says Dewey, artistic endeavor another. Democracy, though tending in its baser forms to emphasize the power of numbers, can also secure this higher moral equality. Democracy testifies, as do science and art, to the "one fact" of human history, the progressive realization of moral unity and the just harmonization of individual and social interests. Science, art, and democratic community are what they are because they require and reward, rather than impede, manifold individual contributions. And the standard for evaluating these contributions is the same in every case, according to Dewey. As he observes regarding art, the distinctions which we actually make are "not comparative, but qualitative. Art is . . . good or bad, sincere or spurious. . . . [E]very honest piece of inquiry is distinctive, individualized. . . ." Admitting, at times, the models of scientific and artistic inquiry to be overintellectualized, Dewey praises democratic community as the simplest but nonetheless most precious embodiment of human experience, association, and intelligent action: "Direct personal relationships," he says, ". . . are [moral equality's] most widespread and available manifestations. . . . No contact of this human sort is replaceable; with reference to it all are equal because all are incommensurable, infinite."[17]

Whether Dewey takes "intelligence" or "experience" as the touchstone for democracy, he accomplishes the same good effect and, not surprisingly, runs the very same risk. Ryan concedes that Dewey expresses more forcefully than almost anyone the relationship between political institutions, narrowly conceived, and the rest of life. He does so, however, in a way that threatens to deny all conflict: between science and faith; between the claims of intelligence, even excellence, and participatory politics; between mastery and piety. The reader is left to decide whether this is effective political theory, or whether its still profound appeal might not be of a "literary kind": "Stylistically," Menand suggests, ". . . Dewey was one of the least novelistic of writers; but he had a novelist's grasp of experience. Whatever else it may have been, his philosophy was a consolation."[18]

CONTENTS

We have attempted to juxtapose theoretical to practical concerns: thus our decision to include short popular essays in which Dewey applies his pragmatic maxims to a specific problem or issue. Part I, "Philosophical

17. See "Individuality, Equality and Superiority" in Part III of this volume, pp. 79–80.
18. Menand, p. 55.

Method," addresses several, intertwined issues: the vices of traditional philosophy, especially its privileging of "knowing" at the expense of "doing"; and the meaning of "truth" in a society dedicated to the democratic resolution of its problems. To illustrate the practical implications of these issues we include Waldo Frank's attack on Dewey's "empiricist" and "naturalist" philosophy for fostering an illiberal contempt for democratic ideals and for morally "disarming" America in the face of fascism. Dewey's response is that naturalistic philosophy is uniquely congenial to democracy and a free society: it is philosophical and political absolutism that robs human values of their significance and effect in the world.

Part II, "Pragmatism and Democracy," explores further the relation between philosophy, understood as a kind of "immanent critique," and the social life criticized. Dewey argues that pragmatic philosophy has important implications for democracy; since pragmatism recognizes the contingent and changing element in life, it accords with the ordinary individual's experience of the world much better than classical philosophy's idealization of unity and timelessness. Pragmatism redeems "active intelligence" against absolute knowledge, making it uniquely suited to a society premised upon progress, rational control, and the more equitable distribution of civilization's fruits. In Dewey's view classical philosophy can only remain the prerogative of a leisure class.

In Part III, "Art, Science, and Moral Progress," Dewey explores the moral and ethical ramifications of "experience," just as in Part II he explored its philosophical and political ones. He suggests that several experiences—art, science, and democratic community—solve the central conundrum of ethics: harmonizing the individual and the whole. Such harmony makes possible a moral equality which, in Dewey's mind, is infinitely more precious than the merely numerical equality to which democracy is reduced by its severest critics and—not coincidentally in his view—its least creative advocates.

"Education for Social Change," Part IV, is devoted to the psychological and ethical principles underlying education. Several of the popular essays reflect Dewey's attempts to distinguish himself from both the "cult of efficiency" and child-centered romanticism, and to reassert a program of education which fuses rather than opposes thinking and doing, innovation and cooperation, and deliberation and intelligent habit. In these writings Dewey makes the case that education is essential to resolving democracy's chief problem: the tension between freedom and responsibility.

Part V, "Pragmatism and the New Deal," presents Dewey's critique of conventional understandings of "liberty." He rejects abstract analyses of liberty as incompatible with any kind of social reform and betterment.

This part closes with three popular essays on economic democracy and the New Deal. These show Dewey struggling, more or less successfully, with the antagonisms which he perceives between capitalism and democracy, reform and restructuring, and expertise and participatory politics. This last was the focus of Reinhold Niebuhr's attack on Dewey, part of which we have included.

Part VI, "'From Absolutism to Experimentalism': The Democratic Public and the War Question," deals with Dewey's understanding of the democratic state, its origins, and its foundations in deliberation and intelligent action. The theoretical material is drawn from *The Public and Its Problems*, the popular arguments from Dewey's essays on the world wars. *The Public and Its Problems* is not only a response to the vehement criticism Dewey suffered for his support of the First World War, it foreshadows his opposition to the second war—leaving the reader to decide which stance is genuinely "pragmatic," and which better exemplifies the possibility for intelligent and concerted action which Dewey never ceased defending (in this case, against authoritarianism).

In part VII, "Reaffirming Democratic Individualism: The Rejection of Communism," Dewey returns to a focus on the individual; this may allay the reader's concerns over, in one critic's words, the "latent *etatisme*" of Dewey's regard for "organized intelligence" and social engineering. In several of these late writings, Dewey evokes his earliest view of philosophy as something which at its best operates to strengthen democratic values. Despite the considerable evolution in many of his commitments over the years, from this he never wavered.

PHILOSOPHICAL METHOD

The Need for a Recovery of Philosophy

Philosophy claims to be one form or mode of knowing. If, then, the conclusion is reached that knowing is a way of employing empirical occurrences with respect to increasing power to direct the consequences which flow from things, the application of the conclusion must be made to philosophy itself. It, too, becomes not a contemplative survey of existence nor an analysis of what is past and done with, but an outlook upon future possibilities with reference to attaining the better and averting the worse. Philosophy must take, with good grace, its own medicine.

It is easier to state the negative results of the changed idea of philosophy than the positive ones. The point that occurs to mind most readily is that philosophy will have to surrender all pretension to be peculiarly concerned with ultimate reality, or with reality as a complete (i.e., completed) whole: with *the* real object. The surrender is not easy of achievement. The philosophic tradition that comes to us from classic Greek thought and that was reinforced by Christian philosophy in the Middle Ages discriminates philosophical knowing from other modes of knowing by means of an alleged peculiarly intimate concern with supreme, ultimate, true reality. To deny this trait to philosophy seems to many to be the suicide of philosophy; to be a systematic adoption of skepticism or agnostic positivism.

The pervasiveness of the tradition is shown in the fact that so vitally a contemporary thinker as Bergson, who finds a philosophic revolution involved in abandonment of the traditional identification of the truly real with the fixed (an identification inherited from Greek thought), does not find it in his heart to abandon the counterpart identification of philosophy with search for the truly Real; and hence finds it necessary to substitute an ultimate and absolute flux for an ultimate and absolute permanence. Thus his great empirical services in calling attention to the fundamental importance of considerations of time for problems of life and mind get compromised with a mystic, non-empirical "Intuition"; and we find him preoccupied with solving, by means of his new idea of ultimate reality, the

[First published in *Creative Intelligence: Essays in the Pragmatic Attitude* (New York: Henry Holt and Co., 1917); reprinted in *The Middle Works*, Vol. 10.]

traditional problems of realities-in-themselves and phenomena, matter and mind, free-will and determinism, God and the world. Is not that another evidence of the influence of the classic idea about philosophy?

Even the new realists are not content to take their realism as a plea for approaching subject-matter directly instead of through the intervention of epistemological apparatus; they find it necessary first to determine the status of *the* real object. Thus they too become entangled in the problem of the possibility of error, dreams, hallucinations, etc., in short, the problem of evil. For I take it that an uncorrupted realism would accept such things as real events, and find in them no other problems than those attending the consideration of any real occurrence—namely, problems of structure, origin, and operation.

It is often said that pragmatism, unless it is content to be a contribution to mere methodology, must develop a theory of Reality. But the chief characteristic trait of the pragmatic notion of reality is precisely that no theory of Reality in general, *überhaupt*, is possible or needed. It occupies the position of an emancipated empiricism or a thoroughgoing naïve realism. It finds that "reality" is a *denotative* term, a word used to designate indifferently everything that happens. Lies, dreams, insanities, deceptions, myths, theories are all of them just the events which they specifically are. Pragmatism is content to take its stand with science; for science finds all such events to be subject-matter of description and inquiry—just like stars and fossils, mosquitoes and malaria, circulation and vision. It also takes its stand with daily life, which finds that such things really have to be reckoned with as they occur interwoven in the texture of events.

The only way in which the term reality can ever become more than a blanket denotative term is through recourse to specific events in all their diversity and thatness. Speaking summarily, I find that the retention by philosophy of the notion of a Reality feudally superior to the events of everyday occurrence is the chief source of the increasing isolation of philosophy from common sense and science. For the latter do not operate in any such region. As with them of old, philosophy in dealing with real difficulties finds itself still hampered by reference to realities more real, more ultimate, than those which directly happen.

I have said that identifying the cause of philosophy with the notion of superior reality is the cause of an *increasing* isolation from science and practical life. The phrase reminds us that there was a time when the enterprise of science and the moral interests of men both moved in a universe invidiously distinguished from that of ordinary occurrence. While all that happens is equally real—since it really happens—happenings are not of equal worth. Their respective consequences, their import, varies tremendously. Counterfeit money, although real (or rather *because* real), is really different from valid circulatory medium, just as disease is really different from health; different in specific structure and so different in consequences. In occidental thought, the Greeks were the first to draw the distinction between the genuine and the spurious in a generalized fashion and to formulate and enforce its tremendous significance for the conduct of life. But since they had at command no technique of experimental analysis and no adequate technique of mathematical analysis, they were compelled to treat the difference of the true and the false, the dependable and the deceptive, as signifying two kinds of existence, the truly real and the apparently real.

Two points can hardly be asserted with too much emphasis. The Greeks were wholly right in the feeling that questions of good and ill, as far as they fall within human control, are bound up with discrimination of the genuine from the spurious, of "being" from what only pretends to be. But because they lacked adequate instrumentalities for coping with this difference in specific situations, they were forced to treat the difference as a wholesale and rigid one. Science was concerned with vision of ultimate and true reality; opinion was concerned with getting along with apparent realities. Each had its appropriate region permanently marked off. Matters of opinion could never become matters of science; their intrinsic nature forbade. When the practice of science went on under such conditions, science and philosophy were one and the same thing. Both had to do with ultimate reality in its rigid and insuperable difference from ordinary occurrences.

We have only to refer to the way in which medieval life wrought the philosophy of an ultimate and supreme reality into the context of practical life to realize that for centuries political and moral interests were bound up with the distinction between the absolutely real and the relatively real. The difference was no matter of a remote technical philosophy, but one which controlled life from the cradle to the grave, from the grave to the endless life after death. By means of a vast institution, which in effect was state as well as church, the claims of ultimate reality were enforced; means of access to it were provided. Acknowledgment of The Reality brought security in this world and salvation in the next. It is not necessary to report the story of the change which has since taken place. It is enough for our purposes to note that none of the modern philosophies of a superior reality, or *the* real object, idealistic or realistic, holds that its insight makes a difference like that between sin and holiness, eternal condemnation and eternal bliss. While in its own context the philosophy of ultimate reality entered into the vital concerns of men, it now tends to be an ingenious dialectic exercised in professorial corners by a few who have retained ancient premises while rejecting their application to the conduct of life.

The increased isolation from science of any philosophy identified with the problem of *the* real is equally marked. For the growth of science has consisted precisely in the invention of an equipment, a technique of appliances and procedures, which, accepting all occurrences as homogeneously real, proceeds to distinguish the authenticated from the spurious, the true from the false, by specific modes of treatment in specific situations. The procedures of the trained engineer, of the competent physician, of the laboratory expert, have turned out to be the only ways of discriminating the counterfeit from the valid. And they have revealed that the difference is not one of antecedent fixity of existence, but one of mode of treatment and of the consequences thereon attendant. After mankind has learned to put its trust in specific procedures in order to make its discriminations between the false and the true, philosophy arrogates to itself the enforcement of the distinction at its own cost.

More than once, this essay has intimated that the counterpart of the idea of invidiously real reality is the spectator notion of knowledge. If the knower, however defined, is set over against the world to be known, knowing consists in possessing a transcript, more or less accurate but otiose, of real things. Whether this transcript is presentative in character (as realists say) or whether it is by means of states of consciousness which represent things (as subjectivists say), is a matter of great importance in its own context. But, in another regard, this difference is negligible in comparison with the point in which both agree. Knowing is viewing from outside. But if it be true that the self or subject of experience is part and parcel of the course of events, it follows that the self *becomes* a knower. It becomes a mind in virtue of a distinctive way of partaking in the course of events. The significant distinction is no longer between the knower *and* the world; it is between different ways of being in and of the movement of things; between a brute physical way and a purposive, intelligent way.

There is no call to repeat in detail the statements which have been advanced. Their net purport is that the directive presence of future possibilities in dealing with existent conditions is what is meant by knowing; that the self becomes a knower or mind when anticipation of future consequences operates as its stimulus. What we are now concerned with is the effect of this conception upon the nature of philosophic knowing.

As far as I can judge, popular response to pragmatic philosophy was moved by two quite different considerations. By some it was thought to provide a new species of sanctions, a new mode of apologetics, for certain religious ideas whose standing had been threatened. By others, it was welcomed because it was taken as a sign that philosophy was about to surrender its otiose and speculative remoteness; that philosophers were beginning to recognize that philosophy is of account only if, like everyday knowing and like science, it affords guidance to action and thereby makes a difference in the event. It was welcomed as a sign that philosophers were willing to have the worth of their philosophizing measured by responsible tests.

I have not seen this point of view emphasized, or hardly recognized, by professional critics. The difference of attitude can probably be easily explained. The epistemological universe of discourse is so highly technical that only those who have been trained in the history of thought think in terms of it. It did not occur, accordingly, to non-technical readers to interpret the doctrine that the meaning and validity of thought are fixed by differences made in consequences and in satisfactoriness to mean consequences in personal feelings. Those who were professionally trained, however, took the statement to mean that consciousness or mind in the mere act of looking at things modifies them. It understood the doctrine of test of validity by consequences to mean that apprehensions and conceptions are true if the modifications effected by them were of an emotionally desirable tone.

Prior discussion should have made it reasonably clear that the source of this misunderstanding lies in the neglect of temporal considerations. The change made in things by the self in knowing is not immediate and, so to say, cross-sectional. It is longitudinal—in the redirection given to changes already going on. Its analogue is found in the changes which take place in the development of, say, iron ore into a watch-spring, not in those of the miracle of transubstantiation. For the static, cross-sectional, non-temporal relation of subject and object, the pragmatic hypothesis substitutes apprehension of a thing in terms of the results in other things which it is tending to effect. For the unique epistemological relation, it substitutes a practical relation of a familiar type:—responsive behavior which changes in time the subject-matter to which it applies. The unique thing about the responsive behavior which constitutes knowing is the specific difference which marks it off from other modes of response, namely, the part played in it by anticipation and prediction. Knowing is the act, stimulated by this foresight, of securing and averting consequences. The success of the achievement measures the standing of the foresight by which response is directed. The popular impression that pragmatic philosophy means that philosophy shall develop ideas relevant to the actual crises of life, ideas influential in dealing with them and tested by the assistance they afford, is correct.

Reference to practical response suggests, however, another misapprehension. Many critics have jumped at the obvious association of the word pragmatic with practical. They have assumed that the intent is to limit all knowledge, philosophic included, to promoting "action," understanding by action either just any bodily movement, or those bodily movements which conduce to the preservation and grosser well-being of the body. James's statement that general conceptions must "cash in" has been taken (especially by European critics) to mean that the end and measure of intelligence lies in the narrow and coarse utilities which it produces. Even an acute American thinker, after first criticizing pragmatism as a kind of idealistic epistemology, goes on to treat it as a doctrine which regards intelligence as a lubricating oil facilitating the workings of the body.

One source of the misunderstanding is suggested by the fact that "cashing in" to James meant that a general idea must always be capable of verification in specific existential cases. The notion of "cashing in" says nothing about the breadth or depth of the specific consequences. As an empirical doctrine, it could not say anything about them in general; the specific cases must speak for themselves. If one conception is verified in terms of eating beefsteak, and another in terms of a favorable credit balance in the bank, that is not because of anything in the theory, but because of the specific nature of the conceptions in question, and because there exist particular events like hunger and trade. If there are also existences in which the most liberal esthetic ideas and the most generous moral conceptions can be verified by specific embodiment, assuredly so much the better. The fact that a strictly empirical philosophy was taken by so many critics to imply an *a priori* dogma about the kind of consequences capable of existence is evidence, I think, of the inability of many philosophers to think in concretely empirical terms. Since the critics were themselves accustomed to get results by manipulating the concepts of "consequences" and of "practice," they assumed that even a would-be empiricist must be doing the same sort of thing. It will, I suppose, remain for a long time incredible to some that a philosopher should really intend to go to specific experiences to determine of what scope and depth practice admits, and what sort of consequences the world permits to come into being. Concepts are so clear; it takes so little time to develop their implications; experiences are so confused, and it requires so much time and energy to lay hold of them. And yet these same critics charge pragmatism with adopting subjective and emotional standards!

As a matter of fact, the pragmatic theory of intelligence means that the function of mind is to project new and more complex ends—to free experience from routine and from caprice. Not the use of thought to accomplish purposes already given either in the mechanism of the body or in that of the existent state of society, but the use of intelligence to liberate and liberalize action, is the pragmatic lesson. Action restricted to given and fixed ends may attain great technical efficiency; but efficiency is the only quality to which it can lay claim. Such action is mechanical (or becomes so), no matter what the scope of the pre-formed end, be it the Will of God or *Kultur.* But the doctrine that intelligence develops within the sphere of action for the sake of possibilities not yet given is the opposite of a doctrine of mechanical efficiency. Intelligence *as* intelligence is inherently forward-looking; only by ignoring its primary function does it become a mere means for an end already given. The latter *is* servile, even when the end is labeled moral, religious, or esthetic. But action directed to ends to which the agent has not previously been attached inevitably carries with it a quickened and enlarged spirit. A pragmatic intelligence is a creative intelligence, not a routine mechanic.

All this may read like a defense of pragmatism by one concerned to make out for it the best case possible. Such is not, however, the intention. The purpose is to indicate the extent to which intelligence frees action from a mechanically instrumental character. Intelligence is, indeed, instrumental *through* action to the determination of the qualities of future experience. But the very fact that the concern of intelligence is with the future, with the as-yet-unrealized (and with the given and the established only as conditions of the realization of possibilities), makes the action in which it takes effect generous and liberal; free of spirit. Just that action which extends and approves intelligence has an intrinsic value of its own in being instrumental:—the intrinsic value of being informed with intelligence in behalf of the enrichment of life. By the same stroke, intelligence becomes truly liberal: knowing is a human undertaking, not an esthetic appreciation carried on by a refined class or a capitalistic possession of a few learned specialists, whether men of science or of philosophy.

More emphasis has been put upon what philosophy is not than upon what it may become. But it is not necessary, it is not even desirable, to set forth philosophy as a scheduled program. There are human difficulties of an urgent, deep-seated kind which may be clarified by trained reflection, and whose solution may be forwarded by the careful development of hypotheses. When it is understood that philosophic thinking is caught up in the actual course of events, having the office of guiding them towards a prosperous issue, problems will abundantly present themselves. Philosophy will not solve these problems; philosophy is vision, imagination, reflection—and these functions, apart from action, modify nothing and hence resolve nothing. But in a complicated and perverse world, action which is not informed with vision, imagination, and reflection, is more likely to increase confusion and conflict than to straighten things out. It is not easy for generous and sustained reflection to become a guiding and illuminating method in action. Until it frees itself from identification with problems which are supposed to depend upon Reality as such, or its distinction from a world of Appearance, or its relation to a Knower as such, the hands of philosophy are tied. Having no chance to link its fortunes with a responsible career by suggesting things to be tried, it cannot identify itself with questions which actually arise in the vicissitudes of life. Philosophy recovers itself when it ceases to be a device for dealing with the problems of philosophers and becomes a method, cultivated by philosophers, for dealing with the problems of men.

Emphasis must vary with the stress and special impact of the troubles which perplex men. Each age knows its own ills, and seeks its own remedies. One does not have to forecast a particular program to note that the central need of any program at the present day is an adequate conception of the nature of intelligence and its place in action. Philosophy cannot disavow responsibility for many misconceptions of the nature of intelligence which now hamper its efficacious operation. It has at least a negative task imposed upon it. It must take away the burdens which it has laid upon the intelligence of the common man in struggling with his difficulties. It must deny and eject that intelligence which is naught but a distant eye, registering in a remote and alien medium the spectacle of nature and life. To enforce the fact that the emergence of imagination and thought is relative to the connexion of the sufferings of men with their doings is of itself to illuminate those sufferings and to instruct those doings. To catch mind in its connexion with the entrance of the novel into the course of the world is to be on the road to see that intelligence is itself the most promising of all novelties, the revelation of the meaning of that transformation of past into future which is the reality of every present. To reveal intelligence as the organ for the guidance of this transformation, the sole director of its quality, is to make a declaration of present untold significance for action. To elaborate these convictions of the connexion of intelligence with what men undergo because of their doings and with the emergence and direction of the creative, the novel, in the world is of itself a program which will keep philosophers busy until something more worth while is forced upon them. For the elaboration has to be made through application to all the disciplines which have an intimate connexion with human conduct:—to logic, ethics, esthetics, economics, and the procedure of the sciences formal and natural.

I also believe that there is a genuine sense in which the enforcement of the pivotal position of intelligence in the world and thereby in control of human fortunes (so far as they are manageable) is the peculiar problem in the problems of life which come home most closely to ourselves— to ourselves living not merely in the early twentieth century but in the United States. It is easy to be foolish about the connexion of thought with national life. But I do not see how any one can question the distinctively national color of English, or French, or German philosophies. And if of late the history of thought has come under the domination of the German dogma of an inner evolution of ideas, it requires but a little inquiry to convince oneself that that dogma itself testifies to a particularly nationalistic need and origin. I believe that philosophy in America will be lost between chewing a historic cud long since reduced to woody fibre, or an apologetics for lost causes (lost to natural science), or a scholastic, schematic formalism, unless it can somehow bring to consciousness America's own needs and its own implicit principle of successful action.

This need and principle, I am convinced, is the necessity of a deliberate control of policies by the method of intelligence, an intelligence which is not the faculty of intellect honored in text-books and neglected elsewhere, but which is the sum-total of impulses, habits, emotions, records, and discoveries which forecast what is desirable and undesirable in future possibilities, and which contrive ingeniously in behalf of imagined good. Our life has no background of sanctified categories upon which we may fall back; we rely upon precedent as authority only to our own undoing—for with us there is such a continuously novel situation that final reliance upon precedent entails some class interest guiding us by the nose whither it will. British empiricism, with its appeal to what has been in the past, is, after all, only a kind of *a priorism.* For it lays down a fixed rule for future intelligence to follow; and only the immersion of philosophy in technical learning prevents our seeing that this is the essence of *a priorism.*

We pride ourselves upon being realistic, desiring a hardheaded cognizance of facts, and devoted to mastering the means of life. We pride ourselves upon a practical idealism, a lively and easily moved faith in possibilities as yet unrealized, in willingness to make sacrifice for their realization. Idealism easily becomes a sanction of waste and carelessness, and realism a sanction of legal formalism in behalf of things as they are—the rights of the possessor. We thus tend to combine a loose and ineffective optimism with assent to the doctrine of take who take can: a deification of power. All peoples at all times have been narrowly realistic in practice and have then employed idealization to cover up in sentiment and theory their brutalities. But never, perhaps, has the tendency been so dangerous and so tempting as with ourselves. Faith in the power of intelligence to imagine a future which is the projection of the desirable in the present, and to invent the instrumentalities of its realization, is our salvation. And it is a faith which must be nurtured and made articulate: surely a sufficiently large task for our philosophy.

The Problem of Truth

To the lay mind it is a perplexing thing that the nature of truth should be a vexed problem. That such is the case seems another illustration of Berkeley's remark about the proneness of philosophers to throw dust in their own eyes and then complain that they cannot see. It is evident enough to the plain man that it takes character to tell the truth habitually; and he has learned, through hard discipline, that it is no easy matter to discover what the truth is in special instances. But such difficulties assume that the nature of truth is perfectly well understood. To be truthful is to make our statements conform to our sincere beliefs, and our beliefs to the facts. Only, so it would seem, some zeal for sophistication can make a topic for philosophic dispute out of such a straightaway situation as this. Whence and why the pother? Before our inquiry ends we may find reason for thinking that some of the difficulties attending the debate are gratuitous. But we must begin by indicating that the conditions which make the nature of truth a problem are found in everyday life, in common sense, so that if to take truth as a problem be a crime, common sense is accessory before the act.

The *prima facie* meaning of truth—of seeing things as they are and reporting them as they are seen—is acceptance of the beliefs that are current, that are authoritative, in a given community or organization. A year or so ago, in reading an article directed against our public and secular schools, I came upon a passage which read substantially as follows: "The child has a right to the Truth, to knowledge of himself, his nature, his origin and his destiny. That Truth the catechism provides." The passage struck me as containing much instruction regarding the popular force of the term truth. There might indeed be serious debate as to whether the residence of the truth is rightly located when it is put in the catechism, but the notion that the truth is the body of beliefs which are of peculiar importance for the guidance of life would go unchallenged. One would not deny that truth might appertain to the enumeration of what one ate for breakfast or the number of flies caught on a piece of flypaper, or the statement of the distance of London from New York, but that sort of thing is not what is popularly meant by truth unless an influencing of the conduct of others is included. It is somewhat forced,

[First published in *Old Penn, Weekly Review of the University of Pennsylvania* 9 (1911); reprinted in *The Middle Works*, Vol. 6.]

from the common-sense point of view, to include such purely descriptive, such as it were, external and irrelevant, matters in a term so dignified as Truth. After all a catalogue is not the truth of things.

At all events, the strong tendency of men to identify truth in the concrete—whatever it may be in the abstract—with beliefs that are so current as to command allegiance and as to place whoever deviates from them under suspicion, may serve as a starting point for our inquiry. One does not require much anthropological lore or much acquaintance with the uncultured portions of present society to perceive that when Truth is, so to say, individualized, when it is spoken of as an integer, dominant political, moral and religious beliefs are indicated. When definitely scientific statements, purely intellectual proportions, come within the scope of the term, it is because, having gained social currency, they are more or less bound up with the collection of authoritative traditions by which the community lives, or because some moral issue is thought to hang upon their acceptance. When a man is not satisfied, in ordinary intercourse, with saying that two and two make four, but finds it necessary to honor this formula with the title of Truth, we have, as a rule, good grounds for believing that the man is speaking neither as a business man nor as a mathematician, but as a preacher, or at least as an educator. And when we hear not that the assassination of Caesar by Brutus was an historic event, but that it is an historic truth, we may safely prepare for the enforcement of a moral, not for the noting of an incident. A popular audience that would be bored by a discussion of truth as a logical or intellectual concept, and that would be chilled and hurt if it realized that such a treatment excluded the ordinary moral associations of the term will—provided of course the proper tone of voice be used—rouse to warmth and to a sense of personal betterment if the Truth is enthusiastically lauded, and it is intimated that this mysterious thing is almost within its own possession. Fantastic popular movements are often instructive as reflexes of matters that are not crude in themselves—that "new-thoughters" and their like play chiefly with the notion of Truth as their fundamental end is as suggestive regarding the popular meaning of the term, as their conjuring with Vibration is indicative of current physical science.

My illustrations may not be very convincing, but, aided by your imaginations, they may remind you that the Truth, as a noun singular, practically always means to the common man a conclusion to which one should pay heed, a general view of things upon which one should regulate one's affairs. Things that are urged upon our attention as the proper objects of attention and as standards of valuation are what we call principles; for all ordinary purposes truths and principles are synonymous terms. And the nature of Principles is evidently an important problem even to the lay mind.

The notion of a comparatively modern moralist that all virtues are a form of regard for truth, or for the logical relationships of things, and that parricide is a violent way of denying the true relation of the case, is no further removed from the attitude of the ordinary man than is the notion that truth is a purely cogitative relation between intelligence and its object. Truth is the sum of beliefs whose acceptance is necessary to salvation, rather than a logical distinction.

If we turn from Truth as a noun singular and absolute to truth as a noun common and distributive, the case is not so different. We forget—I mean philosophers forget—that truth in this aspect is first of all truthfulness, a social virtue, meeting a demand growing out of intercourse, not a logical, much less an epistemological, relation. When mere matters of fact and mere happenings are promoted from the status of fact and event to the category of truth it is because some social consequence is seen to depend on their mode of presentation. The opposite of truth is not error, but lying, the wilful misleading of others.

Since the assigning of blame and liability and the awarding of credit and compensation are among the chief businesses of social intercourse, and since they depend upon the reports of events which men proffer, the ideal of truth, of a certain way of representing facts and occurrences, is bound to arise. Not only is the notion social, rather than logical, in motive, but it is such also in content and criterion more than we are apt to think. Telling the truth, telling a thing the way it is, means designating things in terms that observe the conventions of proper social intercourse. I do not tell the truth to the man about town by addressing him in the formulae of higher mathematics. As it is not the object pictured, but aesthetic custom, which decides whether correct pictorial representation shall or shall not be in terms of perspective,—whether a picture shall be in Chinese or in European symbols—so the genius of the language, reflecting a vast network of social traditions and purposes, enters quite as much as the thing told about in deciding whether what is told is a truthful representation. In spite of the claims of ethical rigorists to the contrary, truth telling has always been a matter of adaptation to a social audience. Not even Plato's identification of Truth as the rational intuition of Pure Being prevented him from recognizing not merely the rightfulness, but the nobility of the lie in communications from superior to inferior. And I imagine that if the enlightened average attitude of to-day has changed, it is not because we have eliminated the socially purposive reference from the meaning of truth, substituting for it a pallid logical or epistemological content, but because we are less sure than was Plato of just who is superior and who inferior.

I do not offer these remarks as a decisive contribution to the problem of what meaning ought to be assigned to the term truth in philosophic analysis, nor even as an account of the entire denotation of the term. On the other hand, I do not regard them as so irrelevant as to require apology. I feel quite sure that these considerations supply the atmosphere which still bathes the concept of truth in philosophy—that it still owes its potency and its supreme interest to its early association with beliefs possessed of social authoritativeness and hence exacting acceptance as principles of conduct. However little the considerations adduced have to do with the real meaning of truth, they have a great deal to do with the fact that we consider it so important to find out what its meaning is. Furthermore, an intelligent discussion of the changed denotation of the term truth, of our present unwillingness to accept "current belief" as an equivalent of truth and of our effort to substitute something more "objective," as we say—less a matter of brute custom—must at least set out from the fact that authoritative belief was once all that truth designated. These two topics shall form, then, the subjects of the remainder of this hour's discussion.

First, then, as to the attitude of plain man as affording the background of the importance of the idea of truth—important far beyond the confines of the logician. Even when we disregard the obvious moral associations with truth, its identification with the virtue of truthfulness, the import of the term remains socially determined. To represent things as they are is to represent them in ways that tend to maintain a common understanding; to misrepresent them is to injure—whether wilfully or no—the conditions of common understanding. An understanding is an agreement; a misunderstanding a disagreement, and understanding is a social necessity because it is a prerequisite of all community of action. It is no accident that the terms communication and community lie so near together; or that intercourse means equally speech and any intimate mode of associated life. Were I to say that representation of things as they are denotes report conforming to current conventions, the phrase would probably give offense. But when I say that it denotes reporting them in accord with the requirements of that mutual understanding which conditions living together I convey the same meaning in a wording that is perhaps less obnoxious. Unless people understand each other, they cannot coadjust their respective acts and offices; all assignment of task, all distribution of labor and cooperation is impossible. To misrepresent is not then to distort or disfigure a thing—which may be funny or may be sacrilegious but which as mere distortion has nothing to do with falsity— but to distort or pervert the conditions of intercourse. To deface a signboard may involve falsification—but that is because it is a signboard or social index. A certain representation of a signature may be falsification, or forgery; but it is not false because of any inaccuracy in likeness—on the contrary, the greater the accuracy the worse the falsification. Only through its function of social direction and instigation, is any report of a thing anything more than just another thing; a discharge or explosion like the report of a cannon. But as things are unless a man reports himself and his acts, from time to time, society cannot keep track of him or utilize him.

To arrive at an understanding is to come to likeness of attitude; or to agreement as to proper diversity of attitude. To create a misunderstanding is to create the probability of action at cross-purposes. And such probability is a quarrel in embryo, for a misunderstanding presumes an understanding, and hence suggests a wilful violation of good faith on the part of somebody. In short, so far as any proposition puts the one to whom it is addressed into the same attitude that his own perception of what is reported ought, according to current prescriptions, to put him, that proposition is true. Similarly error, misrepresentation, is fooling others, or calling out the type of response which current understandings regarding practice frown upon in a given situation. There is a time and a place to see ghosts and there is a time to see the scouts of the enemy; and the great thing is to observe the conveniences about the proper time and place. To think of things rightly or wrongly is to think of them according to or contrary to social demands. Grote's words about "Nomos, King of All," are worth quoting in spite of their familiarity. "The aggregate of beliefs and predispositions to believe, . . . this is an established fact and condition of things, the real origin of which is for the most part unknown, but which each new member of the group is born to and finds subsisting. . . . It becomes a part of each person's nature, a standing habit of mind, or fixed set of mental tendencies, according to which particular experience is interpreted and particular persons appreciated." There is no danger of exaggerating the literal force of these words. There is danger that we restrict their application to the particular concerns that *we* now mark off as moral and political in distinction from those marked off as intellectual. But their meaning is that from the point of view of Nomos the distinction of the intellectual as a separate region, with its own marks and measures, simply has no existence. Either there is *no* rule about observation and judging, and correctness and incorrectness have no application, or else Nomos and Ethos *are* the rule.

How different, then, is any question which may arise regarding the relation of individual mind, or "consciousness," to an object, from the problem—verbally the same—with which the contemporary student is familiar under the name of epistemology! The discipline termed Epistemology assumes, rightly or wrongly, a self-enclosed island of mind on one side, individual and private and only private; over against this is set a world of objects which are physically or cosmically there—and only there. Then it is naturally worried about how the mind can get out of itself to know a world beyond, or how the world out there can creep into "consciousness." But to common sense, the mind of the individual means those attitudes of observance—or acknowledgment—and of reaching conclusions which have an effect, through intercourse, upon common practice and welfare. And objects mean only the materials, the tools and obstacles, which are familiar in this practice.

If the individual's state of mind comes into play at all, it is only on the practical basis. One man's perceptions communicated in reports afford reliable signs; he is a social asset. Another man's perceptions yield reports that are confusing and harmful; he is a social liability. But the difference is the same in kind as between a skilful tracker and a poor one; between one whose eyesight makes him a good pilot and one whose eyesight is so defective that he is to be avoided as a lookout. State of mind, in other words, means a practical attitude or capacity of the individual judged from the standpoint of definite social use and results. So far as a person's way of feeling, observing and imagining and stating things are not connected with social consequences, so far they have no more to do with truth or falsity than his dreams or reveries. A man's private affairs are his private affairs, and that is all that there is to be said of them. Being nobody else's business, it is absurd to regard them as either true or false.

If we shift the question from the relation of individual mind to the world of objects, over to the logical relation which propositions as propositions sustain to each other, the contrast of the presuppositions of the contemporary student of logic with those of the layman is almost equally marked. It is a demand of common sense that statements hang together, that they give a consistent report or narrative. But to hang together denotes no thing of a uniquely intellectual nature; it denotes the reinforcement which statements furnish one another in calling out a certain attitude of practical response. To give an incoherent account of anything is to prompt a number of incompatible and mutually destructive reactions. When a man's statements contradict one another, he contradicts *himself* and thereby destroys his social utility; he is divided against himself and therefore unreliable.

This exposition involves more than acknowledging that representation is primarily—from the common-sense standpoint—a fact of social intercourse, or that truth is important because of social interests. The bearing of social interests does not cease with making truth valued and an object of demand. They affect also the proper subject-matter of correct representation. To say, as I have said (speaking, of course, from this particular point of view), that a given statement is true when it throws its hearer into the same disposition toward behavior that his own observation or opinion of the same matter ought, *according to current prescription*, to throw him, is to proclaim that these prescriptions, not the things themselves, furnish the standard of truthful representation. How, indeed, could it be otherwise? The report, the communication, is not the thing over again; it is an account, a taking stock, of the thing. This story, or elucidation, must necessarily be in terms of something beyond the thing itself; this something beyond is the place the thing occupies in the current scheme of social customs. It is not, so to say, the object alone which decides what is the proper and authorized account of itself; but the object as a term and factor in established social practice. To observe a thing rightly is perforce to observe social prescription; that "observe" is used in both senses may be a poor philosophic pun but is nevertheless a description of a basic fact.

If a plant is tribally tabu, then the truth about that plant is that it is unfit, even a poisonous, article of diet. Supernatural vengeance will overtake the one who slyly partakes of it—not because the gods have chosen to attach evil consequences to a plant which "in itself" is innocent and nutritious, but because this is the sort of consequence that does as matter of fact follow upon eating poisonous food. To say that the plant "in itself" is edible means only that it tempts a hungry young man to eat it. No matter how much a given noise tends to excite fear and flight in a young man, if social custom decrees that that noise ought not to frighten the warrior class to which the youth is destined, the truth about that object is that it is indifferent or contemptible. The scope of these illustrations is, I think, unlimited. Either there is no social way in which it is fitting to conceive and state to others and hence to oneself objects, and then the matter is wholly outside the sphere of truth and falsity; or the objects have a social status and office, which are authoritative for all statements about them. If, in other words, it be objected that our illustrations owe their force to the fact that we have cunningly selected instances where social valuations of conduct are implied—such as the right to eat or the virtue of bravery—the objection, when analyzed, confirms the point made. To common sense there is absolutely no such thing as being a plant or noise, only that and nothing more. The plant, the noise, is a thing of a certain kind, a thing of traits and qualities; and what *we* might and should mark off as traits belonging to the thing as thing, in contrast to traits belonging in virtue of social custom, blend indissolubly into each other. To make this distinction between the plant or noise as physical, or even natural, and the plant or noise in some relation is to take precisely the step that carries us out of and to conduct beyond the common-sense point of view into an abstract and scientific view. To my mind, Mr. Santayana simplified, instead of complicating, philosophic discussion, when he added tertiary qualities to things over and above the conventionally recognized primary and secondary qualities; tertiary qualities being, you will recall, the pleasant or sad or feeble or splendid or wicked traits of things. Well, the introduction of another distinction may also tend to clarification: we may speak of quaternary qualities, meaning the qualities that custom prescribes as properly belonging to objects in virtue of their being factors in a social life that is naught but the maintenance of custom. Now these qualities interfuse the others. Just because observation has been socially trained, fixed by education, and because classifications and appraisals deposited in language have, from the very beginning, woven themselves into every perception and opinion, socially determined qualities are an inextricable part of any object. And whenever the notion of truth or falsity comes into play, the socially prescribed feature stands out as the rightful, the authoritative, definition of the object, in contrast with the tendency of the individual to regard it in an interest which is not merely private, but, according to current convention, illicit—anti-social. From the standpoint of practical common sense, to say that truth involves a distinction of the thing as it is in itself, the "real" thing, from the thing as it appears or is merely conceived to be, is to insist precisely upon the contrast between a social prescription as authoritative and a personal regard as tempting but forbidden.

I will venture to sum up this account in a series of formal statements: First, Representation of a thing denotes, to the plain man, presenting a thing from the standpoint of its meaning, not copying the thing, as a thing. Secondly, Meaning is conceived in terms of social procedure and social consequences. Thirdly, Right or correct meaning is that which social custom prescribes and sanctions. In fulfilling one part of our original undertaking—that of finding out what representing things as they are means to common sense—we have also, if I mistake not, virtually carried out our implied promise to show that the conception of the plain man carries within itself the conditions which make the meaning of truth a general and urgent problem. If representation of things in accordance with their own nature denotes in effect representation according to the requirements of social traditions, then as soon as the validity of these traditions is seriously called into question, we are committed to a search for the nature and standard of truth. And it is obvious to us, with the advantage of a historic perspective, that to find the ultimate authority as to truth in institutions as they exist is to locate truth in a territory bound to become the focus of hostile attack. Who shall guard the guardian? What guarantees the guarantee? What so sanctifies custom that custom may shed sanctity upon special ways of regarding and reporting things? From the standpoint of custom itself, of tradition, the question is easy to answer. Custom is divine, supernatural in origin and ultimate intent. But the moment custom is suspected and criticized, this answer fails to be satisfactory just because it so flagrantly expresses just the customs that are doubted.

The situation regarding truth and its standard is aggravated, moreover, because, as soon as men permit themselves to look at custom with a questioning eye, custom undergoes such a tremendous shift of value. When it ceases to be the authoritative guardian of truth, it becomes the reservoir and responsible author of error. For the essence of a critical attitude towards custom is the perception that custom not only includes absurd and evil methods of overt action, but that it involves corruption of men's modes of viewing and valuing things; any way you take it, once you venture to criticize it at all, it is irrational in itself, and tends to pervert rationality in all specific cases of belief.

In effect then, to query the worth of custom as a standard of action and judgment is to seek beyond custom for a measure of custom. But where and how shall the required measure be found? How in the world shall accepted beliefs be corrected, once we regard them as incorrect? Where is the point of truth? What is there to which to appeal? We cannot recur to objects just as they present themselves, for these objects are thoroughly infected with the influence of just those customs which have become suspected. They, so to speak, only exhibit in detail, or specify, what the questioned beliefs convey in collective fashion. If we retain our notion of truth as conformity of belief to objects as they really are, the essential point, hereafter, is to discover that type of object of which it may be said that it "really" is. The situation in which custom is seriously questioned as a final authority of behavior thus admits of alternative treatments. Perception of the conflict, the incompatibility, of customs and conviction that their opposition is hopeless beyond remedy, may induce wholesale scepticism. Truth is not, or if it is, it is unattainable. And this scepticism may take the form of an easy poise, of suspense, as to all beliefs, a condescending superiority and tolerance; or of an arbitrary seizure upon some one tradition which is to be asserted as truth—that form of scepticism which goes currently by the name of "faith." Or, seeing that the difficulty resides in the faculty of statement, in the function of viewing and regarding objects, men may decide to avoid error by abrogating this function and relapsing into sheer acceptance of things as they come. Or men seek for an object which, transcending the sources of error that attend the objects implicated in customary belief, is finally and indubitably "Real" so that it may stand as adequate measure of the truth of all other perceptions and beliefs. Such a "Real Object" and such a truth must transcend experience. . . .

In short, from the standpoint of scientific inquiry, truth indicates not just accepted beliefs, but beliefs accepted in virtue of a certain method. Without trenching, at this point, upon recent controversy as to the relation of truth and verification, one may fairly say that, to science, truth *denotes* verified beliefs, propositions that have emerged from a certain procedure of inquiry and testing. By that I mean that if a scientific man were asked to point to samples of what he meant by truth, he would pick out neither dogmas, no matter how strong their hold, nor transcendental beings no matter how esthetically sublime, but beliefs which were the outcome of the best technique of inquiry available in some particular field; and he would do this no matter what his abstract conception of the Nature of Truth. The effect of this new method of designating truth upon the social, or common-sense, conception of truth is worth noting. To the person equipped with the tools of experimental inquiry, truth designates not the object asserted or content believed in just as object or content, but that object asserted or believed on account of the prior employ of a certain method. To the layman in that field, not acquainted with the dependence of that proposition upon a technique of science, the belief itself is the truth. Common sense, by education and like methods, takes up into itself the results of scientific inquiry quite apart from what gives them their authority to the scientific man. Moreover, by all kinds of applications and inventions, the results of these methods become an integral part of current social practice; the bridge, the railway, the light, the loom, embody scientific verifications into the very substance of common sense itself. By assimilating in such ways the fruits of inquiry into its own beliefs and standards, common sense has no great difficulty in maintaining unchanged its own complacently dogmatic view of truth as a fixed body of authoritative doctrines. And it should not be forgotten that pretty much everyone is a layman in every field but his own specialty. The philosopher who is quite aware that *his* truths denote only the best results that he has been able to get by the best methods at his command, accepts the results of the physicist on faith, and treats them as truths because of their own inherent content. The experimental physicist, aware of the provisional, because experimental, nature of *his* truths, gladly hands over truth absolute and unalloyed to the keeping of the pure mathematician, who perhaps completes the circle by accepting the trust, because he in turn takes on authority the results of some transcendental philosopher. . . .

Our Guilt in Fascism

Waldo Frank

"For they sow the wind, and they shall reap the whirlwind."—*Hosea.*

I

Here is my thesis: This war, from which we dream to immunize ourselves, is but a symptom of a revolution: a revolution whose deep roots in the past, and whose flowerings for life or for death in the future, we share; as we share the cultures and the civilization of Europe. This revolution takes the form of war because of the ignorance of its true causes in the peoples, in their leaders, in their prominent opposers. And the trend both of the symptomatic war and of the deeper revolution becomes regressive, *Fascist,* because this universal ignorance chokes the vitalities of men, denies them creative channels forward from the crisis, forces them into violence, impotence, despair, and into desperate remedies compounded of their darkness. Of this modern ignorance—what Reinhold Niebuhr calls our "ignorance of ignorance"—the intellectuals are the most guilty. And there is no ground for the tenacious American idea that we are exempt, either from the objective conditions of revolution and war or from the subjective causes which, unless known, will turn them, here too, inevitably fascist. There is no ground for our complacence; but ground indeed, if only we can overcome it! for hope; because of the time and the still virgin energies which make us today the most favored, the most challenged, the most responsible of the nations. . . .

Superficially, this revolution of ours will mean the liquidation of the modern state, of modern society, after their three brief centuries of splendor. More deeply, it will mean the liquidation of the basic human value, of the ruling sense of man's meaning to himself as an individual within the mystery of life, which has subsumed and shaped the modern era. To "blame" this on the machine is shallow. The machine itself came of a shift in man's self-meaning which *had* to be temporary; since it was absolutely false although—for a time—pragmatically useful. The true victors of the old Thirty Years' War were no generals, no armies; but Copernicus, Bacon, above all Descartes. The struggle was against the political-social forms of the dry-rotted scholasticism of medieval Europe which could no longer hold or feed the vitalities of men; although the

[First published in *The New Republic* (6 May 1940).]

truth must not be overlooked that this same scholasticism in an earlier age fed them and gave them the power to supersede their forms. For a while, now they swirled upon themselves, and Europe retched in a reaction not unlike today's. Perhaps the men who best symbolized Europe's renewal by giving the forces of men once more an at least transitional proto-channel in the direction of growth were Luther and Calvin: perhaps *these* are the true fathers of the machine age. The economics, politics, technics, of the modern era could not have found the energies and the forms to be realized at all—which means, *to be*—without the psychological factors of the new religion.

The point to be made here is that the western world has a religion *now* which is playing an analogous role with that once played by the decadent scholastics. It calls itself by the best names (as did the degenerate churchmen): calls itself "the modern mind," "progressive," "scientific," "instrumentalist"—calls itself anything but a religion. It, too, is dark and decadent; but, unlike its analogue in the earlier cycle, it was rotten ere it was half ripe (the eighteenth century). And it stands today against the vitalities of man seeking life within the forms of living which three centuries have builded—stands as desperately against these vitalities as did the half-dead scholasticism of the fifteenth and sixteenth centuries against Renaissance, Reformation and the birth of science.

II

And now we can approach our modern "religion" which had its clearest form in the eighteenth century. It took over most of the ethical values and energies of the medieval synthesis, dispensing with the organic vision of man embodied in the Great Tradition, from which these values and energies had issued. This it discarded, because it could not successfully dissociate the sense of God in man from the three *premises* of the medieval Republic against which it justifiably reacted: the premise of the Christian revelation in literal form which a Copernican (succeeding a Ptolemaic) view of the cosmos appeared to destroy; the premise of social status which the rising city classes and a vastly expanding world and the new horizontal dynamics of the individual will had rendered hateful; the premise of justice and salvation focused *beyond* the grave, which the enriched mind and technics of the West had turned into a reactionary interpretation of Christian ethics. The medieval method of rationalism, the new religion took over, discarding, however, the intuitive, organic myth by which reason issued from and could touch universal truth: the myth of divine revelation.

Nevertheless, the modern rationalism was also based on revelation.

The Judeo-Platonic Christian myth which premised the medieval rationales of theology and politics and art, stored within it the profoundest
intuitive treasures of man's self-knowledge: the vision of the prophets, the
seers, the poets; the creative acts whereby for thirty centuries in a hundred climes the men and women of the West had kept alive our Great
Tradition. All this, the modern rationalism consciously discarded, substituting for it as its "revelation" *the facts* discoverable by inductive logic
in the world of natural science and the *method* of the logic itself which it
unconsciously turned into an idol, to take the place of God as the Truth-
giver.

This empirical rationalism is our modern religion. It is far more unan-
imously followed in all cogent centers of modern life: political, intellectual, industrial, social, esthetic, than was the scholastic religion from
which, by the sixteenth century, mystics, moralists, logicians, artists, even
theologians, all over Europe, were departing. This religion of ours is
nameless to itself; it shrinks from the word as from such words as
tragedy, sin, God, which would treacherously lead it back into the organic
realm of the mystery of human freedom. It is an implicit religion; and as
such has been able to insinuate itself even into the churches, where it
countervails against the rhetoric of pastors, priests and rabbis, from whose
rituals of the Great Tradition the oxygen of life has long since vanished.

Empirical rationalism appears to be a theory of reality based exclusively on reports of the senses. What do they report? Things and states,
from which the rational process induces other things and states, categories, laws, adding nothing. The approximate sum of them all is supposed
to be reality; and man is scornfully advised not to transcend its limit—
what, twenty years ago, I called "the comfort of the limit," lest he fall in
the abyss of "fantasy . . . indulgence in this fantasy marks a manner of
yearning and not a principle of construction" (John Dewey). Now, what
these things and states of things and categories and laws of things are, is
WORDS. There is no separate entity, table: that is why there must be a
word, table. Words are pointers. I am within a continuum of both substance and experience with the table and need to get into a specific
relationship with the table. But to know truth even about the table, I must
subsume that things and states are joined indissolubly in reality. Then,
my words pointing to things and states make the reality functionable for
me within it. Thus, words have ever been used in cultures; although the
organic continuity of things they pointed to was expressed perhaps in
clumsy myths, as of pantheism or of personal godmakers. Now, empirical
rationalism came along to tell us that the words only, the categories and
sums of words only, are the real. . . .

Every great religion, every great culture, specifically those of the Christian medieval Republic, were premised on myths that embodied the organic intuition of the race and of the whole man of the race. And from this intuition, articulated by poet, artist, seer, the vitalities of life could flow into the rationales or rationalisms of the culture; conversely, the acts of the culture could constantly be related with the vitality—the reality— of the intuition. That was how conceptions like Democracy, Brotherhood of Man, Justice, etc., were born and grew; and how reason became cogent. Now, the modern religion and the society based on it cuts away the life-giving source. Having filched rationalism from a myth which was, at the very lowest estimate, an esthetic form of deep and organic knowledge, it presumes to base its reason on contingent "things," actually on symbols and pointers of illusory and ephemeral events within the flux of its own process!

That is why we are choking to death under a superstructure which arrogantly precludes from our conscious life the experience of the organic real: the superstructure so imperiously dominant in our schools and graduate schools, our newspapers, radios, critical journals, our popular and highbrow arts, our laboratories, our legislatures, that it is *atmospheric*—invisible as air. *A religion that leaves life out.*

What, in this asphyxiation, happens to our modern values: to Democracy, Freedom, Justice, Reason? Without their pre-rational, organic premise, they become unreal idols . . . abstractions from the Whole that alone could give them breath. What happens to the individual ego? Exiled from its cosmic dimension, it becomes a cancer in the blind social body; adds up into the destructive ego-nation, the passive herd or the regimented egomaniac horde. What happens to our huge deposits, heaped by science, of factual knowledge about the natural world, about the human being? Without the intuitive conduit to the organic real, the dynamic indwelling of man's spirit with the universe, whereby alone man touches the realm of freedom that dwells within necessity, the science-heaps add up into ignorance, into arrogance and complacence—finally into that supreme symbol of our disease; the armaments which are fast becoming the total modern nations.

III

Fascism gained steady ground in Europe, because it had no effective foes in Europe. Britain has political genius: why was it not applied to the grimly visible problem of preventing the war? Britain and France were real political democracies; why did their toiling majorities, with the power in their hands, drop their hands to lose it? Why did they flinch when the hour struck to consolidate a century's gains? Somehow, vitality and strong good will were not within the progressive movements. Where were they? The truth is that these organized opposers to the imperialists and exploiters have the same fundamental values as their foes. Maybe Mr. Chamberlain (like Mr. Roosevelt) prays every night. No matter: he doesn't believe a thing except *things*—except the heaping up of *things*. His notion of the proper heap differs from Clem Atlee's, from Léon Blum's, from Josef Stalin's, from Leon Trotsky's, from John Dewey's notions. But they've all got the same essential values of empirical rationalism, which leave man out . . . the same religion (with variations) which leaves life out.

But life won't stay out. Its vital conduits are the emotions. In a culture with a creative religion, the emotions rise from the depths of men, their body and their spirit, into social, esthetic, intellectual and institutional forms; the emotions *inform* the home, the cities, the landside, the arts, the sciences, the crafts, the schools, the amusements of the people. The modern religion, tacitly and implicitly clamped upon the world, freezes the cultural superstructure, so that the emotions of men and women, conductors of their creative energies, of their loves and dreams communal and personal, cannot flow up and make the superstructure living. Not into our government, not into our labor and intellectual oppositions, not into our arts and entertainments, not into our trades, crafts, schools and homes. Not even into the sterilized and vitiated churches. Life, denied these normative expressions, swirls in subterranean anger; seeks pretexts of rebellion, becomes insanely and demonically destructive: creates *antimen* like Hitler, and by the millions, the tens of millions, creates in the democracies his passive, self-censored lovers. . . .

Under all, empirical rationalism blots out the possibility of human freedom. The intellect, in its own measures, can conceive only the necessity of strict determinism, after the image of its processes. The intellect requires, and rationalism requires, the *pre-rational* premise of the intuition to recognize the mystic truth that men—only within experienced necessity—can be free. Without the pre-rational premise, reason falls into unreason. Wherefore, the Fascist fury against freedom, its glorification of the dark, absolute necessity of the herd, is our modern religion's most sardonic fulfilment. And the irony of the Fascist hate of the artists—the priests of freedom—is that so few of us deserve it. . . .

Anti-Naturalism in Extremis

In a book G. K. Chesterton wrote after a visit to this country, he spoke as follows of the prospects of democracy in this country. "As far as that democracy becomes or remains Catholic and Christian, that democracy will remain democratic. . . . Men will more and more realise that there is no meaning in democracy if there is no meaning in anything; and that there is no meaning in anything if the universe has not a centre of significance and an authority that is the basis of our rights."

I should not have supposed that advance was to have been expected in greater realization of the truism that if there is no meaning in anything, there is no meaning in democracy. The nub of the passage clearly resides in assertion that the rights and freedom which constitute democracy have no validity or significance save as they are referable to some centre and authority entirely outside nature and outside men's connections with one another in society. This intrinsically sceptical, even cynical and pessimistic, view of human nature is at the bottom of all the asseverations that naturalism is destructive of the values associated with democracy, including belief in the dignity of man and the worth of human life. This disparaging view (to put it mildly) is the basis upon which rests the whole enterprise of condemning naturalism, no matter in what fine philosophical language the condemnation is set forth. The fact of the case is that naturalism finds the values in question, the worth and dignity of men and women, founded in human nature itself, in the connections, actual and potential, of human beings with one another in their natural social relationships. Not only that, but it is ready at any time to maintain the thesis that a foundation within man and nature is a much sounder one than is one alleged to exist outside the constitution of man and nature.

I do not suppose it is a matter of just expediency or policy in winning adherents that keeps in the dim background the historic origin of the view that human nature is inherently too depraved to be trusted. But it is well to recall that its source is the Pauline (and Augustinian) interpretation of an ancient Hebrew legend about Adam and Eve in the Paradise of Eden. Adherents of the Christian faith who have been influenced by geology, history, anthropology, and literary criticism prefer, quite understandably, to relegate the story to the field of symbolism. But the view that

[First published in *Partisan Review* 10 (January–February 1943); reprinted in *The Later Works*, Vol. 15.]

all nature was somehow thoroughly corrupted and that mankind is collectively and individually in a fallen estate, is the only ground upon which there can be urged the necessity of redemption by extra-natural means. And the diluted philosophic version of historic supernaturalism which goes by the name of rationalistic metaphysical spiritualism or idealism has no basis upon which to erect its "higher" non-natural organs and faculties, and the supernatural truths they are said to reveal, without a corresponding thoroughly pessimistic view of human nature.

I now come to the question of the moral and social consequences that flow from the base and degrading view of nature in general and of human nature in particular that inheres in every variety of anti-naturalistic philosophy. I begin with the fact that the whole tendency of this view has been to put a heavy discount upon resources that are potentially available for betterment of human life. In the case of any candid clear-eyed person, it is enough to ask one simple question: What is the inevitable effect of holding that anything remotely approaching a basic and serious amelioration of the human estate must be based upon means and methods that lie outside the natural and social world, while human capacities are so low that reliance upon them only makes things worse? Science cannot help; industry and commerce cannot help; political and jural arrangements cannot help; ordinary human affections, sympathies and friendships cannot help. Place these natural resources under the terrible handicap put upon them by every mode of anti-naturalism, and what is the outcome? Not that these things have not accomplished anything in fact, but that their operation has always been weakened and hampered in just the degree in which supernaturalism has prevailed.

Take the case of science as a case of "natural" knowledge obtained by "natural" means and methods; together with the fact that after all, from the extra-naturalistic point of view, science is *mere* natural knowledge which must be put in stark opposition to a higher realm of truths accessible to extra-natural organs. Does any one believe that where this climate of opinion prevails, scientific method and the conclusions reached by its use can do what they are capable of? Denial of reasonable freedom and attendant responsibility to any group produces conditions which can then be cited as reasons why such group cannot be entrusted with freedom or given responsibility. Similarly, the low estimate put upon science, the idea that because it is occupied with the natural world, it is incapacitated from exercising influence upon values to which the adjectives "ideal" and "higher," (or any adjectives of eulogistic connotation) can be applied, restricts its influence. *The fruit of anti-naturalism is then made the ground of attack upon naturalism.*

If I stated that this low opinion of science in its natural state tended to lower the intellectual standards of anti-naturalists, to dull their sense of the importance of evidence, to blunt their sensitivity to the need of accuracy of statement, to encourage emotional rhetoric at the expense of analysis and discrimination, I might seem to be following too closely the model set by the aspersions (such as have been quoted) of anti-naturalists. It may be said, however, that while some writers of the anti-naturalistic school say a good deal, following Aristotle, about the "intellectual virtues," I fail to find any evidence that they have a perception of the way in which the rise of scientific methods has enlarged the range and sharpened the edge of these virtues. How could they, when it is a necessary part of their scheme to depreciate scientific method, in behalf of higher methods and organs of attaining extra-natural truths said to be of infinitely greater import?

Aside from displaying systematic disrespect for scientific method, supernaturalists deny the findings of science when the latter conflict with a dogma of their creed. The story of the conflict of theology and science is the result. It is played down at the present time. But, as already indicated, it throws a flood of light on the charge, brought in the manifesto previously quoted, that it is the naturalists who are endangering free scholarship. Philosophic anti-naturalists are ambiguous in their treatment of certain scientific issues. For example, competent scientific workers in the biological field are agreed in acceptance of some form of genetic development of all species of plants and animals, mankind included. This conclusion puts man definitely and squarely within the natural world. What, it may be asked, is the attitude of non-theological anti-naturalists toward this conclusion? Do those, for example, who sign a statement saying that naturalists regard man as "simply a highly developed animal" mean to deny the scientific biological conclusion? Do they wish to hold that philosophical naturalism and not scientific inquiry originated and upholds the doctrine of development? Or, do they wish to take advantage of the word "animal" to present naturalistic philosophers in a bad light?

Since the latter accept without discount and qualification facts that are authenticated by careful and thorough inquiry, they recognize in their full force observed facts that disclose the differences existing between man and other animals, as well as the strands of continuity that are discovered in scientific investigation. The idea that there is anything in naturalism that prevents acknowledgment of differential traits in their full significance, or that compels their "reduction" to traits characteristic of worms, clams, cats, or monkeys has no foundation. Lack of foundation is probably the reason why anti-naturalist critics find it advisable to represent naturalism as simply a variety of materialism. For the view at-

tributed to naturalism is simply another instance of a too common procedure in philosophical controversy: Namely, representation of the position of an opponent in the terms it would have *if* the critic held it; that is,
the meaning it has not in its own terms but after translation into the
terms of an opposed theory. Upon the whole, the non-supernatural anti-
naturalists are in such a dilemma that we should extend sympathetic pity
to them. If they presented the naturalistic position in its own terms, they
would have to take serious account of scientific method and its conclusions.

But if they should do that, they would inevitably be imbued with some
of the ideas of the very philosophy they are attacking. Under these
circumstances, the ambivalence of their own attitude is readily understood.

Lack of respect for scientific method, which after all is but systematic,
extensive and carefully controlled use of alert and unprejudiced observation and experimentation in collecting, arranging and testing facts to
serve as evidence, is attended by a tendency toward finalism and dogmatism. Non-theological anti-naturalists would probably deny that their
views are marked by that quality of fanaticism which has marked the
supernatural brand. And they have not displayed it in anything like the
same intensity. But from the standpoint of logic, it must be said that their
failure to do so is more creditable to their hearts than to their heads. For
it is an essential part of their doctrine that above the inquiring, patient,
ever-learning and tentative method of science there exists some organ or
faculty which reveals ultimate and immutable truths, and that apart from
the truths thus obtained there is no sure foundation for morals and for a
humane order of society. As one critic of naturalism remarked (somewhat
naively indeed), without these absolute and final truths, there would be in
morals only the kind of certainty that exists in physics and chemistry.

Non-theological anti-naturalists write and speak as if there were complete agreement on the part of all absolutists as to standards, rules, and
ideals with respect to the specific content of ultimate truths. Supernaturalists know better. They are aware of the conflict that exists; they
are aware that conflict between truths claiming ultimate and complete
authority is the most fundamental kind of discord that can exist. Hence,
their claim to supernatural guidance; and hence fanaticism in carrying
on a campaign to wipe out heresies which are dangerous in the degree
they claim to rest on possession of ultimate truths. The non-supernatural
variety in the more human attitude it usually takes is living upon a capital
which is inherited from the modern liberal developments professedly
repudiated. Were its adherents to yield to the demands of logic, they
would see how much more secure is the position of those who hold that

given a body of ultimate and immutable truths, without which there is only moral and social confusion and conflict, a special institution is demanded which will make known and enforce these truths.

During periods in which social customs were static, and isolation of groups from one another was the rule, it was comparatively easy for men to live in complacent assurance as to the finality of their own practices and beliefs. That time has gone. The problem of attaining mutual understanding and a reasonable degree of amicable cooperation among different peoples, races, classes, is bound up with the problem of reaching by peaceful and democratic means some workable adjustment of the values, standards, and ends which are now in a state of conflict. Dependence upon the absolutist and totalitarian element involved in every form of anti-naturalism adds to the difficulty of this already extremely difficult undertaking.

To represent naturalistic morals as if they involved denial of the existence and the legitimacy of any sort of regulative end and standard is but another case of translation of a position into the terms of the position of its opponents. The idea that unless standards and rules are eternal and immutable they are not rules and criteria at all is childish. If there is anything confirmed by observation it is that human beings naturally cherish certain things and relationships, they naturally institute values. Having desires and having to guide themselves by aims and purposes, no other course is possible. It is also an abundantly confirmed fact of observation that standards and ends grew up and obtained their effectiveness over human behavior in all sorts of relatively accidental ways. Many of them reflect conditions of geographical isolation, social segregation, and absence of scientific methods. These conditions no longer obtaining, it requires a good deal of pessimism to assume that vastly improved knowledge of nature, human nature included, cannot be employed or will not be employed to render human relationships more humane, just and liberal. The notion that such knowledge and such application, the things for which naturalism stands, will increase misunderstanding and conflict is an extraordinary "reversed charge" of results produced by dogmatic absolutism in appeal to extra-natural authority.

Reference to the pessimism which is involved reminds one of the chorus of voices now proclaiming that naturalism is committed to a dangerously romantic, optimistic, utopian view of human nature. This claim might be looked at as a welcome variation of the charge that naturalism looks upon everything human as "merely" animal. But it happens also to be aside from the mark. It is probably "natural" for those who engage in sweeping rationalistic generalizations to match their own pessimism by attributing an equally unrestrained optimism to their opponents. But since naturalists are committed to basing conclusions upon evidence, they give equal weight to observed facts that point in the direction of both non-social behavior and that of amity and cooperation. In neither case, however, are facts now existing taken to be final and fixed. They are treated as indications of things to be done.

Naturalism is certainly hopeful enough to reject the view expressed by Cardinal Newman when he said "She (the Church) regards this world and all that is in it, as dust and ashes, compared with the value of a single soul. . . . She considers the action of this world and the action of the soul simply incommensurate." Naturalism rejects this view because the "soul and its action" as supernatural are put in opposition to a natural world and its action, the latter being regarded as thoroughly corrupt. But naturalism does not fly to the opposite extreme. It holds to the possibility of discovering by natural means the conditions in human nature and in the environment which work in detail toward the production of concrete forms of both social health and social disease—as the possibility of knowledge and corresponding control in action by adequate knowledge is in process of actual demonstration in the case of medicine. The chief difficulty in the road is that in social and moral matters we are twenty-five hundred years behind the discovery of Hippocrates as to the natural quality of the cause of disease and health. We are also behind his dictum that all events are equally sacred and equally natural.

I mention one further instance of the contrast between the relative bearings of anti-naturalism and naturalism in connection with social problems. Because of the influence of a low view of human nature and of matter a sharp line has been drawn and become generally current between what is called *economic* and what is called *moral:*—and this in spite of facts which demonstrate that at present industry and commerce have more influence upon the actual relation of human groups to one another than any other single factor. The "economic" was marked off as a separate compartment because on the one hand it was supposed to spring from and to satisfy appetites and desires that are bodily and carnal, and on the other hand economic activities have to do with mere "matter."

Whether or not Karl Marx originated the idea that economic factors are the only ultimate causative factors in production of social changes, he did not originate the notion that such factors are "materialistic." He accepted that notion from the current and classic Greek-medieval-Christian tradition. I know of no way to judge how much of the remediable harshness and brutal inhumanity of existing social relationships is connected with denial of intrinsic moral significance to the activities by means of which men live. I do not mean that anti-naturalism is the original source of the evils that exist. But I do mean that the belief that whatever is natural is sub-normal and in tendency is anti-moral, has a great deal to do with perpetuating this state of affairs after we have natural means at command for rendering the situation more humane. Moreover, on the political side we fail to note that so-called laissez-faire individualism, with its extreme separatism and isolation of human beings from one another, is in fact a secularized version of the doctrine of a supernatural soul which has intrinsic connection only with God.

Fear and hate for that which is feared accompany situations of great stress and strain. The philosophic attempt to hold the rise of naturalism accountable for the evils of the present situation, as the ideological incarnation of the enemy democratic peoples are fighting, is greatly accentuated by the emotional perturbations that attend the present crisis. Intense emotion is an all-or-none event. It sees things in terms of only blackest black and purest shining white. Hence, persons of scholastic cultivation can write as if brutality, cruelty, and savage intolerance were unknown until the rise of naturalism. A *diabolus ex machina* is the natural emotionalized dramatic counterpart of the *deus ex machina* of supernaturalism. A naturalistic writer being human may yield to the influence of fear and hate. But in so far he abandons his humanistic naturalism. For it calls for observation of concrete natural causal conditions, and for projection of aims and methods that are consonant with the social conditions disclosed in inquiry. His philosophy commits him to continued use of all the methods of intelligent operation that are available. It commits him to aversion to the escapism and humanistic defeatism inherent in anti-naturalism.

As the war is a global war, so the peace must be a peace that has respect for all the peoples and "races" of the world. I mentioned earlier the provincialism which regards the non-Christians of the world, especially of Asia (and later Africa will come into the scene) as outside the fold, and which philosophical non-supernaturalism admits within the truly human compass only upon conditions its own metaphysics dictates. A philosophic naturalist cannot approve nor go along with those whose beliefs and whose actions, if the latter cohere with their theories, weaken dependence upon the natural agencies, cultural, scientific, economic, political, by which a more humane and friendly world must be built. On the contrary, to him the present tragic scene is a challenge to employ courageously, patiently, persistently and with wholehearted devotion all the *natural* resources that are now potentially at our command.

PRAGMATISM
AND
DEMOCRACY

Philosophy and
Civilization

Philosophy, like politics, literature, and the plastic arts, is itself a phenomenon of human culture. Its connection with social history, with civilization, is intrinsic. There is current among those who philosophize the conviction that, while past thinkers have reflected in their systems the conditions and perplexities of their own day, present-day philosophy in general, and one's own philosophy in particular, is emancipated from the influence of that complex of institutions which forms culture. Bacon, Descartes, Kant, each thought with fervor that he was founding philosophy anew because he was placing it securely upon an exclusive intellectual basis, exclusive, that is, of everything but intellect. The movement of time has revealed the illusion; it exhibits as the work of philosophy the old and ever new undertaking of adjusting that body of traditions which constitute the actual mind of man to scientific tendencies and political aspirations which are novel and incompatible with received authorities. Philosophers are parts of history, caught in its movement; creators perhaps in some measure of its future, but also assuredly creatures of its past.

Those who assert in the abstract definition of philosophy that it deals with eternal truth or reality, untouched by local time and place, are forced to admit that philosophy as a concrete existence is historical, having temporal passage and a diversity of local habitations. Open your histories of philosophy, and you find written throughout them the same periods of time and the same geographical distributions which provide the intellectual scheme of histories of politics, industry, or the fine arts. I cannot imagine a history of philosophy which did not partition its material between the Occident and the Orient; which did not find the former falling into ancient, mediaeval, and modern epochs; which in setting forth Greek thought did not specify Asiatic and Italian colonies and Athens. On the other hand, those who express contempt for the enterprise of philosophy as a sterile and monotonous preoccupation with unsolvable or unreal problems, cannot, without convicting themselves of Philistinism, deny that, however it may stand with philosophy as a revela-

[First published in *Philosophical Review* 36 (1927); from an address to the Sixth International Congress of Philosophy, Harvard University, 15 Sept. 1926; reprinted in *The Later Works*, Vol. 3.]

tion of eternal truths, it is tremendously significant as a revelation of the predicaments, protests, and aspirations of humanity.

The two views of the history of thought are usually proffered as unreconcilable opposites. According to one, it is the record of the most profound dealings of the reason with ultimate being; according to the other, it is a scene of pretentious claims and ridiculous failures. Nevertheless, there is a point of view from which there is something common to the two notions, and this common denominator is more significant than the oppositions. Meaning is wider in scope as well as more precious in value than is truth, and philosophy is occupied with meaning rather than with truth. Making such a statement is dangerous; it is easily misconceived to signify that truth is of no great importance under any circumstances; while the fact is that truth is so infinitely important when it is important at all, namely, in records of events and descriptions of existences, that we extend its claims to regions where it has no jurisdiction. But even as respects truths, meaning is the wider category; truths are but one class of meanings, namely, those in which a claim to verifiability by their consequences is an intrinsic part of their meaning. Beyond this island of meanings which in their own nature are true or false lies the ocean of meanings to which truth and falsity are irrelevant. We do not inquire whether Greek civilization was true or false, but we are immensely concerned to penetrate its meaning. We may indeed ask for the truth of Shakespeare's *Hamlet* or Shelley's "Skylark," but by truth we now signify something quite different from that of scientific statement and historical record.

In philosophy we are dealing with something comparable to the meaning of Athenian civilization or of a drama or a lyric. Significant history is lived in the imagination of man, and philosophy is a further excursion of the imagination into its own prior achievements. All that is distinctive of man, marking him off from the clay he walks upon or the potatoes he eats, occurs in his thought and emotions, in what we have agreed to call consciousness. Knowledge of the structure of sticks and stones, an enterprise in which, of course, truth is essential, apart from whatever added control it may yield, marks in the end but an enrichment of consciousness, of the area of meanings. Thus scientific thought itself is finally but a function of the imagination in enriching life with the significance of things; it is of its peculiar essence that it must also submit to certain tests of application and control. Were significance identical with existence, were values the same as events, idealism would be the only possible philosophy.

It is commonplace that physically and existentially man can but make a superficial and transient scratch upon the outermost rind of the world. It has become a cheap intellectual pastime to contrast the infinitesimal pettiness of man with the vastnesses of the stellar universes. Yet all such comparisons are illicit. We cannot compare existence and meaning; they are disparate. The characteristic life of man is itself the meaning of vast stretches of existences, and without it the latter have no value or significance. There is no common measure of physical existence and conscious experience because the latter is the only measure there is for the former. The significance of being, though not its existence, is the emotion it stirs, the thought it sustains.

It follows that there is no specifiable difference between philosophy and its role in the history of civilization. Discover and define the right characteristic and unique function in civilization, and you have defined philosophy itself. To try to define philosophy in any other way is to search for a will-o'-the-wisp; the conceptions which result are of purely private interpretation for they only exemplify the particular philosophies of their authorship and interpretation. Take the history of philosophy from whatever angle and in whatever cross-section you please, Indian, Chinese, Athenian, the Europe of the twelfth or the twentieth century, and you find a load of traditions proceeding from an immemorial past. You find certain preoccupying interests that appear hypnotic in their rigid hold upon imagination and you also find certain resistances, certain dawning rebellions, struggles to escape and to express some fresh value of life. The preoccupations may be political and artistic as in Athens; they may be economic and scientific as today. But in any case, there is a certain intellectual work to be done; the dominant interest working throughout the minds of masses of men has to be clarified, a result which can be accomplished only by selection, elimination, reduction, and formulation; the interest has to be intellectually forced, exaggerated, in order to be focused. Otherwise it is not intellectually in consciousness, since all clear consciousness by its very nature marks a wrenching of something from its subordinate place to confer upon it a centrality which is existentially absurd. Where there is sufficient depth and range of meanings for consciousness to arise at all, there is a function of adjustment, of reconciliation of the ruling interest of the period with preoccupations which had a different origin and an irrelevant meaning. Consider, for example, the uneasy, restless effort of Plato to adapt his new mathematical insights and his political aspirations to the traditional habits of Athens; the almost humorously complacent union of Christian supernaturalism in the Middle Ages with the naturalism of pagan Greece; the still fermenting effort of the recent age to unite the new science of nature with inherited classic and mediaeval institutions. The life of all thought is to effect a junction at some point of the new and the old, of deepsunk customs and unconscious dispositions, that are brought to the light of attention by some conflict with newly emerging directions of activity. Philosophies which emerge at distinctive periods define the larger patterns of continuity which are woven in effecting the enduring junctions of a stubborn past and an insistent future.

Philosophy thus sustains the closest connection with the history of culture, with the succession of changes in civilization. It is fed by the streams of tradition, traced at critical moments to their sources in order that the current may receive a new direction; it is fertilized by the ferment of new inventions in industry, new explorations of the globe, new discoveries in science. But philosophy is not just a passive reflex of civilization that persists through changes, and that changes while persisting. It is itself a change; the patterns formed in this junction of the new and the old are prophecies rather than records; they are policies, attempts to forestall subsequent developments. The intellectual registrations which constitute a philosophy are generative just because they are selective and eliminative exaggerations. While purporting to say that such and such is and always *has* been the purport of the record of nature, in effect they proclaim that such and such *should* be the significant value to which mankind should loyally attach itself. Without evidence adduced in its behalf such a statement may seem groundless. But I invite you to examine for yourselves any philosophical idea which has had for any long period a significant career and find therein your own evidence. Take, for example, the Platonic patterns of cosmic design and harmony; the Aristotelian perpetually recurrent ends and grooved potentialities; the Kantian fixed forms of intellectual synthesis; the conception of nature itself as it figured in seventeenth and eighteenth century thought. Discuss them as revelations of eternal truth, and something almost childlike or something beyond possibility of decision enters in; discuss them as selections from existing culture by means of which to articulate forces which the author believed should and would dominate the future, and they become preciously significant aspects of human history.

Thus philosophy marks a change of culture. In forming patterns to be conformed to in future thought and action, it is additive and transforming in its role in the history of civilization. Man states anything at his peril; once stated, it occupies a place in a new perspective; it attains a permanence which does not belong to its existence; it enters provokingly into wont and use; it points in a troubling way to need of new endeavors. I do not mean that the creative element in the role of philosophy is necessarily the dominant one; obviously its formulations have been often chiefly conservative, justificatory of selected elements of traditions and received institutions. But even these preservative systems have had a transforming if not exactly a creative effect; they have lent the factors which were selected a power over later human imagination and sentiment which they would otherwise have lacked. And there are other periods, such as those of the seventeenth and eighteenth centuries in Europe, when philosophy is overtly revolutionary in attitude. To their authors, the turn was just from complete error to complete truth; to later generations looking back, the alteration in strictly factual content does not compare with that in desire and direction of effort. . . .

In the historic role of philosophy, the scientific factor, the element of correctness, of verifiable applicability, has a place, but it is a negative one. The meanings delivered by confirmed observation, experimentation, and calculation, scientific facts and principles, serve as tests of the values which tradition transmits and of those which emotion suggests. Whatever is not compatible with them must be eliminated in any sincere philosophizing. This fact confers upon scientific knowledge an incalculably important office in philosophy. But the criterion is negative; the exclusion of the inconsistent is far from being identical with a positive test which demands that only what has been scientifically verifiable shall provide the entire content of philosophy. It is the difference between an imagination that acknowledges its responsibility to meet the logical demands of ascertained facts, and a complete abdication of all imagination in behalf of a prosy literalism.

Finally, it results from what has been said that the presence and absence of native born philosophies is a severe test of the depth of unconscious tradition and rooted institutions among any people, and of the productive force of their culture. For sake of brevity, I may be allowed to take our own case, the case of civilization in the United States. Philosophy, we have been saying, is a conversion of such culture as exists into consciousness, into an imagination which is logically coherent and is not incompatible with what is factually known. But this conversion is itself a further movement of civilization; it is not something performed upon the body of habits and tendencies from without, that is, miraculously. If American civilization does not eventuate in an imaginative formulation of itself, if it merely re-arranges the figures already named and placed, in playing an inherited European game, that fact is itself the measure of the culture which we have achieved. A deliberate striving for an American Philosophy as such would be only another evidence of the same emptiness and impotency. There is energy and activity among us, enough and to spare. Not an inconsiderable part of the vigor that once went into industrial accomplishment now finds its way into science; our scientific "plant" is coming in its way to rival our industrial plants. Especially in psychology and the social sciences an amount of effort is putting forth which is hardly equalled in any one other part of the world. He would be a shameless braggart who claimed that the result is as yet adequate to the activity. What is the matter? It lies, I think, with our lack of imagination in generating leading ideas. Because we are afraid of speculative ideas, we do, and do over and over again, an immense amount of dead, specialized work in the region of "facts." We forget that such facts are only data; that is, are only fragmentary, uncompleted meanings, and unless they are rounded out into complete ideas—a work which can only be done by hypotheses, by a free imagination of intellectual possibilities—they are as helpless as are all maimed things and as repellent as are needlessly thwarted ones. . . .

Philosophy and Democracy

Why such a title as Philosophy and Democracy? Why Philosophy and Democracy, any more than Chemistry and Oligarchy, Mathematics and Aristocracy, Astronomy and Monarchy? Is not the concern of philosophy with truth, and can truth vary with political and social institutions any more than with degrees of latitude and meridians of longitude? Is there one ultimate reality for men who live where suffrage is universal and another and different reality where limited suffrage prevails? If we should become a socialistic republic next week would that modify the nature of the ultimates and absolutes with which philosophy deals any more than it would affect the principles of arithmetic or the laws of physics? . . .

. . . Let us consider the matter not theoretically but historically. In point of fact, nobody would deny that there has been a German, a French, an English philosophy in a sense in which there have not been national chemistries or astronomies. Even in science there is not the complete impersonal detachment which some views of it would lead us to expect. There is difference in color and temper, in emphasis and preferred method characteristic of each people. But these differences are inconsiderable in comparison with those which we find in philosophy. There the differences have been differences in standpoint, outlook and ideal. They manifest not diversities of intellectual emphasis so much as incompatibilities of temperament and expectation. They are different ways of construing life. They indicate different practical ethics of life, not mere variations of intellectual assent. In reading Bacon, Locke, Descartes, Comte, Hegel, Schopenhauer, one says to oneself this could have proceeded only from England, or France, or Germany, as the case may be. The parallelisms with political history and social needs are obvious and explicit.

Take the larger divisions of thought. The conventional main division of philosophy is into ancient, medieval and modern. We may make a similar division in the history of science. But there the meaning is very different. We either mean merely to refer to the stage of ignorance and of knowledge found in certain periods, or we mean not science at all but certain phases of philosophy. When we take science proper, astronomy or

[First published in *University* [of California] *Chronicle* 21 (1919); from an address to the Philosophical Union of the University of California, 29 November 1918. Republished in *Characters and Events*, ed. Joseph Ratner (New York: Henry Holt and Co., 1929); reprinted in *The Middle Works*, Vol. 11.]

geometry, we do not find Euclid especially Greek in his demonstrations. No, ancient, medieval, modern, express in philosophy differences of interest and of purpose characteristic of great civilizations, great social epochs, differences of religious and social desire and belief. They are applicable to philosophy only because economic, political and religious differences manifest themselves in philosophy in fundamentally the same ways that they are shown in other institutions. The philosophies embodied not colorless intellectual readings of reality, but men's most passionate desires and hopes, their basic beliefs about the sort of life to be lived. They started not from science, not from ascertained knowledge, but from moral convictions, and then resorted to the best knowledge and the best intellectual methods available in their day to give the form of demonstration to what was essentially an attitude of will, or a moral resolution to prize one mode of life more highly than another, and the wish to persuade other men that this was the wise way of living.

And this explains what is meant by saying that love of wisdom is not after all the same thing as eagerness for scientific knowledge. By wisdom we mean not systematic and proved knowledge of fact and truth, but a conviction about moral values, a sense for the better kind of life to be led. Wisdom is a moral term, and like every moral term refers not to the constitution of things already in existence, not even if that constitution be magnified into eternity and absoluteness. As a moral term it refers to a choice about something to be done, a preference for living this sort of life rather than that. It refers not to accomplished reality but to a desired future which our desires, when translated into articulate conviction, may help bring into existence.

There are those who think such statements give away the whole case for philosophy. Many critics and foes of philosophy coming from the camp of science would doubtless claim they were admissions of the claims that philosophy has always been a false light, a pretentious ambition; and that the lesson is that philosophers should sit down in humility and accept the ascertainments of the special sciences, and not go beyond the task of weaving these statements into a more coherent fabric of expression. Others would go further and find in such statements a virtual confession of the futility of all philosophizing.

But there is another way of taking the matter. One might rather say that the fact that the collective purpose and desire of a given generation and people dominates its philosophy is evidence of the sincerity and vitality of that philosophy; that failure to employ the known facts of the period in support of a certain estimate of the proper life to lead would show lack of any holding and directing force in the current social ideal. Even wresting facts to a purpose, obnoxious as it is, testifies to a certain ardency in the vigor with which a belief about the right life to be led is held. It argues moral debility if the slave Epictetus and the Emperor Aurelius entertain just the same philosophy of life, even though both belong to the same Stoic school. "A community devoted to industrial pursuits, active in business and commerce, is not likely to see the needs and possibilities of life in the same way as a country with high aesthetic culture and little enterprise in turning the energies of nature to mechanical account. A social group with a fairly continuous history will respond mentally to a crisis in a very different way from one which has felt the shock of distinct breaks." Different hues of philosophic thought are bound to result. Women have as yet made little contribution to philosophy. But when women who are not mere students of other persons' philosophy set out to write it, we cannot conceive that it will be the same in viewpoint or tenor as that composed from the standpoint of the different masculine experience of things. Institutions, customs of life, breed certain systematized predilections and aversions. The wise man reads historic philosophies to detect in them intellectual formulations of men's habitual purposes and cultivated wants, not to gain insight into the ultimate nature of things or information about the make-up of reality. As far as what is loosely called reality figures in philosophies, we may be sure that it signifies those selected aspects of the world which are chosen because they lend themselves to the support of men's judgment of the worth-while life, and hence are most highly prized. In philosophy, "reality" is a term of value or choice.

To deny however that philosophy is in any essential sense a form of science or of knowledge, is not to say that philosophy is a mere arbitrary expression of wish or feeling or a vague suspiration after something, nobody knows what. All philosophy bears an intellectual impress because it is an effort to convince some one, perhaps the writer himself, of the reasonableness of some course of life which has been adopted from custom or instinct. Since it is addressed to man's intelligence, it must employ knowledge and established beliefs, and it must proceed in an orderly way, logically. The art of literature catches men unaware and employs a charm to bring them to a spot whence they see vividly and intimately some picture which embodies life in a meaning. But magic and immediate vision are denied the philosopher. He proceeds prosaically along the highway, pointing out recognizable landmarks, mapping the course, and labeling with explicit logic the stations reached. This means of course that philosophy must depend upon the best science of its day. It can intellectually recommend its judgments of value only as it can select relevant material from that which is recognized to be established truth, and can persuasively use current knowledge to drive home the reasonableness of its conception of life. It is this dependence upon the method of logical presentation and upon scientific subject matter which confers upon philosophy the garb, though not the form, of knowledge.

Scientific form is a vehicle for conveying a non-scientific conviction, but the carriage is necessary, for philosophy is not mere passion but a passion that would exhibit itself as a reasonable persuasion. Philosophy is therefore always in a delicate position, and gives the heathen and Philistine an opportunity to rage. It is always balancing between sophistry, or pretended and illegitimate knowledge, and vague, incoherent mysticism—not of necessity mysticism in its technical definition, but in that sense of the mysterious and misty which affects the popular meaning of the word. When the stress is too much on intellectual form, when the original moral purpose has lost its vitality, philosophy becomes learned and dialectical. When there is cloudy desire, unclarified and unsustained by the logical exhibition of attained science, philosophy becomes hortatory, edifying, sentimental, or fantastic and semi-magical. The perfect balance may hardly be attained by man, and there are few indeed who can even like Plato rhythmically alternate with artistic grace from one emphasis to the other. But what makes philosophy hard work and also makes its cultivation worth while, is precisely the fact that it assumes the responsibility for setting forth some ideal of a collective good life by the methods which the best science of the day employs in its quite different task, and with the use of the characteristic knowledge of its day. The philosopher fails when he avoids sophistry, or the conceit of knowledge, only to pose as a prophet of miraculous intuition or mystic revelation or a preacher of pious nobilities of sentiment.

Perhaps we can now see why it is that philosophers have so often been led astray into making claims for philosophy which when taken literally are practically insane in their inordinate scope, such as the claim that philosophy deals with some supreme and total reality beyond that with which the special sciences and arts have to do. Stated sincerely and moderately, the claim would take the form of pointing out that no knowledge as long as it remains just knowledge, just apprehension of fact and truth, is complete or satisfying. Human nature is such that it is impossible that merely finding out that things are thus and so can long content it. There is an instinctive uneasiness which forces men to go beyond any intellectual grasp or recognition, no matter how extensive. Even if a man had seen the whole existent world and gained insight into its hidden and complicated structure, he would after a few moments of ecstasy at the marvel thus revealed to him become dissatisfied to remain at that point. He would begin to ask himself what of it? What is it all about? What does it all mean? And by these questions he would not signify the absurd search for a knowledge greater than all knowledge, but would indicate the need for projecting even the completest knowledge upon a realm of another dimension—namely, the dimension of action. He would mean: What am I to do about it? What course of activity does this state of things require of me? What possibilities to be achieved by my own thought turned over into deed does it open up to me? What new responsibilities does this knowledge impose? To what new adventures does it invite? All knowledge in short makes a difference. It opens new perspectives and releases energy to new tasks. This happens anyway and continuously, philosophy or no philosophy. But philosophy tries to gather up the threads into a central stream of tendency, to inquire what more fundamental and general attitudes of response the trend of knowledge exacts of us, to what new fields of action it calls us. It is in this sense, a practical and moral sense, that philosophy can lay claim to the epithets of universal, basic and superior. Knowledge *is* partial and incomplete, any and all knowledge, till we have placed it in the context of a future which cannot be known, but only be speculated about and resolved upon. It is, to use in another sense a favorite philosophical term, a matter of *appearance,* for it is not self-enclosed, but an indication of something to be done.

As was intimated at the outset, considerable has been said about philosophy, but nothing as yet about democracy. Yet, I hope, certain implications are fairly obvious. There has been, roughly speaking, a coincidence in the development of modern experimental science and of democracy. Philosophy has no more important question than a consideration of how far this may be mere coincidence, and how far it marks a genuine correspondence. Is democracy a comparatively superficial human expedient, a device of petty manipulation, or does nature itself, as that is uncovered and understood by our best contemporaneous knowledge, sustain and support our democratic hopes and aspirations? Or, if we choose to begin arbitrarily at the other end, if to construct democratic institutions is our aim, how then shall we construe and interpret the natural environment and natural history of humanity in order to get an intellectual warrant for our endeavors, a reasonable persuasion that our undertaking is not contradicted by what science authorizes us to say about the structure of the world? How shall we read what we call reality (that is to say the world of existence accessible to verifiable inquiry) so that we may essay our deepest political and social problems with a conviction that they are to a reasonable extent sanctioned and sustained by the nature of things? Is the world as an object of knowledge at odds with our purposes and efforts? Is it merely neutral and indifferent? Does it lend itself equally to all our social ideals, which means that it gives itself to none, but stays aloof, ridiculing as it were the ardor and earnestness with which we take our trivial and transitory hopes and plans? Or is its nature such that it is at least willing to cooperate, that it not only does not say us nay, but gives us an encouraging nod?

Is not this, you may ask, taking democracy too seriously? Why not ask the question about say presbyterianism or free verse? Well, I would not wholly deny the pertinency of similar questions about such movements. All deliberate action of mind is in a way an experiment with the world to see what it will stand for, what it will promote and what frustrate. The world is tolerant and fairly hospitable. It permits and even encourages all sorts of experiments. But in the long run some are more welcomed and assimilated than others. Hence there can be no difference save one of depth and scope between the questions of the relation of the world to a scheme of conduct in the form of church government or a form of art and that of its relation to democracy. If there be a difference, it is only because democracy is a form of desire and endeavor which reaches further and condenses into itself more issues.

This statement implies a matter of definition. What is meant by democracy? It can certainly be defined in a way which limits the issue to matters which if they bear upon philosophy at all affect it only in limited and technical aspects. Anything that can be said in the way of definition in the remaining moments must be, and confessedly is, arbitrary. The arbitrariness may however, be mitigated by linking up the conception with the historic formula of the greatest liberal movement of history—the formula of liberty, equality and fraternity. In referring to this, we only exchange arbitrariness for vagueness. It would be hard indeed to arrive at any consensus of judgment about the meaning of any one of the three terms inscribed on the democratic banner. Men did not agree in the eighteenth century and subsequent events have done much to accentuate their differences. Do they apply purely politically, or do they have an economic meaning?—to refer to one great cleavage which in the nineteenth century broke the liberal movement into two factions, now opposed to one another as liberal and conservative were once opposed.

Let us then take frank advantage of the vagueness and employ the terms with a certain generosity and breadth. What does the demand for liberty imply for philosophy, when we take the idea of liberty as conveying something of decided moral significance? Roughly speaking, there are two typical ideas of liberty. One of them says that freedom is action in accord with the consciousness of fixed law; that men are free when they are rational, and they are rational when they recognize and consciously conform to the necessities which the universe exemplified. As Tolstoi says, even the ox would be free if it recognized the yoke about its neck and took the yoke for the law of its own action instead of engaging in a vain task of revolt which escapes no necessity but only turns it in the direction of misery and destruction. This is a noble idea of freedom embodied, both openly and disguisedly, in classic philosophies. It is the only view consistent with any form of absolutism whether materialistic or idealistic, whether it considers the necessary relations which form the universe to be physical in character or spiritual. It holds of any view which says that reality exists under the form of eternity, that it is, to use a technical term, a *simul totum*, an all at once and forever affair, no matter whether the all at once be of mathematical-physical laws and structures, or a comprehensive and exhaustive divine consciousness. Of such a conception one can only say that however noble, it is not one which is spontaneously congenial to the idea of liberty in a society which has set its heart on democracy.

A philosophy animated, be it unconsciously or consciously, by the strivings of men to achieve democracy will construe liberty as meaning a universe in which there is real uncertainty and contingency, a world which is not all in, and never will be, a world which in some respect is incomplete and in the making, and which in these respects may be made this way or that according as men judge, prize, love and labor. To such a philosophy any notion of a perfect or complete reality, finished, existing always the same without regard to the vicissitudes of time, will be abhorrent. It will think of time not as that part of reality which for some strange reason has not yet been traversed, but as a genuine field of novelty, of real and unpredictable increments to existence, a field for experimentation and invention. It will indeed recognize that there is in things a grain against which we cannot successfully go, but it will also insist that we cannot even discover what that grain is except as we make this new experiment and that fresh effort, and that consequently the mistake, the effort which is frustrated in direct execution, is as true a constituent of the world as is the act which most carefully observes law. For it is the grain which is rubbed the wrong way which more clearly stands out. It will recognize that in a world where discovery is genuine, error is an inevitable ingredient of reality, and that man's business is not to avoid it—or to cultivate the illusion that it is mere appearance—but to turn it to account, to make it fruitful. Nor will such a philosophy be mealy-mouthed in admitting that where contingency is real and experiment is required, good fortune and bad fortune are facts. It will not construe all accomplishment in terms of merit and virtue, and all loss and frustration in terms of demerit and just punishment. Because it recognizes that contingency cooperates with intelligence in the realization of every plan, even the one most carefully and wisely thought out, it will avoid conceit and intellectual arrogance. It will not fall into the delusion that consciousness is or can be everything as a determiner of events. Hence it will be humbly grateful that a world in which the most extensive and accurate thought and reason can only take advantage of events is also a world which gives room to move about in, and which offers the delights of consummations that are new revelations, as well as those defeats that are admonishments to conceit.

The evident contrast of equality is inequality. Perhaps it is not so evident that inequality means practically inferiority and superiority. And that this relation works out practically in support of a regime of authority or feudal hierarchy in which each lower or inferior element depends upon, holds from, one superior from which it gets direction and to which it is responsible. Let one bear this idea fully in mind and he will see how largely philosophy has been committed to a metaphysics of feudalism. By this I mean it has thought of things in the world as occupying certain grades of value, or as having fixed degrees of truth, ranks of reality. The traditional conception of philosophy to which I referred at the outset, which identifies it with insight into supreme reality or ultimate and comprehensive truth, shows how thoroughly philosophy has been committed to a notion that inherently some realities are superior to others, are better than others. Now any such philosophy inevitably works in behalf of a regime of authority, for it is only right that the superior should lord it over the inferior. The result is that much of philosophy has gone to justifying the particular scheme of authority in religion or social order which happened to exist at a given time. It has become unconsciously an apologetic for the established order, because it has tried to show the rationality of this or that existent hierarchical grading of values and schemes of life. Or when it has questioned the established order it has been a revolutionary search for some rival principle of authority. How largely indeed has historic philosophy been a search for an indefeasible seat of authority. Greek philosophy began when men doubted the authority of custom as a regulator of life; it sought in universal reason or in the immediate particular, in being or in flux, a rival source of authority, but one which as a rival was to be as certain and definite as ever custom had been. Medieval philosophy was frankly an attempt to reconcile authority with reason, and modern philosophy began when man doubting the authority of revelation began a search for some authority which should have all the weight, certainty and inerrancy previously ascribed to the will of God embodied in the divinely instituted church.

Thus for the most part the democratic practice of life has been at an immense intellectual disadvantage. Prevailing philosophies have unconsciously discountenanced it. They have failed to furnish it with articulation, with reasonableness, for they have at bottom been committed to the principle of a single, final and unalterable authority from which all lesser authorities are derived. The men who questioned the divine right of kings did so in the name of another absolute. The voice of the people was mythologized into the voice of God. Now a halo may be preserved about the monarch. Because of his distance, he can be rendered transcendentally without easy detection. But the people are too close at hand, too obviously empirical, to be lent to deification. Hence democracy has ranked for the most part as an intellectual anomaly, lacking philosophical basis and logical coherency, but upon the whole to be accepted because somehow or other it works better than other schemes and seems to develop a more kindly and humane set of social institutions. For when it has tried to achieve a philosophy it has clothed itself in an atomistic individualism, as full of defects and inconsistencies in theory as it was charged with obnoxious consequences when an attempt was made to act upon it.

Now whatever the idea of equality means for democracy, it means, I take it, that the world is not to be construed as a fixed order of species, grades or degrees. It means that every existence deserving the name of existence has something unique and irreplaceable about it, that it does not exist to illustrate a principle, to realize a universal or to embody a kind or class. As philosophy it denies the basic principle of atomistic individualism as truly as that of rigid feudalism. For the individualism traditionally associated with democracy makes equality quantitative, and hence individuality something external and mechanical rather than qualitative and unique. In social and moral matters, equality does not mean mathematical equivalence. It means rather the inapplicability of considerations of greater and less, superior and inferior. It means that no matter how great the quantitative differences of ability, strength, position, wealth, such differences are negligible in comparison with something else—the fact of individuality, the manifestation of something irreplaceable. It means, in short, a world in which an existence must be reckoned with on its own account, not as something capable of equation with and transformation into something else. It implies, so to speak, a metaphysical mathematics of the incommensurable in which each speaks for itself and demands consideration on its own behalf.

If democratic equality may be construed as individuality, there is nothing forced in understanding fraternity as continuity, that is to say, as association and interaction without limit. Equality, individuality, tends to isolation and independence. It is centrifugal. To say that what is specific and unique can be exhibited and become forceful or actual only in relationship with other like beings is merely, I take it, to give a metaphysical version to the fact that democracy is concerned not with freaks or geniuses or heroes or divine leaders but with associated individuals in which each by intercourse with others somehow makes the life of each more distinctive.

All this, of course, is but by way of intimation. In spite of its form it is not really a plea for a certain kind of philosophizing. For if democracy be a serious, important choice and predilection it must in time justify itself by generating its own child of wisdom, to be justified in turn by its children, better institutions of life. It is not so much a question as to whether there will be a philosophy of this kind as it is of just who will be the philosophers associated with it. . . .

Science and Free Culture

It is no longer possible to hold the simple faith of the Enlightenment that assured advance of science will produce free institutions by dispelling ignorance and superstition:—the sources of human servitude and the pillars of oppressive government. The progress of natural science has been even more rapid and extensive than could have been anticipated. But its technological application in mass production and distribution of goods has required concentration of capital; it has resulted in business corporations possessed of extensive legal rights and immunities; and, as is a commonplace, has created a vast and intricate set of new problems. It has put at the disposal of dictators means of controlling opinion and sentiment of a potency which reduces to a mere shadow all previous agencies at the command of despotic rulers. For negative censorship it has substituted means of propaganda of ideas and alleged information on a scale that reaches every individual, reiterated day after day by every organ of publicity and communication, old and new. In consequence, for practically the first time in human history, totalitarian states exist claiming to rest upon the active consent of the governed. While despotic governments are as old as political history, this particular phenomenon is as startlingly unexpected as it is powerful.

One of the earlier arguments for democracy is countered in the most disturbing way. Before the industrial revolution had made much headway it was a commonplace that oppressive governments had the support of only a relatively small class. Republican government, it was assumed, would have the broad support of the masses, so that the "people" who, as Rousseau expressed it, had been nothing would become everything. We are now told the contrary. Democracy is said to be but a numerical contrivance, resting upon shifting combinations of individuals who happen at a given time to make up a majority of voters. We are told that the moral consensus which exists only when there is unity of beliefs and aims, is conspicuously lacking in democracies, and is of the very essence of totalitarian states. The claim stands side by side with that of Marxist communists who say that since their views are inherently scientific, false opinions have no legitimate standing as against the authority of The Truth. But in a way the Fascist claim goes deeper since it pretends to

[From *Freedom and Culture* (New York: G.P. Putnam's Sons, 1939); reprinted in *The Later Works*, Vol. 13.]

extend below merely intellectual loyalties, to which science appeals, and lay hold of fundamental emotions and impulses.

There is an argument about science which so far has found comparatively little response in democratic countries, but which nevertheless puts a problem so basic that it will receive more and more attention as time goes by. It is said that the principles of laissez-faire individualism have governed the conduct of scientific inquiry; that the tastes and preferences of individual investigators have been allowed to regulate its course to such an extent that present intellectual confusion and moral chaos of the world exists because of tacit connivance of science with uncontrolled individualistic activity in industry.

The position is so extreme and goes so contrary to all we had come to believe that it is easily passed over as an aberration. But the view, because of its extreme character, may be taken to point to a genuine issue: just what are the social consequences of science? Are they not so important, because of technological applications, that the social interest is paramount over intellectual interest? Can the type of social control of industry urged by socialists be carried through without some kind of public regulation of the scientific investigations that are the source of the inventions determining the course of industry? And might not such regulation throttle the freedom of science? Those who say that the social effect of inventions (which exist only because of the findings of scientific inquiry) is so unsettling that the least which can be done is to declare a moratorium on science express the same problem with more moderation.

The claim is made in Russia that the direction taken by science has in the last hundred and fifty years been so determined by the interest of the dominant economic class, that science has been upon the whole an organ of bourgeois democracy:—not so consciously perhaps as in the case of government, the police and the army, but yet in substantial effect. Since it is impossible to draw any fixed line between the physical and the social sciences, and since the latter—both with respect to investigation and teaching—must be regulated in the interest of the politics of the new social order, it is impossible to allow the physical sciences to go their way apart without political regulation. Nazi Germany decrees what is scientific truth in anthropology regarding race, and Moscow determines that Mendelism is scientifically false, and dictates the course to be pursued by Genetics. Both countries look askance at the theory of Relativity, although on different grounds. Quite aside, however, from special cases, a general atmosphere of control of opinion cannot exist without reacting in pretty fundamental ways upon every form of intellectual activity—art too as well as science.

Even if we hold that extreme views are so extreme as to be distorted caricatures, there remains an actual problem. Can society, especially a democratic society, exist without a basic consensus and community of beliefs? If it cannot, can the required community be achieved without regulation of scientific pursuits exercised by a public authority in behalf of social unity?

In this connection the accusation of irresponsibility as to social consequences is brought against scientific men, and it is in this context that the underlying issue takes shape. It is argued (and some who take the position are themselves scientists) that the main directions of physical science during the past hundred years, increasingly so in the last half century, have been set, indirectly and directly, by the requirements of industry carried on for private profit. Consideration of the *problems* which have not received attention in comparison with those which have absorbed expenditure of intellectual energies will, it is said, prove the proposition.

Direct control has been exercised for the most part by governments. They have subsidized the kind of investigations that promise increased national power, either by promoting manufacturing and commerce as against other national states, or by fostering researches that strengthen military prowess. Indirect control has been exercised in subtler ways. The place of industry is so central in modern life that quite apart from questions handed directly over to scientific laboratories by industrial enterprises, it is psychologically impossible for men engaged in scientific research not to be most sensitive and most responsive to the *type* of problems presented in practical effort to control natural energies;—which in the concrete means manufacturing and distributing goods. Moreover, a kind of positive halo surrounds scientific endeavors. For it has been held, not without grounds, that general social—or at least national— welfare is thereby promoted. Germany led other countries in physical research; and it was in Germany that scientific advances could be shown to have contributed most directly to national strength and prestige. It was thus possible for some intellectual observers, not particularly naïve, to hold up German universities as models to follow in our own country. . . .

I referred above to the role of nationalism in deciding the direction taken by science. The striking instance is of course the organization of scientific men for aid to a nation in time of war. The instance brings to a head tendencies that are going on in less overt and more unconscious ways pretty much all the time, even in times of nominal peace. Increase of the scope of governmental activities in all industrialized countries, going on for some years at an accelerated pace, has reinforced the alliance between national interest and scientific inquiry. It is certainly arguable that when the choice at hand in between regulation of science by private economic interests and by nationalist interest, the latter should have preference. It may be inferred that the open control of science exercised in totalitarian states is but a culmination of tendencies that have been going on in more or less covert ways for some time—from which it follows that the problem presented extends beyond the borders of those particular states.

Strangely enough, at first sight, the demand for direct social control of scientific inquiries and conclusion is unwittingly reinforced by an attitude quite commonly taken by scientific men themselves. For it is commonly said and commonly believed that science is completely neutral and indifferent as to the ends and values which move men to act: that at most it only provides more efficient means for realization of ends that are and must be due to wants and desires completely independent of science. It is at this point that the present climate of opinion differs so widely from that which marked the optimistic faith of the Enlightenment; the faith that human science and freedom would advance hand in hand to usher in an era of indefinite human perfectibility.

That the popular esteem of science is largely due to the aid it has given to men for attainment of things they wanted independently of what they had learned from science is doubtless true. Russell has stated in a vivid way the sort of thing that has enabled science to displace beliefs that had previously been held: "The world ceased to believe that Joshua caused the sun to stand still, because Copernican astronomy was useful in navigation; it abandoned Aristotle's physics, because Galileo's theory of falling bodies made it possible to calculate the trajectory of a cannonball. It rejected the theory of the flood because geology is useful in mining and so on."[1] That the quotation expresses the sort of thing that gave the conclusions of the new science prestige and following at a time when it badly needed some outside aid in getting a hearing can hardly be doubted. As illustrative material it is especially impressive because of the enormous authority enjoyed by the doctrines of Aristotle and of the Church. If even in the case where all the advantage was on the side of old doctrines, the demonstrated serviceability of science gave it the victory, we can easily judge the enhancement of the esteem in which science was held in matters where it had no such powerful foe to contend with.

Quite apart from the antagonism to science displayed by entrenched institutional interests that had previously obtained a monopoly over beliefs in, say, astronomy, geology and some fields of history, history proves the existence of so much indifference on the part of mankind to the quality of its beliefs and such lethargy towards methods that disturb old

1. Bertrand Russell, *Power*, p. 138.

beliefs, that we should be glad that the new science has had such powerful adventitious aid. But it leaves untouched the question as to whether
scientific knowledge has power to modify the ends which men prize and
strive to attain. Is it proved that the findings of science—the best authenticated knowledge we have—add only to our power to realize desires
already in existence? Or is this view derived from some previous theory
about the constitution of human nature? Can it be true that desires and
knowledge exist in separate non-communicating compartments? Do the
facts which can undoubtedly be cited as evidence, such as the use of
scientific knowledge indifferently to heal disease and prolong human life
and to provide the instruments for wholesale destruction of life, really
prove the case? Or are they specially selected cases that support a doctrine that originated on other grounds than the evidence of facts? Is
there such a complex separation of human ends from human beliefs as
the theory assumes?

   The shock given old ideas by the idea that knowledge is incapable of
modifying the quality of desires (and hence cannot affect the formation
of ends and purposes) is not of course in itself a ground for denying it is
sound. It may be that the old view is totally false. Nevertheless, the point
is worth discussion. We do not have to refer to the theory of Plato that
knowledge, or what passes as knowledge, is the sole final determinant of
man's ideas of the Good and hence of their actions. Nor is it needful to
refer to Bacon's vision of the organization of scientific knowledge as the
prospective foundation of future social policies directed exclusively to
the advance of human well-being. The simple fact is that all the deliberately liberal and progressive movements of modern times have based
themselves on the idea that action is determined by ideas, up to the time
when Hume said that reason was and should be the "slave of the passions"; or, in contemporary language, of the emotions and desires. Hume's
voice was a lonely one when he uttered the remark. The idea is now
echoed and re-echoed from almost every quarter. The classic economic
school made wants the prime motors of human action, reducing reason
to a power calculating the means best fitted to satisfy the wants. The first
effect of biology upon psychology was to emphasize the primacy of
appetites and instincts. Psychiatrists have enforced the same conclusion
by showing that intellectual disturbances originate in emotional malad-
justments, and by exhibiting the extent of dictation of belief by desire.

   It is one thing, however, to recognize that earlier theories neglected the
importance of emotions and habits as determinants of conduct and exaggerated that of ideas and reason. It is quite another thing to hold that
ideas (especially those warranted by competent inquiry) and emotions
(with needs and desires) exist in separate compartments so that no inter-

action between them exists. When the view is as baldly stated it strikes one as highly improbable that there can be any such complete separation in the constitution of human nature. And while the idea must be accepted if the evidence points that way, no matter into what plight human affairs are forever plunged, the implications of the doctrine of complete separation of desire and knowledge must be noted. The assumption that desires are rigidly fixed is not one on its face consistent with the history of man's progress from savagery through barbarism to even the present defective state of civilization. If knowledge, even of the most authenticated kind, cannot influence desires and aims, if it cannot determine what is of value and what is not, the future outlook as to formation of desires is depressing. Denial that they can be influenced by knowledge points emphatically to the non-rational and anti-rational forces that will form them. One alternative to the power of ideas is habit or custom, and then when the rule of sheer habit breaks down—as it has done at the present time—all that is left is competition on the part of various bodies and interests to decide which shall come out ahead in a struggle, carried on by intimidation, coercion, bribery, and all sorts of propaganda, to shape the desires which shall predominantly control the ends of human action. The prospect is a black one. It leads one to consider the possibility that Bacon, Locke, and the leaders of the Enlightenment—typified by the act of Condorcet, writing, while imprisoned and waiting for death, about the role of science in the future liberation of mankind—were after all quite aware of the actual influence of appetite, habit, and blind desire upon action, but were engaged in holding up another and better way as the alternative to follow in the future.

That the course they anticipated has not come to fruition is obvious without argument. Bacon's action in using his own knowledge as a servant of the Crown in strengthening Great Britain in a military way against other nations now seems more prophetic of what has happened than what he put down in words. The power over Nature which he expected to follow the advance of science has come to pass. But in contradiction to his expectations, it has been largely used to increase, instead of reduce, the power of Man over Man. Shall we conclude that the early prophets were totally and intrinsically wrong? Or shall we conclude that they immensely underestimated the obduracy of institutions and customs antedating the appearance of science on the scene in shaping desires in their image? Have events after all but accentuated the problem of discovering the means by which authenticated beliefs shall influence desires, the formation of ends, and thereby the course of events? Is it possible to admit the power of propaganda to shape ends and deny that of science?

Looked at from one angle, the question brings us back to our fundamental issue: the relation of culture and human nature. For the fact
which is decisive in answering the question whether verified knowledge is
or is not capable of shaping desires and ends (as well as means) is
whether the desires that are effective in settling the course of action are
innate and fixed, or are themselves the product of a certain culture. If the
latter is the case, the practical issue reduces itself to this: Is it possible for
the scientific attitude to become such a weighty and widespread constituent of culture that, through the medium of culture, it may shape human
desires and purposes?

To state the question is a long way from ability to answer it. But it is
something to have the issue before us in its actual instead of in its
factitious form. The issue ceases to be the indeterminate one of the
relation of knowledge and desires in the native psychological constitution
of man—indeterminate, among other reasons, because it is disputable
whether there is any such thing as the latter apart from native biological
constitution. It becomes the determinate one of the institution of the
kind of culture in which scientific method and scientific conclusions are
integrally incorporated.

The problem stated in this way puts in a different light the esteem
gained by science because of its serviceability. That there are individuals
here and there who have been influenced to esteem science because of
some obvious contribution to satisfaction of their merely personal desires
may well be a fact. That there are groups similarly influenced must be
admitted. But the reasons why men have been willing to accept conclusions derived from science in lieu of older ideas are not exclusively or
even mainly those of direct personal and class benefit. Improvements in
navigation and mining have become part of the state of culture. It is in
this capacity they have tended to displace beliefs that were congenial to
an earlier state of culture. By and large the same thing is true of the
application of physics and chemistry in more effective satisfaction of
wants and in creation of new wants. While their application to produce
increased efficiency in carrying on war has doubtlessly recommended
those sciences to persons like rulers and generals, who otherwise would
have been indifferent, the mass of persons have been moved to an attitude of favorable esteem by what has happened in the arts of peace. The
decisive factor would seem to be whether the arts of war or of peace are
to be in the future the ones that will control culture, a question that
involves the need of discovering why war is such an important constituent
of present culture.

I should be on controversial ground if I held up as evidence the belief
that the technologies, which are the practical correlates of scientific
theories, have now reached a point in which they can be used to create an

era of abundance instead of the deficit-economics that existed before natural science developed, and that with an era of abundance and security the causes of conflict would be reduced. It may be mentioned as a hypothetical illustration. The kind of serviceability which is capable of generating high esteem for science *may* possibly be serviceability for general and shared, or "social," welfare. If the economic regime were so changed that the resources of science were employed to maintain security for all, the present view about the limitation of science might fade away. I imagine there are not many who will deny that esteem for science, even when placed upon the ground of serviceability alone, is produced at least in part by an admixture of general with private serviceability. If there is a skeptic let him consider the contribution made by science both actually and still more potentially to agriculture, and the social consequences of the change in production of foods and raw materials, thereby effected.

The other side of the ledger is marked by such a debit entry as the following from the English chemist Soddy: "So far the pearls of science have been cast before swine, who have given us in return millionaires and slums, armaments and the desolation of war." The contrast is real. If its existence seems to support the doctrine that science only supplies means for more efficient execution of already existing desires and purposes, it is because it points to the division which exists in our culture. The war that mobilizes science for wholesale destruction mobilizes it, also, for support of life and for healing the wounded. The desires and ends involved proceed not from native and naked human nature but from modifications it has undergone in interaction with a complex of cultural factors of which science is indeed one, but one which produces social consequences only as it is affected by economic and political traditions and customs formed before its rise. . . .

We have been considering science as a body of conclusions. We have ignored science in its quality of an attitude embodied in habitual will to employ certain methods of observation, reflection, and test rather than others. When we look at science from this point of view, the significance of science as a constituent of culture takes on a new color. The great body of scientific inquirers would deny with indignation that they are actuated in *their* esteem for science by its material serviceability. If they use words sanctioned by long tradition, they say they are moved by love of the truth. If they use contemporary phraseology, less grandiloquent in sound but of equivalent meaning, they say they are moved by a controlling interest in inquiry, in discovery, in following where the evidence of discovered facts points. Above all they say that this kind of interest excludes interest in reaching any conclusion not warranted by evidence, no matter how personally congenial it may be.

In short, it is a fact that a certain group of men, perhaps relatively not very numerous, have a "disinterested" interest in scientific inquiry. This interest has developed a morale having its own distinctive features. Some of its obvious elements are willingness to hold belief in suspense, ability to doubt until evidence is obtained; willingness to go where evidence points instead of putting first a personally preferred conclusion; ability to hold ideas in solution and use them as hypotheses to be tested instead of as dogmas to be asserted; and (possibly the most distinctive of all) enjoyment of new fields for inquiry and of new problems.

Every one of these traits goes contrary to some human impulse that is naturally strong. Uncertainty is disagreeable to most persons; suspense is so hard to endure that assured expectation of an unfortunate outcome is usually preferred to a long-continued state of doubt. "Wishful thinking" is a comparatively modern phrase; but men upon the whole have usually believed what they wanted to believe, except as very convincing evidence made it impossible. Apart from a scientific attitude, guesses, with persons left to themselves, tend to become opinions and opinions dogmas. To hold theories and principles in solution, awaiting confirmation, goes contrary to the grain. Even today questioning a statement made by a person is often taken by him as a reflection upon his integrity, and is resented. For many millennia opposition to views widely held in a community was intolerable. It called down the wrath of the deities who are in charge of the group. Fear of the unknown, fear of change and novelty, tended, at all times before the rise of scientific attitude, to drive men into rigidity of beliefs and habits; they entered upon unaccustomed lines of behavior— even in matters of minor moment—with qualms which exacted rites of expiation. Exceptions to accepted rules have either been ignored or systematically explained away when they were too conspicuous to ignore. Baconian idols of the tribe, the cave, the theater, and den have caused men to rush to conclusions, and then to use all their powers to defend from criticism and change the conclusions arrived at. The connection of common law with custom and its resistance to change are familiar facts. Even religious beliefs and rites which were at first more or less heretical deviations harden into modes of action it is impious to question, after once they have become part of the habits of a group.

If I mention such familiar considerations it is in part to suggest that we may well be grateful that science has had undeniable social serviceability, and that to some extent and in some places strong obstructions to adoption of changed beliefs have been overcome. But the chief reason for calling attention to them is the proof they furnish that in some persons and to some degree science has already created a new morale—which is equivalent to the creation of new desires and new ends. The existence of the scientific attitude and spirit, even upon a limited scale, is proof that science is capable of developing a distinctive type of disposition and purpose: a type that goes far beyond provision of more effective means for realizing desires which exist independently of any effect of science.

It is not becoming, to put it moderately, for those who are themselves animated by the scientific morale to assert that other persons are incapable of coming into possession of it and being moved by it.

Such an attitude is saved from being professional snobbery only when it is the the result of sheer thoughtlessness. When one and the same representative of the intellectual class denounces any view that attaches inherent importance to the consequences of science, claiming the view is false to the spirit of science—and also holds that it is impossible for science to do anything to affect desires and ends, the inconsistency demands explanation.

A situation in which the fundamental dispositions and ends of a few are influenced by science while that of most persons and most groups is not so influenced proves that the issue is cultural. The difference sets a social problem: what are the causes for the existence of this great gap, especially since it has such serious consequences? If it is possible for persons to have their beliefs formed on the ground of evidence, procured by systematic and competent inquiry, nothing can be more disastrous socially than that the great majority of persons should have them formed by habit, accidents of circumstance, propaganda, personal and class bias. The existence, even on a relatively narrow scale, of a morale of fairmindedness, intellectual integrity, of will to subordinate personal preference to ascertained facts and to share with others what is found out, instead of using it for personal gain, is a challenge of the most searching kind. Why don't a great many more persons have this attitude?

The answer given to this challenge is bound up with the fate of democracy. The spread of literacy, the immense extension of the influence of the press in books, newspapers, periodicals, make the issue peculiarly urgent for a democracy. The very agencies that a century and a half ago were looked upon as those that were sure to advance the cause of democratic freedom, are those which now make it possible to create pseudo-public opinion and to undermine democracy from within. Callousness due to continuous reiteration may produce a certain immunity to the grosser kinds of propaganda. But in the long run negative measures afford no assurance. While it would be absurd to believe it desirable or possible for every one to become a scientist when science is defined from the side of subject matter, the future of democracy is allied with spread of the scientific attitude. It is the sole guarantee against wholesale misleading by propaganda. More important still, it is the only assurance of the possibility of a public opinion intelligent enough to meet present social problems.

To become aware of the problem is a condition of taking steps toward its solution. The problem is in part economic. The nature of control of the means of publicity enters directly; sheer financial control is not a favorable sign. The democratic belief in free speech, free press and free assembly is one of the things that exposes democratic institutions to attack. For representatives of totalitarian states, who are the first to deny such freedom when they are in power, shrewdly employ it in a democratic country to destroy the foundations of democracy. Backed with the necessary financial means, they are capable of carrying on a work of continuous sapping and mining. More dangerous, perhaps, in the end is the fact that all economic conditions tending toward centralization and concentration of the means of production and distribution affect the public press, whether individuals so desire or not. The causes which require large corporate capital to carry on modern business, naturally influence the publishing business.

The problem is also an educative one. A book instead of a paragraph could be given to this aspect of the topic. That the schools have mostly been given to imparting information ready-made, along with teaching the tools of literacy, cannot be denied. The methods used in acquiring such information are not those which develop skill in inquiry and in test of opinions. On the contrary, they are positively hostile to it. They tend to dull native curiosity, and to load powers of observation and experimentation with such a mass of unrelated material that they do not operate as effectively as they do in many an illiterate person. The problem of the common schools in a democracy has reached only its first stage when they are provided for everybody. Until what shall be taught and how it is taught is settled upon the basis of formation of the scientific attitude, the so-called educational work of schools is a dangerously hit-or-miss affair as far as democracy is concerned. . . .

ART, SCIENCE, AND MORAL PROGRESS

The Ethics of Democracy

Democracy, like any other polity, has been finely termed the memory of an historic past, the consciousness of a living present, the ideal of the coming future. Democracy, in a word, is a social, that is to say, an ethical conception, and upon its ethical significance is based its significance as governmental. Democracy is a form of government only because it is a form of moral and spiritual association.

But so is aristocracy. What is the difference? What distinguishes the ethical basis and ideal of one from that of the other? It may appear a roundabout way to reach a simple end, to refer to Plato and to Greek life to get data for an answer; but I know of no way in which I can so easily bring out what seems to me the truth. The Platonic Republic is a splendid and imperishable formulation of the aristocratic ideal. If it had no value for philosophical reasons, if its theory of morals, of reality and of knowledge had disappeared as utterly as the breezes which swept the grasses under the plane tree by which Plato and his disciples sat and talked, the Republic would be immortal as the summary of all that was best and most permanent in Greek life, of its ways of thinking and feeling, and of its ideals. But the Republic is more; it seizes upon the heart of the ethical problem, the relation of the individual to the universal, and states a solution. The question of the Republic is as to the ideal of men's conduct; the answer is such a development of man's nature as brings him into complete harmony with the universe of spiritual relations, or, in Platonic language, the state. This universe, in turn, is man writ large; it is the manifestation, the realization of the capacities of the individual. Such a development of the individual that he shall be in harmony with all others in the state, that is, that he shall possess as his own the unified will of the community; that is the end both of politics and of ethics. Nothing could be more aside from the mark than to say that the Platonic ideal subordinates and sacrifices the individual to the

[First published as No. 1, Second Series, University of Michigan Philosophical Papers (Ann Arbor: Andrews & Co., 1888); reprinted in *The Early Works*, Vol. 1.]

state. It does, indeed, hold that the individual can be what he ought to be, can become what, in idea, he is, only as a member of a spiritual organism, called by Plato the state, and, in losing his own individual will, acquiring that of this larger reality. But this is not loss of selfhood or personality, it is its realization. The individual is not sacrificed; he is brought to reality in the state.

We certainly cannot find here any ground upon which to distinguish the aristocratic from the democratic idea. But we have not asked how this unity of the individual and the universe, this perfect man in the perfect state, is to be brought about. Here lies the distinction sought for; it is not a question of end, but of means. According to Plato (and the aristocratic idea everywhere), the multitude is incapable of forming such an ideal and of attempting to reach it. Plato is the true author of the doctrine of the "remnant." There is, in his words, "no chance of perfection either in states or in individuals until a necessity is laid upon the *small* class of caring for the state." It is to the one wise man, or to the few, that Plato looks for redemption. Once found these are to be given absolute control, and are to see to it that each individual is placed in such a position in the state that he may make perfect harmony with the others, and at the same time perform that for which he is best fitted, and thus realize the goal of life—"Justice," in Plato's word.

Such is the barest outline of the most perfect picture of the aristocratic ideal which history affords. The few best, the aristoi; these know and are fitted for rule; but they are to rule not in their own interests but in that of society as a whole, and, therefore, in that of every individual in society. They do not bear rule *over* the others; they show them what they can best do, and guide them in doing it. There is no need to dwell upon the charm, upon the attractiveness of the aristocratic ideal. The best witness to it is in the long line of great men who have reiterated with increasing emphasis that all will go wrong, until the few who know and are strong, are put in power, while others, foregoing the assertion of their individuality, submit to superior wisdom and goodness.

But history has been making the other way. If history be, as Strauss said, a sound aristocrat, then history is committing suicide. It is working towards something which is not history. The aristocratic ideal, spite of all its attractions, is not equal to reality; it is not equal to the actual forces animating men as they work in history. It has failed because it is found that the practical consequence of giving the few wise and good power is that they cease to remain wise and good. They become ignorant of the needs and requirement of the many; they leave the many outside the pale with no real share in the commonwealth. Perchance they even willfully use their wisdom and strength for themselves, for the assertion of priv-

ilege and status and to the detriment of the common good. The aristocratic society always limits the range of men who are regarded as par-
ticipating in the state, in the unity of purpose and destiny; and it always
neglects to see that those theoretically included really obtain their well
being. Every forward democratic movement is followed by the broaden-
ing of the circle of the state, and by more effective oversight that every
citizen may be insured the rights belonging to him.

But even were it possible to find men so wise as not to ignore the
misery and degradation beyond their immediate ken, men so good as to
use their power only for the community, there is another fact which is
the condemnation of the aristocratic theory. The ethical idea is not satisfied merely when all men sound the note of harmony with the highest
social good, so be it that they have not worked it out for themselves. Were
it granted that the rule of the aristoi would lead to the highest external
development of society and the individual, there would still be a fatal
objection. Humanity cannot be content with a good which is procured
from without, however high and otherwise complete that good. The
aristocratic idea implies that the mass of men are to be inserted by
wisdom, or, if necessary, thrust by force, into their proper positions in the
social organism. It is true, indeed, that when an individual has found that
place in society for which he is best fitted and is exercising the function
proper to that place, he has obtained his completest development, but it is
also true (and this is the truth omitted by aristocracy, emphasized by
democracy) that he must find this place and assume this work in the
main for himself. Democracy does not differ from aristocracy in its goal.
The end is not mere assertion of the individual will as individual; it is
not disregard of law, of the universal; it is complete realization of the law,
namely of the unified spirit of the community. Democracy differs as to its
means. This universal, this law, this unity of purpose, this fulfilling of
function in devotion to the interests of the social organism, is not to be
put into a man from without. It must begin in the man himself, however
much the good and the wise of society contribute. Personal responsibility,
individual initiation, these are the notes of democracy. Aristocracy and
democracy both imply that the actual state of society exists for the sake of
realizing an end which is ethical, but aristocracy implies that this is to be
done primarily by means of special institutions or organizations within
society, while democracy holds that the ideal is already at work in every
personality, and must be trusted to care for itself. There is an individualism in democracy which there is not in aristocracy; but it is an ethical,
not a numerical individualism; it is an individualism of freedom, of
responsibility, of initiative to and for the ethical ideal, not an individualism of lawlessness. In one word, democracy means that *personality* is the

first and final reality. It admits that the full significance of personality can be learned by the individual only as it is already presented to him in objective form in society; it admits that the chief stimuli and encouragements to the realization of personality come from society; but it holds, none the less, to the fact that personality cannot be procured for any one, however degraded and feeble, by any one else, however wise and strong. It holds that the spirit of personality indwells in every individual and that the choice to develop it must proceed from that individual. From this central position of personality result the other notes of democracy, liberty, equality, fraternity,—words which are not mere words to catch the mob, but symbols of the highest ethical idea which humanity has yet reached—the idea that personality is the one thing of permanent and abiding worth, and that in every human individual there lies personality.

By way of illustration (and what is said in the remainder of this paper is only by way of illustration), let us take the notion of liberty. Plato gives a vivid illustration of what he means by democratic freedom. It is doing as one likes. It is ordering life as one pleases. It is thinking and acting as one has a mind to. Liberty in a democracy can have no limit. Its result is loss of reverence and of order. It is the denial of moderation, of the principle of limit. Democratic liberty is the following out of individual wills, of particular desires, to the utmost degree. It has no order or law (*Republic* viii. 557–563). In a word, it is the extreme assertion of individualism, resulting in anarchy. In this conception of liberty he has been followed by all of the anti-democratic school. But from the democratic standpoint, it must be remembered that the individual is something more than the individual, namely, a personality. His freedom is not mere self-assertion, nor unregulated desire. You cannot say that he knows no law; you must say that he knows no law but his own, the law of personality; no law, in other words, externally imposed, however splendid the authority, and undoubted the goodness of those that impose it. Law is the objective expression of personality. It is not a limitation upon individual freedom; it is correlative with it. Liberty is not a numerical notion of isolation; it is the ethical idea that personality is the supreme and only law, that every man is an absolute end in himself. The democratic ideal includes liberty, because democracy without initiation from within, without an ideal chosen from within and freely followed from within, is nothing.

Again, for illustration, take the notion of equality. If we heed the aristocratic school, we learn that equality means numerical equality, that one number one is just as good as any other number one. Conceiving it to refer to bald individuality, they think its inevitable outcome, logical if not historical, is an equal division of all things from virtue to wealth. Democracy is condemned because it regards as equal the worst and the best of men, the wisest and the most ignorant. It is condemned because it is said to aim at an equal distribution of wealth and of the happiness that grows from material possessions and surroundings. It is said that it is both foolish and wicked to attempt by the lie of equality to blind one's eyes to the differences of men in wisdom, virtue, and industry; that upon these differences, indeed, rests the whole structure of society with its necessary grades of subordination and service; and that the only society which is either stable or progressive is one in which the motives of inequality, both political and industrial, have fair play. As Maine says, the motives which have always impelled mankind to the production of increasing industrial resources are such as infallibly entail inequality in its distribution. It is the never-ending struggle for existence, the private war which makes one man strive to climb upon the shoulders of another and stay there, which have been the springs to action. Take them away, introduce equality, and you have no motive to progress.

What shall we say to this indictment? Simply that it is beside the mark. As relates to democracy, it corresponds to no reality. Equality is not an arithmetical, but an ethical conception. Personality is as universal as humanity; it is indifferent to all distinctions which divide men from men. Wherever you have a man, there you have personality, and there is no trace by which one personality may be distinguished from another so as to be set above or below. It means that in every individual there lives an infinite and universal possibility; that of being a king and priest. Aristocracy is blasphemy against personality. It is the doctrine of the elect few applied not to some life in the future, but to all relations of humanity. Hero-worship means man despised. The true meaning of equality is synonymous with the definition of democracy given by James Russell Lowell. It is the form of society in which every man has a chance and knows that he has it—and we may add, a chance to which no possible limits can be put, a chance which is truly infinite, the chance to become a person. Equality, in short, is the ideal of humanity; an ideal in the consciousness of which democracy lives and moves.

One aspect of the indictment remains to be touched—the nature of industrial equality, or the supposed tendency of democracy towards socialism, if not communism. And there is no need to beat about the bush in saying that democracy is not in reality what it is in name until it is industrial, as well as civil and political. Such a condition is indeed far enough away; on this point, democracy is an ideal of the future, not a starting point. In this respect, society is still a sound aristocrat. And the reflex influence of this upon our civil and political organization is such that they are only imperfectly democratic. For their sakes, therefore, as well as for that of industrial relations, a democracy of wealth is a necessity.

All that makes such assertions seem objectionable is that this democracy of wealth is represented, often by its adherents, always by its opponents, as if it meant the numerical division into equal portions of all wealth, and its numerical redistribution. But all that has been said in this paper has been said in vain, unless it be now recognized that democracy is anything but a numerical notion; and that the numerical application of it is as much out of place here as it is everywhere else. What is meant in detail by a democracy of wealth we shall not know until it is more of a reality than it is now. In general, however, it means and must mean that all industrial relations are to be regarded as subordinate to human relations, to the law of personality. Numerical identity is not required, it is not even allowed; but it is absolutely required that industrial organization shall be made a *social* function. And if this expression again seems objectionable, it is because it is interpreted to mean that in some way society, as a whole, to the abolition of all individual initiative and result, is to take charge of all those undertakings which we call economic. It seems to imply socialism in the sense in which that mode of life destroys that individual responsibility and activity which are at the very heart of modern life. But when we are told that the family is a social institution, and that life in the family is a social function, do we understand this to mean that it is a form of existence in which all individuality is renounced, and an artificial entity created which absorbs the rightful activities of the individual? I think not; we mean that the family is an ethical community, and that life in the family conforms to its idea only when the individual realizes oneness of interest and purpose with it.

And this, in kind, is precisely what is meant when we speak of industrial relations as being necessarily social; we mean that they are to become the material of an ethical realization; the form and substance of a community of good (though not necessarily of goods) wider than any now known: that as the family, largely in its best examples, the state somewhat, though in a less degree, mean unity of purpose and interest, so economic society must mean unity of interest and purpose. The truth is that in these matters we are still largely in the intellectual bounds which bound pre-Christian thought. We still think of life as having two parts, one animal, the other truly human and therefore truly ethical. The getting and distributing of the material benefits of life are regarded as indeed a *means* to the possibility of the higher life, the life of men in their distinctively human relations, but as in themselves wholly outside of that life. Both Plato and Aristotle, for example, always take it as a matter of course, that everything which is industrial, which concerns the getting or distributing of wealth, lies wholly outside, nay, is opposed to the life of the citizen, that is, of the member of an ethical community. Plato's attacks upon the Sophists for receiving money for teaching were on the ground that they thus degraded a personal (that is, a moral) relation, that of teacher and pupil, to an industrial; as if the two were necessarily hostile. Aristotle denies that an artisan can have virtue, i.e., the qualities pertaining to the fulfillment of social functions. Mechanics are, indeed, indispensable to the state, "but not all who are indispensable to the state are citizens." (And we must remember that the terms "citizen" and "state" have, in Aristotle, always an ethical bearing.) It was necessary that there should be some who should give themselves to that which is purely material, the industrial, in order that others might have the leisure to give themselves to the social and political, the ethical. We have, nominally, at least, given up the idea that a certain body of men are to be set aside for the doing of this necessary work; but we still think of this work, and of the relations pertaining to it, as if they were outside of the ethical realm and wholly in the natural. We admit, nay, at times we claim, that ethical rules are to be *applied* to this industrial sphere, but we think of it as an external application. That the economic and industrial life is *in itself* ethical, that it is to be made contributory to the realization of personality through the formation of a higher and more complete unity among men, this is what we do not recognize; but such is the meaning of the statement that democracy must become industrial.

I have used these illustrations simply for the sake of showing what I understand the conception of democracy to mean, and to show that the ordinary objections to democracy rest upon ideas which conceive of it after the type of an individualism of a numerical character; and have tried to suggest that democracy is an ethical idea, the idea of a personality, with truly infinite capacities, incorporate with every man. Democracy and the one, the ultimate, ethical ideal of humanity are to my mind synonyms. The idea of democracy, the ideas of liberty, equality, and fraternity, represent a society in which the distinction between the spiritual and the secular has ceased, and as in Greek theory, as in the Christian theory of the Kingdom of God, the church and the state, the divine and the human organization of society are one. But this, you will say, is idealism. In reply, I can but quote James Russell Lowell once more and say that "it is indeed idealism, but that I am one of those who believe that the real will never find an irremovable basis till it rests upon the ideal"; and add that the best test of any form of society is the ideal which it proposes for the forms of its life, and the degree in which it realizes this ideal.

Intelligence and Morals

The division of mankind into the two camps of the redeemed and the condemned had not needed philosophy to produce it. But the Greek cleavage of men into separate kinds on the basis of their position within or without the city-state was used to rationalize this harsh intolerance. The hierarchic organization of feudalism, within church and state, of those possessed of sacred rule and those whose sole excellence was obedience, did not require moral theory to generate or explain it. But it took philosophy to furnish the intellectual tools by which such chance episodes were emblazoned upon the cosmic heavens as a grandiose spiritual achievement. No; it is all too easy to explain bitter intolerance and desire for domination. Stubborn as they are, it was only when Greek moral theory had put underneath them the distinction between the irrational and the rational, between divine truth and good and corrupt and weak human appetite, that intolerance on system and earthly domination for the sake of eternal excellence were philosophically sanctioned. The health and welfare of the body and the securing for all of a sure and a prosperous livelihood were not matters for which medieval conditions fostered care in any case. But moral philosophy was prevailed upon to damn the body on principle, and to relegate to insignificance as merely mundane and temporal the problem of a just industrial order. Circumstances of the times bore with sufficient hardness upon successful scientific investigation; but philosophy added the conviction that in any case truth is so supernal that it must be supernaturally revealed, and so important that it must be authoritatively imparted and enforced. Intelligence was diverted from the critical consideration of the natural sources and social consequences of better and worse into the channel of metaphysical subtleties and systems, acceptance of which was made essential to participation in the social order and in rational excellence. Philosophy bound the once erect form of human endeavor and progress to the chariot wheels of cosmology and theology.

Since the Renaissance, moral philosophy has repeatedly reverted to the Greek ideal of natural excellence realized in social life, under the fostering care of intelligence in action. The return, however, has taken place under the influence of democratic polity, commercial expansion

[First published as *Ethics* (New York: Columbia University Press, 1908). Revised and reprinted in *The Influence of Darwin on Philosophy* (New York: Henry Holt and Co., 1910); reprinted in *The Middle Works*, Vol. 4.]

and scientific reorganization. It has been a liberation more than a reversion. This combined return and emancipation, having transformed our practice of life in the last four centuries, will not be content till it has written itself clear in our theory of that practice. Whether the consequent revolution in moral philosophy be termed pragmatism or be given the happier title of the applied and experimental habit of mind is of little account. What is of moment is that intelligence has descended from its lonely isolation at the remote edge of things, whence it operated as unmoved mover and ultimate good, to take its seat in the moving affairs of men. Theory may therefore become responsible to the practices that have generated it; the good be connected with nature, but with nature naturally, not metaphysically, conceived, and social life be cherished in behalf of its own immediate possibilities, not on the ground of its remote connections with a cosmic reason and an absolute end.

There is a notion, more familiar than correct, that Greek thought sacrificed the individual to the state. None has ever known better than the Greek that the individual comes to himself and to his own only in association with others. But Greek thought subjected, as we have seen, both state and individual to an external cosmic order; and thereby it inevitably restricted the free use in doubt, inquiry and experimentation, of the human intelligence. The *anima libera*, the free mind of the sixteenth century, of Galileo and his successors, was the counterpart of the disintegration of cosmology and its animistic teleology. The lecturer on political economy reminded us that his subject began, in the Middle Ages, as a branch of ethics, though, as he hastened to show, it soon got into better association. Well, the same company was once kept by all the sciences, mathematical and physical as well as social. According to all accounts it was the integrity of the number one and the rectitude of the square that attracted the attention of Pythagoras to arithmetic and geometry as promising fields of study. Astronomy was the projected picture book of a cosmic object lesson in morals, Dante's transcript of which is none the less literal because poetic. If physics alone remained outside the moral fold, while noble essences redeemed chemistry, occult forces blessed physiology, and the immaterial soul exalted psychology, physics is the exception that proves the rule: matter was so inherently immoral that no high-minded science would demean itself by contact with it.

If we do not join with many in lamenting the stripping from nature of those idealistic properties in which animism survived, if we do not mourn the secession of the sciences from ethics, it is because the abandonment by intelligence of a fixed and static moral end was the necessary precondition of a free and progressive science of both things and morals; because the emancipation of the sciences from ready-made, remote and abstract values was necessary to make the sciences available for creating and maintaining more and specific values here and now. The divine comedy of modern medicine and hygiene is one of the human epics yet to be written; but when composed it may prove no unworthy companion of the medieval epic of other-worldly beatific visions. The great ideas of the eighteenth century, that expansive epoch of moral perception which ranks in illumination and fervor along with classic Greek thought, the great ideas of the indefinitely continuous progress of humanity and of the power and significance of freed intelligence, were borne by a single mother—experimental inquiry.

The growth of industry and commerce is at once cause and effect of the growth in science. Democritus and other ancients conceived the mechanical theory of the universe. The notion was not only blank and repellent, because it ignored the rich social material which Plato and Aristotle had organized into their rival idealistic views; but it was scientifically sterile, a piece of dialectics. Contempt for machines as the accoutrements of despised mechanics kept the mechanical conception aloof from these specific and controllable experiences which alone could fructify it. This conception, then, like the idealistic, was translated into a speculative cosmology and thrown like a vast net around the universe at large, as if to keep it from coming to pieces. It is from respect for the lever, the pulley and the screw that modern experimental and mathematical mechanics derives itself. Motion, traced through the workings of a machine, was followed out into natural events and studied just as motion, not as a poor yet necessary device for realizing final causes. So studied, it was found to be available for new machines and new applications, which in creating new ends also promoted new wants, and thereby stimulated new activities, new discoveries and new inventions. The recognition that natural energy can be systematically applied, through experimental observation, to the satisfaction and multiplication of concrete wants is doubtless the greatest single discovery ever imported into the life of man—save perhaps the discovery of language. Science, borrowing from industry, repaid the debt with interest, and has made the control of natural forces for the aims of life so inevitable that for the first time man is relieved from overhanging fear, with its wolflike scramble to possess and accumulate, and is freed to consider the more gracious question of securing to all an ample and liberal life. The industrial life had been condemned by Greek exaltation of abstract thought and by Greek contempt for labor as representing the brute struggle of carnal appetite for its own satiety. The industrial movement, offspring of science, restored it to its central position in morals. When Adam Smith made economic activity the moving spring of man's unremitting effort, from the cradle to the grave, to better his own lot, he recorded this change. And when he made sympathy the central spring in man's conscious moral endeavor, he reported the effect which the increasing intercourse of men, due primarily to commerce, had in breaking down suspicion and jealousy and in liberating man's kindlier impulses.

Democracy, the crucial expression of modern life, is not so much an addition to the scientific and industrial tendencies as it is the perception of their social or spiritual meaning. Democracy is an absurdity where faith in the individual as individual is impossible; and this faith is impossible when intelligence is regarded as a cosmic power, not an adjustment and application of individual tendencies. It is also impossible when appetites and desires are conceived to be the dominant factor in the constitution of most men's characters, and when appetite and desire are conceived to be manifestations of the disorderly and unruly principle of nature. To put the intellectual centre of gravity in the objective cosmos, outside of men's own experiments and tests, and then to invite the application of individual intelligence to the determination of society is to invite chaos. To hold that want is mere negative flux and hence requires external fixation by reason, and then to invite the wants to give free play to themselves in social construction and intercourse is to call down anarchy. Democracy is estimable only through the changed conception of intelligence, that forms modern science, and of want, that forms modern industry. It is essentially a changed psychology. The substitution, for *a priori* truth and deduction, of fluent doubt and inquiry meant trust in human nature in the concrete; in individual honesty, curiosity and sympathy. The substitution of moving commerce for fixed custom meant a view of wants as the dynamics of social progress, not as the pathology of private greed. The nineteenth century indeed turned sour on that somewhat complacent optimism in which the eighteenth century rested: the ideas that the intelligent self-love of individuals would conduce to social cohesion, and competition among individuals usher in the kingdom of social welfare. But the conception of a social harmony of interests in which the achievement by each individual of his own freedom should contribute to a like perfecting of the powers of all, through a fraternally organized society, is the permanent contribution of the industrial movement to morals—even though so far it be but the contribution of a problem.

Intellectually speaking, the centuries since the fourteenth are the true middle ages. They mark the transitional period of mental habit, as the so-called medieval period represents the petrifaction, under changed outward conditions, of Greek ideas. The conscious articulation of genuinely modern tendencies has yet to come, and till it comes the ethic of our own life must remain undescribed. But the system of morals which has come nearest to the reflection of the movements of science, democracy and commerce, is doubtless the utilitarian. Scientific, after the modern mode, it certainly would be. Newton's influence dyes deep the moral thought of the eighteenth century. The arrangements of the solar system had been described in terms of a homogeneous matter and motion, worked by two opposed and compensating forces: all because a method of analysis, of generalization by analogy, and of mathematical deduction back to new empirical details had been followed. The imagination of the eighteenth century was a Newtonian imagination; and this no less in social than in physical matters. Hume proclaims that morals is about to become an experimental science. Just as, almost in our own day, Mill's interest in a method for social science led him to reformulate the logic of experimental inquiry, so all the great men of the Enlightenment were in search for the organon of morals which should repeat the physical triumphs of Newton. Bentham notes that physics has had its Bacon and Newton; that morals has had its Bacon in Helvétius, but still awaits its Newton; and he leaves us in no doubt that at the moment of writing he was ready, modestly but firmly, to fill the waiting niche with its missing figure.

The industrial movement furnished the concrete imagery for this ethical renovation. The utilitarians borrowed from Adam Smith the notion that through industrial exchange in a free society the individual pursuing his own good is led, under the guidance of the "invisible hand," to promote the general good more effectually than if he had set out to do it. This idea was dressed out in the atomistic psychology which Hartley built out from Locke—and was returned at usurious rates to later economists.

From the great French writers who had sought to justify and promote democratic individualism, came the conception that, since it is perverted political institutions which deprave individuals and bring them into hostility, nation against nation, class against class, individual against individual, the great political problem is such a reform of law and legislation, civil and criminal, of administration, and of education as will force the individual to find his own interests in pursuits conducing to the welfare of others.

Tremendously effective as a tool of criticism, operative in abolition and elimination, utilitarianism failed to measure up to the constructive needs of the time. Its theoretical equalization of the good of each with that of every other was practically perverted by its excessive interest in the middle and manufacturing classes. Its speculative defect of an atomistic psychology combined with this narrowness of vision to make light of the constructive work that needs to be done by the state, before all can have, otherwise than in name, an equal chance to count in the common good. Thus the age-long subordination of economics to politics was revenged in the submerging of both politics and ethics in a narrow theory of economic profit; and utilitarianism, in its orthodox descendants, proffered the disjointed pieces of a mechanism, with a monotonous reiteration that looked at aright they form a beautifully harmonious organism.

Prevision, and to some extent experience, of this failure, conjoined with differing social traditions and ambitions, evoked German idealism, the transcendental morals of Kant and his successors. German thought strove to preserve the traditions which bound culture to the past, while revising these traditions to render them capable of meeting novel conditions. It found weapons at hand in the conceptions borrowed by Roman law from Stoic philosophy, and in the conceptions by which protestant humanism had re-edited scholastic catholicism. Grotius had made the idea of natural law, natural right and obligation, the central idea of German morals, as thoroughly as Locke had made the individual desire for liberty and happiness the focus of English and then of French speculation. Materialized idealism is the happy monstrosity in which the popular demand for vivid imagery is most easily reconciled with the equally strong demand for supremacy of moral values; and the complete idealistic materialism of Stoicism has always given its ideas a practical influence out of all proportion to their theoretical vogue as a system. To the Protestant, that is the German, humanist, Natural Law, the bond of harmonious reason in nature, the spring of social intercourse among men, the inward light of individual conscience, united Cicero, St. Paul and Luther in blessed union; gave a rational, not superrational basis for morals, and provided room for social legislation which at the same time could easily be held back from too ruthless application to dominant class interests.

Kant saw the mass of empirical and hence irrelevant detail that had found refuge within this liberal and diffusive reason. He saw that the idea of reason could be made self-consistent only by stripping it naked of these empirical accretions. He then provided, in his critiques, a somewhat cumbrous moving van for transferring the resultant pure or naked reason out of nature and the objective world, and for locating it in new quarters, with a new stock of goods and new customers. The new quarters were particular subjects, individuals; the stock of goods were the forms of perception and the functions of thought by which empirical flux is woven into durable fabrics; the new customers were a society of individuals in which all are ends in themselves. There ought to be an injunc-

tion issued that Kant's saying about Hume's awakening of him should not
be quoted save in connection with his other saying that Rousseau brought
him to himself, in teaching him that the philosopher is of less account
than the laborer in the fields unless he contributes to human freedom.
But none the less, the new tenant, the universal reason, and the old
homestead, the empirical tumultuous individual, could not get on together. Reason became a mere voice which, having nothing in particular
to say, said Law, Duty, in general, leaving to the existing social order of
the Prussia of Frederick the Great the congenial task of declaring just
what was obligatory in the concrete. The marriage of freedom and authority was thus celebrated with the understanding that sentimental primacy went to the former and practical control to the latter.

The effort to force a universal reason that had been used to the broad
domains of the cosmos into the cramped confines of individuality conceived as merely "empirical," a highly particularized creature of sense,
could have but one result: an explosion. The products of that explosion
constitute the Post-Kantian philosophies. It was the work of Hegel to
attempt to fill in the empty reason of Kant with the concrete contents of
history. The voice sounded like the voice of Aristotle, Thomas of Aquino
and Spinoza translated into Swabian German; but the hands were as the
hands of Montesquieu, Herder, Condorcet and the rising historical school.
The outcome was the assertion that history is reason, and reason is
history: the actual is rational, the rational is the actual. It gave the pleasant appearance (which Hegel did not strenuously discourage) of being
specifically an idealization of the Prussian nation, and incidentally a
systematized apologetic for the universe at large. But in intellectual and
practical effect, it lifted the idea of process above that of fixed origins and
fixed ends, and presented the social and moral order, as well as the
intellectual, as a scene of becoming, and it located reason somewhere
within the struggles of life.

Unstable equilibrium, rapid fermentation and a succession of explosive
reports are thus the chief notes of modern ethics. Scepticism and tradition-
alism, empiricism and rationalism, crude naturalisms and all-embracing
idealisms, flourish side by side—all the more flourish, one suspects,
because side by side. Spencer exults because natural science reveals that
a rapid transit system of evolution is carrying us automatically to the goal
of perfect man in perfect society; and his English idealistic contemporary, Green, is so disturbed by the removal from nature of its moral
qualities, that he tries to show that this makes no difference, since nature
in any case is constituted and known through a spiritual principle which
is as permanent as nature is changing. An Amiel genteelly laments the
decadence of the inner life, while his neighbor Nietzsche brandishes in

rude ecstasy the banner of brute survival as a happy omen of the final victory of nobility of mind. The reasonable conclusion from such a scene is that there is taking place a transformation of attitude towards moral theory rather than mere propagation of varieties among theories. The classic theories all agreed in one regard. They all alike assumed the existence of *the* end, the *summum bonum,* the final goal; and of *the* separate moral force that moves to that goal. Moralists have disputed as to whether the end is an aggregate of pleasurable state of consciousness, enjoyment of the divine essence, acknowledgment of the law of duty, or conformity to environment. So they have disputed as to the path by which the final goal is to be reached: fear or benevolence? reverence for pure law or pity for others? self-love or altruism? But these very controversies implied that there was but the one end and the one means.

The transformation in attitude, to which I referred, is the growing belief that the proper business of intelligence is discrimination of multiple and present goods and of the varied immediate means of their realization; not search for the one remote aim. The progress of biology has accustomed our minds to the notion that intelligence is not an outside power presiding supremely but statically over the desires and efforts of man, but is a method of adjustment of capacities and conditions within specific situations. History, as the lecturer on that subject told us, has discovered itself in the idea of process. The genetic standpoint makes us aware that the systems of the past are neither fraudulent impostures nor absolute revelations; but are the products of political, economic and scientific conditions whose change carries with it change of theoretical formulations. The recognition that intelligence is properly an organ of adjustment in difficult situations makes us aware that past theories were of value so far as they helped carry to an issue the social perplexities from which they emerged. But the chief impact of the evolutionary method is upon the present. Theory having learned what it cannot do, is made responsible for the better performance of what needs to be done, and what only a broadly equipped intelligence can undertake: study of the conditions out of which come the obstacles and the resources of adequate life, and developing and testing the ideas that, as working hypotheses, may be used to diminish the causes of evil and to buttress and expand the sources of good. This program is indeed vague, but only unfamiliarity with it could lead one to the conclusion that it is less vague than the idea that there is a single moral ideal and a single moral motive force.

From this point of view there is no separate body of moral rules; no separate system of motive powers; no separate subject-matter of moral knowledge, and hence no such thing as an isolated ethical science. If the business of morals is not to speculate upon man's final end, and upon an ultimate standard of right, it is to utilize physiology, anthropology and psychology to discover all that can be discovered of man, his organic powers and propensities. If its business is not to search for the one separate moral motive, it is to converge all the instrumentalities of the social arts, of law, education, economics and political science upon the construction of intelligent methods of improving the common lot.

If we still wish to make our peace with the past, and to sum up the plural and changing goods of life in a single word, doubtless the term happiness is the one most apt. But we should again exchange free morals for sterile metaphysics, if we imagine that "happiness" is any less unique than the individuals who experience it; any less complex than the constitution of their capacities, or any less variable than the objects upon which their capacities are directed.

To many timid, albeit sincere, souls of an earlier century, the decay of the doctrine that all true and worthful science is knowledge of final causes seemed fraught with danger to science and to morals. The rival conception of a wide open universe, a universe without bounds in time or space, without final limits of origin or destiny, a universe with the lid off, was a menace. We now face in moral science a similar crisis and like opportunity, as well as share in a like dreadful suspense. The abolition of a fixed and final goal and causal force in nature did not, as matter of fact, render rational conviction less important or less attainable. It was accompanied by the provision of a technique of persistent and detailed inquiry in all special fields of fact, a technique which led to the detection of unsuspected forces and the revelation of undreamed of uses. In like fashion we may anticipate that the abolition of *the* final goal and *the* single motive power and *the* separate and infallible faculty in morals, will quicken inquiry into the diversity of specific goods of experience, fix attention upon their conditions and bring to light values now dim and obscure. The change may relieve men from responsibility for what they cannot do, but it will promote thoughtful consideration of what they may do and the definition of responsibility for what they do amiss because of failure to think straight and carefully. Absolute goods will fall into the background, but the question of making more sure and extensive the share of all men in natural and social goods will be urgent, a problem not to be escaped nor evaded. . . .

No, nature is not an unchangeable order, unwinding itself majestically from the reel of law under the control of deified forces. It is an indefinite congeries of changes. Laws are not governmental regulations which limit change, but are convenient formulations of selected portions of change followed through a longer or shorter period of time, and then registered in statistical forms that are amenable to mathematical manipulation. That this device of shorthand symbolization presages the subjection of man's intelligent effort to fixity of law and environment is interesting as a culture survival, but is not important for moral theory. Savage and child delight in creating bogeys from which, their origin and structure being conveniently concealed, interesting thrills and shudders may be had. Civilized man in the nineteenth century outdid these bugaboos in his image of a fixed universe hung on a cast-iron framework of fixed, necessary and universal laws. Knowledge of nature does not mean subjection to predestination, but insight into courses of change; an insight which is formulated in "laws," that is, methods of subsequent procedure.

Knowledge of the process and conditions of physical and social change through experimental science and genetic history has one result with a double name: increase of control and increase of responsibility; increase of power to direct natural change, and increase of responsibility for its equitable direction toward fuller good. Theory located within progressive practice instead of reigning statically supreme over it, means practice itself made responsible to intelligence; to intelligence which relentlessly scrutinizes the consequences of every practice, and which exacts liability by an equally relentless publicity. As long as morals occupies itself with mere ideals, forces and conditions as they are will be good enough for "practical" men, since they are then left free to their own devices in turning these to their own account. As long as moralists plume themselves upon possession of the domain of the categorical imperative with its bare precepts, men of executive habits will always be at their elbows to regulate the concrete social conditions through which the form of law gets its actual filling of specific injunctions. When freedom is conceived to be transcendental, the coercive restraint of immediate necessity will lay its harsh hand upon the mass of men.

In the end, men do what they can do. They refrain from doing what they cannot do. They do what their own specific powers in conjunction with the limitations and resources of the environment permit. The effective control of their powers is not through precepts, but through the regulation of their conditions. If this regulation is to be not merely physical or coercive, but moral, it must consist of the intelligent selection and determination of the environments in which we act; and in an intelligent exaction of responsibility for the use of men's powers. Theorists inquire after the "motive" to morality, to virtue and the good, under such circumstances. What then, one wonders, is their conception of the make-up of human nature and of its relation to virtue and to goodness? The pessimism that dictates such a question, if it be justified, precludes any consideration of morals.

The diversion of intelligence from discrimination of plural and concrete goods, from noting their conditions and obstacles, and from devising methods for holding men responsible for their concrete use of powers and conditions, has done more than brute love of power to establish inequality and injustice among men. It has done more, because it has confirmed with social sanctions the principle of feudal domination. All men require moral sanctions in their conduct: the consent of their kind. Not getting it otherwise, they go insane to feign it. No man ever lived with the exclusive approval of his own conscience. Hence the vacuum left in practical matters by the remote irrelevancy of transcendental morals has to be filled in somehow. It is filled in. It is filled in with class-codes, class-standards, class-approvals—with codes which recommend the practices and habits already current in a given circle, set, calling, profession, trade, industry, club or gang. These class-codes always lean back upon and support themselves by the professed ideal code. This latter meets them more than half-way. Being in its pretense a theory for regulating practice, it must demonstrate its practicability. It is uneasy in isolation, and travels hastily to meet with compromise and accommodation the actual situation in all its brute unrationality. Where the pressure is greatest—in the habitual practice of the political and economic chieftains—there it accommodates the most.

Class-codes of morals are sanctions, under the caption of ideals, of uncriticized customs; they are recommendations, under the head of duties, of what the members of the class are already most given to doing. If there are to obtain more equable and comprehensive principles of action, exacting a more impartial exercise of natural power and resource in the interests of a common good, members of a class must no longer rest content in responsibility to a class whose traditions constitute its conscience, but be made responsible to a society whose conscience is its free and effectively organized intelligence.

In such a conscience alone will the Socratic injunction to man to know himself be fulfilled.

Individuality, Equality
and Superiority

What do these words mean? Professors have one measure of superior ability; captains of industry another. One class esteems aptitude for learning academic subjects; the other class appraises in terms of power in execution. Suppose that investigators and artists were so socially dominant that they were effectively articulate. Should we not then employ quite other standards of measurement? . . .

There are as many modes of superiority and inferiority as there are consequences to be attained and works to be accomplished. And until society becomes static new modes of activity are continually developing, each of which permits and exacts its own specific inferiorities and superiorities. There is doubtless some degree of correlation between traits which promote superiority in more than one direction. But the idea of abstract, universal superiority and inferiority is an absurdity. The current loose use of these conceptions suggests overcompensation on the part of those who assume that they belong to a superior class. It appears like an attempt to escape from the limitations and incapacities which we all know, subconsciously at least, that we possess. . . .

The irony of the situation is that this course is usually taken in the name of aristocracy, even of intellectual aristocracy, and as part of an attack upon the tendencies of democracy to ignore individuality. It may be that the word democracy has become so intimately associated with a particular political order, that of general suffrage and elective officials, which does not work very satisfactorily, that it is impossible to recover its basic moral and ideal meaning. But the meaning remains whatever name is given it. It denotes faith in individuality, in uniquely distinctive qualities in each normal human being; faith in corresponding unique modes of activity that create new ends, with willing acceptance of the modifications of the established order entailed by the release of individualized capacities.

Democracy in this sense denotes, one may say, aristocracy carried to its limit. It is a claim that every human being as an individual may be the

[First published in *New Republic* 33 (1922). Republished in *Characters and Events,* ed. Joseph Ratner (New York: Henry Holt and Co., 1929), and in *Education Today,* ed. Joseph Ratner (New York: G. P. Putnam's Sons, 1940); reprinted in *The Middle Works,* Vol. 13.]

best for some particular purpose and hence be the most fitted to rule, to lead, in that specific respect. The habit of fixed and numerically limited classifications is the enemy alike of true aristocracy and true democracy. It is because our professed aristocrats surrender so gladly to the habit of quantitative or comparative classifications that it is easy to detect snobbery of greater or less refinement beneath their professed desire for a régime of distinction. For only the individual is ultimately distinctive; the rest is a matter of common qualities differing merely in degree. Even in the crudest pioneer democracy there was something more distinctive, more aristocratic, than in that smoothed-off communal worship of qualities belonging to certain classes which is characteristic of present day critics of democracy.

The most ardent of the early advocates of equality never fell into the stupidity of alleging that all persons are qualitatively alike. Rousseau was one of the first to insist upon natural differences, psychological and physical. It was his profound conviction of the intensity and scope of these differences which made him so insistent upon political, legal and, within certain limits, economic equality. Otherwise some form of native superior energy would result in the enslavement of the masses, adding artificial enfeeblement to their natural deficiencies, while corrupting those of superior ability by giving them an artificial mastery over others and a cruel, contemptuous disregard for their welfare.

In our own earlier history, John Adams is perhaps the chief proponent of the unavoidable necessity of recognizing the aristocratic principle in politics because of inequality of natural endowments. But Adams was a realist. He did not assume that superiority of gifts meant intellectual superiority or that aristocracy in practice means the rule of the mentally and morally superior. He saw that the native superiorities which were bound in any political system to find outlet and to warp institutions to their ends are of indefinitely many kinds—power, power to command and influence the action of others, being their only common divisor. In his own realistic words: "An aristocrat is any man who can command two votes, one besides his own." And this superior influence may be due, he points out, to virtue, talent or intrigue and debauchery; to loquacity or taciturnity, to frankness or reserve, to goodfellowship or fraud, violence and treachery, to deism or atheism. Powerful is as powerful does. Adams never fell into that mealy-mouthed sentimentalism of contemporary defenders of aristocracy who assume that native superiorities are all in the direction of talent and virtue, and inferiorities all in the opposite direction.

Thomas Jefferson is associated with the democratic school. But he writes to John Adams: "I agree with you that there is a natural aristocracy among men. . . . The natural aristocracy of virtue and talents is the most precious gift of nature. . . . That government is best which provides the most effectively for selection of these natural aristocrats into the offices of government." And he proceeds to state that the differences between Adams and himself concern the means which are best calculated to secure this result. Adams thought that some express and definite institution was necessary; Jefferson thought that such explicit recognition would encourage the "tinsel" aristocracy of wealth and birth at the expense of natural aristocracy; for the wealthy will manage to protect themselves anyway and need no artificial protection against the feebleness of the poor. Both agreed that equality is moral, a matter of justice socially secured, not of physical or psychological endowment.

No intelligent defender of democratic equality has ever believed anything else. Today he is not as sure as men were a century ago that any legal and political system can of itself prevent the untoward working of native differences of power. He sees very clearly that a régime of economic anarchy like the present overstimulates many of the least desirable forms of superior native power, and that the result overrides the legal and political bulwarks of moral equality. In consequence he sees that moral equality cannot be conceived on the basis of legal, political and economic arrangements. For all of these are bound to be classificatory; to be concerned with uniformities and statistical averages. Moral equality means incommensurability, the inapplicability of common and quantitative standards. It means intrinsic qualities which require unique opportunities and differential manifestation; superiority in finding a specific work to do, not in power for attaining ends common to a class of competitors, which is bound to result in putting a premium on mastery over others. Our best, almost our only, models of this kind of activity are found in art and science. There are indeed minor poets and painters and musicians. But the real standard of art is not comparative, but qualitative. Art is not greater and less, it is good or bad, sincere or spurious. Not many intellectual workers are called to be Aristotles or Newtons or Pasteurs or Einsteins. But every honest piece of inquiry is distinctive, individualized; it has its own incommensurable quality and performs its own unique service.

Upon reflection, however, it is apparent that there is something academic in confining the models of moral equality to art and intellectual pursuits. Direct personal relationships, the affections and services of human companionship are its most widespread and available manifestations. The snobbery of the snobbish, who call themselves aristocrats, is nowhere as evident as in their neglect of the superior gifts and attainments of the humble of the earth in these respects. No contact of this human sort is replaceable; with reference to it all are equal because all are incommensurable, infinite. Democracy will not be democracy until education makes it its chief concern to release distinctive aptitudes in art, thought and companionship. At present the intellectual obstacle in the way is the habit of classification and quantitative comparisons. Our pseudo-aristocrats with their flourishing of abstract and uniform superiority and inferiority are now the main defendants of a concept of classes which means only the mass divided into smaller portions. The democrat with his faith in moral equality is the representative of aristocracy made universal. His equality is that of distinction made universal.

Individuality in Our Day

Most attacks on the mechanistic character of science are caused by the survival of philosophies and religions formed when nature was the grim foe of man. The possibility of the present, and therefore its problem, is that through and by science, nature may become the friend and ally of man. I have rarely seen an attack on science as hostile to humanism which did not rest upon a conception of nature formed long before there was any science. That there is much at any time in environing nature which is indifferent and hostile to human values is obvious to any serious mind. When natural knowledge was hardly existent, control of nature was impossible. Without power of control, there was no recourse save to build places of refuge in which man could live in imagination, although not in fact. There is no need to deny the grace and beauty of some of these constructions. But when their imaginary character is once made apparent, it is futile to suppose that men can go on living and sustaining life by them. When they are appealed to for support, the possibilities of the present are not perceived, and its constructive potentialities remain unutilized.

In reading many of the literary appreciations of science, one would gather that until the rise of modern science, men had not been aware that living in nature entails death and renders fortune precarious and uncertain; "science" is even treated as if it were responsible for the revelation of the fact that nature is often a foe of human interests and goods. But the very nature of the creeds that men have entertained in the past and of the rites they have practiced is proof that men were overwhelmingly conscious of this fact. If they had not been, they would not have resorted to magic, miracles, myth and the consolations and compensations of another world and life. As long as these things were sincerely believed in, dualism, anti-naturalism, had a meaning, for the "other world" was then a reality. To surrender the belief and retain the dualism is temporarily possible for bewildered minds. It is a condition which it is impossible to maintain permanently. The alternative is to accept what science tells us of the world in which we live and to resolve to use the agencies it puts within our power to render nature more amenable to human desire and more contributory to human good. "Naturalism" is a word with all kinds

[First published as "Individuality in Our Day. The Sixth and Final Article in Professor Dewey's Series, 'Individualism, Old and New,'" in *New Republic* 62 (2 April 1930); reprinted in *The Later Works*, Vol. 5.]

of meanings. But a naturalism which perceives that man with his habits, institutions, desires, thoughts, aspirations, ideals and struggles, is within nature, an integral part of it, has the philosophical foundation and the practical inspiration for effort to employ nature as an ally of human ideals and goods such as no dualism can possibly provide.

There are those who welcome science provided it remain "pure"; they see that as a pursuit and contemplated object it is an addition to the enjoyed meaning of life. But they feel that its applications in mechanical inventions are the cause of many of the troubles of modern society. Undoubtedly these applications have brought new modes of unloveliness and suffering. I shall not attempt the impossible task of trying to strike a net balance of ills and enjoyments between the days before and after the practical use of science. The significant point is that application is still restricted. It touches our dealings with things but not with one another. We use scientific method in directing physical but not human energies. Consideration of the full application of science must accordingly be prophetic rather than a record of what has already taken place. Such prophecy is not however without foundation. Even as things are there is a movement in science which foreshadows, if its inherent promise be carried out, a more humane age. For it looks forward to a time when all individuals may share in the discoveries and thoughts of others, to the liberation and enrichment of their own experience.

No scientific inquirer can keep what he finds to himself or turn it to merely private account without losing his scientific standing. Everything discovered belongs to the community of workers. Every new idea and theory has to be submitted to this community for confirmation and test. There is an expanding community of cooperative effort and of truth. It is true enough that these traits are now limited to small groups having a somewhat technical activity. But the existence of such groups reveals a possibility of the present—one of the many possibilities that are a challenge to expansion, and not a ground for retreat and contraction.

Suppose that what now happens in limited circles were extended and generalized. Would the outcome be oppression or emancipation? Inquiry is a challenge, not a passive conformity; application is a means of growth, not of repression. The general adoption of the scientific attitude in human affairs would mean nothing less than a revolutionary change in morals, religion, politics and industry. The fact that we have limited its use so largely to technical matters is not a reproach to science, but to the human beings who use it for private ends and who strive to defeat its social application for fear of destructive effects upon their power and profit. A vision of a day in which the natural sciences and the technologies that flow from them are used as servants of a humane life constitutes the imagination that is relevant to our own time. A humanism that flees from science as an enemy denies the means by which a liberal humanism might become a reality.

The scientific attitude is experimental as well as intrinsically communicative. If it were generally applied, it would liberate us from the heavy burden imposed by dogmas and external standards. Experimental method is something other than the use of blow-pipes, retorts and reagents. It is the foe of every belief that permits habit and wont to dominate invention and discovery, and ready-made system to override verifiable fact. Constant revision is the work of experimental inquiry. By revision of knowledge and ideas, power to effect transformation is given us. This attitude, once incarnated in the individual mind, would find an operative outlet. If dogmas and institutions tremble when a new idea appears, this shiver is nothing to what would happen if the idea were armed with the means for the continuous discovery of new truth and the criticism of old belief. To "acquiesce" in science is dangerous only for those who would maintain affairs in the existing social order unchanged because of lazy habit or self-interest. For the scientific attitude demands faithfulness to whatever is discovered and steadfastness in adhering to new truth.

The "given" which science calls upon us to accept is not fixed; it is in process. A chemist does not study the elements in order to bow down before them; ability to produce transformations is the outcome. It is said, and truly, that we are now oppressed by the weight of science. But why? Some allowance has to be made, of course, for the time it takes to learn the uses of new means and to appropriate their potentialities. When these means are as radically new as is experimental science, the time required is correspondingly long. But aside from this fact, the multiplication of means and materials is an increase of opportunities and purposes. It marks a release of individuality for affections and deeds more congenial to its own nature. Even the derided bathtub has its individual uses; an individual is not perforce degraded because he has the chance to keep himself clean. The radio will make for standardization and regimentation only as long as individuals refuse to exercise the selective reaction that is theirs. The enemy is not material commodities, but the lack of the will to use them as instruments for achieving preferred possibilities. Imagine a society free from pecuniary domination, and it becomes self-evident that material commodities are invitations to individual taste and choice, and occasions for individual growth. If human beings are not strong and steadfast enough to accept the invitation and take advantage of the proffered occasion, let us put the blame where it belongs.

There is at least this much truth in economic determinism. Industry is not outside of human life, but within it. The genteel tradition shuts its eyes to this fact; emotionally and intellectually it pushes industry and its material phase out into a region remote from human values. To stop with mere emotional rejection and moral condemnation of industry and trade as materialistic is to leave them in this inhuman region where they operate as the instruments of those who employ them for private ends. Exclusion of this sort is an accomplice of the forces that keep things in the saddle. There is a subterranean partnership between those who employ the existing economic order for selfish pecuniary gain and those who turn their backs upon it in the interest of personal complacency, private dignity, and irresponsibility. . . .

The destructive effect of science upon beliefs long cherished and values once prized is, and quite naturally so, a great cause of dread of science and its applications in life. The law of inertia holds of the imagination and its loyalties as truly as of physical things. I do not suppose that it is possible to turn suddenly from these negative effects to possible positive and constructive ones. But as long as we refuse to make an effort to change the direction in which imagination looks at the world, as long as we remain unwilling to reexamine old standards and values, science will continue to wear its negative aspect. Take science (including its application to the machine) for what it is, and we shall begin to envisage it as a potential creator of new values and ends. We shall have an intimation, on a wide and generous scale, of the release, the increased initiative, independence and inventiveness, which science now brings in its own specialized fields to the individual scientist. It will be seen as a means of originality and individual variation. Even to those sciences which delight in calling themselves "pure," there is a significant lesson in the instinct that leads us to speak of Newton's and Einstein's law.

Because the free working of mind is one of the greatest joys open to man, the scientific attitude, incorporated in individual mind, is something which adds enormously to one's enjoyment of existence. The delights of thinking, of inquiry, are not widely enjoyed at the present time. But the few who experience them would hardly exchange them for other pleasures. Yet they are now as restricted in quality as they are in the number of those who share them. That is to say, as long as "scientific" thinking confines itself to technical fields, it lacks full scope and varied material. Its subject-matter is technical in the degree in which application in human life is shut out. The mind that is hampered by fear lest something old and precious be destroyed is the mind that experiences fear of science. He who has this fear cannot find reward and peace in the discovery of new truths and the projection of new ideals. He does not walk the earth freely, because he is obsessed by the need of protecting some private possession of belief and taste. For the love of private possessions is not confined to material goods.

It is a property of science to find its opportunities in problems, in questions. Since knowing is inquiring, perplexities and difficulties are the meat on which it thrives. The disparities and conflicts that give rise to problems are not something to be dreaded, something to be endured with whatever hardihood one can command; they are things to be grappled with. Each of us experiences these difficulties in the sphere of his personal relations, whether in his more immediate contacts or in the wider associations conventionally called "society." At present, personal frictions are one of the chief causes of suffering. I do not say all suffering would disappear with the incorporation of scientific method into individual disposition; but I do say that it is now immensely increased by our disinclination to treat these frictions as problems to be dealt with intellectually. The distress that comes from being driven in upon ourselves would be largely relieved; it would in part be converted into the enjoyment that attends the free working of mind, if we took them as occasions for the exercise of thought, as problems having an objective direction and outlet. . . .

Because science starts with questions and inquiries it is fatal to all social system-making and programs of fixed ends. In spite of the bankruptcy of past systems of belief, it is hard to surrender our faith in system and in some wholesale belief. We continually reason as if the difficulty were in the particular system that has failed and as if we were on the point of now finally hitting upon one that is true as all the others were false. The real trouble is with the attitude of dependence upon any of them. Scientific method would teach us to break up, to inquire definitely and with particularity, to seek solutions in the terms of concrete problems as they arise. It is not easy to imagine the difference which would follow from the shift of thought to discrimination and analysis. Wholesale creeds and all-inclusive ideals are impotent in the face of actual situations; for doing always means the doing of something in particular. They are worse than impotent. They conduce to blind and vague emotional states in which credulity is at home, and where action, following the lead of overpowering emotion, is easily manipulated by the self-seekers who have kept their heads and wits. Nothing would conduce more, for example, to the elimination of war than the substitution of specific analysis of its causes for the wholesale love of "liberty, humanity, justice and civilization."

All of these considerations would lead to the conclusion that depression of the individual is the individual's own liability, were it not for the time it takes for a new principle to make its way deeply into individual mind on a large scale. But as time goes on, the responsibility becomes an individual one. For individuality is inexpugnable and it is of its nature to assert itself. The first move in recovery of an integrated individual is accordingly with the individual himself. In whatever occupation he finds himself and whatever interest concerns him, he is himself and no other, and he lives in situations that are in some respect flexible and plastic.

We are given to thinking of society in large and vague ways. We should forget "society" and think of law, industry, religion, medicine, politics, art, education, philosophy—and think of them in the plural. For points of contact are not the same for any two persons, and hence the questions which the interests and occupations pose are never twice the same. There is no contact so immutable that it will not yield at some point. All these callings and concerns are the avenues through which the world acts upon us and we upon the world. There is no society at large, no business in general. Harmony with conditions is not a single and monotonous uniformity, but a diversified affair requiring individual attack.

Individuality is inexpugnable because it is a manner of distinctive sensitivity, selection, choice, response and utilization of conditions. For this reason, if for no other, it is impossible to develop integrated individuality by any all-embracing system or program. No individual can make the determination for anyone else; nor can he make it for himself all at once and forever. A native manner of selection gives direction and continuity, but definite expression is found in changing occasions and varied forms. The selective choice and use of conditions have to be continually made and remade. Since we live in a moving world and change with our interactions in it, every act produces a new perspective that demands a new exercise of preference. If, in the long run, an individual remains lost, it is because he has chosen irresponsibility; and if he remains wholly depressed it is because he has chosen the course of easy parasitism.

Acquiescence, in the sense of drifting, is not something to be achieved; it is something to be overcome, something that is "natural" in the sense of being easy. But it assumes a multitude of forms, and Rotarian applause for present conditions is only one of these forms. A different form of submission consists in abandoning the values of a new civilization for those of the past. To assume the uniform of some dead culture is only another means of regimentation. True integration is to be found in relevancy to the present, in active response to conditions as they present themselves, in the effort to make them over according to some consciously chosen possibility.

Individuality is at first spontaneous and unshaped; it is a potentiality, a capacity of development. Even so, it is a unique manner of acting in and with a world of objects and persons. It is not something complete in itself, like a closet in a house or a secret drawer in a desk, filled with treasures that are waiting to be bestowed on the world. Since individuality is a distinctive way of feeling the impacts of the world and of showing a preferential bias in response to these impacts, it develops into shape and form only through interaction with actual conditions; it is no more complete in itself than is a painter's tube of paint without relation to a canvas. The work of art is the truly individual thing; and it is the result of the interaction of paint and canvas through the medium of the artist's distinctive vision and power. In its determination, the potential individuality of the artist takes on visible and enduring form. The imposition of individuality as something made in advance always gives evidence of a mannerism, not of a manner. For the latter is something original and creative; something formed in the very process of creation of other things.

The future is always unpredictable. Ideals, including that of a new and effective individuality, must themselves be framed out of the possibilities of existing conditions, even if these be the conditions that constitute a corporate and industrial age. The ideals take shape and gain a content as they operate in remaking conditions. We may, in order to have continuity of direction, plan a program of action in anticipation of occasions as they emerge. But a program of ends and ideals if kept apart from sensitive and flexible method becomes an encumbrance. For its hard and rigid character assumes a fixed world and a static individual; and neither of these things exists. It implies that we can prophesy the future—an attempt which terminates, as someone has said, in prophesying the past or in its reduplication.

The same Emerson who said that "society is everywhere in conspiracy against its members" also said, and in the same essay, "accept the place the divine providence has found for you, the society of your contemporaries, the connection of events." Now, when events are taken in disconnection and considered apart from the interactions due to the selecting individual, they conspire against individuality. So does society when it is accepted as something already fixed in institutions. But "the connection of events," and "the society of your contemporaries" as formed of moving and multiple associations, are the only means by which the possibilities of individuality can be realized.

Psychiatrists have shown how many disruptions and dissipations of the individual are due to his withdrawal from reality into a merely inner world. There are, however, many subtle forms of retreat, some of which are erected into systems of philosophy and are glorified in current literature. "It is in vain," said Emerson, "that we look for genius to reiterate its miracles in the old arts; it is its instinct to find beauty and holiness in

new and necessary facts, in the field and road-side, in the shop and mill."
To gain an integrated individuality, each of us needs to cultivate his own
garden. But there is no fence about this garden: it is no sharply marked-
off enclosure. Our garden is the world, in the angle at which it touches
our own manner of being. By accepting the corporate and industrial
world in which we live, and by thus fulfilling the pre-condition for
interaction with it, we, who are also parts of the moving present, create
ourselves as we create an unknown future.

Art and Civilization

The possibility of the occurrence of genuine communication is a broad problem . . . It is a fact that it takes place, but the nature of community of experience is one of the most serious problems of philosophy—so serious that some thinkers deny the fact. The existence of communication is so disparate to our physical separation from one another and to the inner mental lives of individuals that it is not surprising that supernatural force has been ascribed to language and that communication has been given sacramental value.

Moreover, events that are familiar and customary are those we are least likely to reflect upon; we take them for granted. They are also, because of their closeness to us, through gesture and pantomime, the most difficult to observe. Communication through speech, oral and written, is the familiar and constant feature of social life. We tend, accordingly, to regard it as just one phenomenon among others of what we must in any case accept without question. We pass over the fact that it is the foundation and source of all activities and relations that are distinctive of internal union of human beings with one another. A vast number of our contacts with one another are external and mechanical. There is a "field" in which they take place, a field defined and perpetuated by legal and political institutions. But the consciousness of this field does not enter our conjoint action as its integral and controlling force. Relations of nations to one another, relations of investors and laborers, of producers and consumers, are interactions that are only to a slight degree forms of communicative intercourse. There are interactions between the parties involved, but they are so external and partial that we undergo their consequences without integrating them into an experience.

We hear speech, but it is almost as if we were listening to a babel of tongues. Meaning and value do not come home to us. There is in such cases no communication and none of the result of community of experience that issues only when language in its full import breaks down physical isolation and external contact. Art is a more universal mode of language than is the speech that exists in a multitude of mutually unintelligible forms. The language of art has to be acquired. But the language of art is not affected by the accidents of history that mark off different modes of human speech. The power of music in particular to merge different individualities in a common surrender, loyalty and inspiration, a power

[From *Art as Experience* (New York: Minton, Balch & Co., 1934); reprinted in *The Later Works*, Vol. 10.]

utilized in religion and in warfare alike, testifies to the relative universality of the language of art. The differences between English, French
and German speech create barriers that are submerged when art speaks.

Philosophically speaking, the problem with which we are confronted is
the relation of the discrete and the continuous. Both of them are stubborn facts and yet they have to meet and blend in any human association
that rises above the level of brute intercourse. In order to justify continuity, historians have often resorted to a falsely named "genetic" method,
wherein there is no genuine genesis, because everything is resolved into
what went before. But Egyptian civilization and art were not just a preparation for Greek, nor were Greek thought and art mere reedited versions
of the civilizations from which they so freely borrowed. Each culture has
its own individuality and has a pattern that binds its parts together.

Nevertheless, when the art of another culture enters into attitudes that
determine our experience genuine continuity is effected. Our own experience does not thereby lose its individuality but it takes unto itself and
weds elements that expand its significance. A community and continuity
that do not exist physically are created. The attempt to establish continuity by methods which resolve one set of events and one of institutions
into those which preceded it in time is doomed to defeat. Only an expansion of experience that absorbs into itself the values experienced because
of life-attitudes, other than those resulting from our own human environment, dissolves the effect of discontinuity.

The problem in question is not unlike that we daily undergo in the
effort to understand another person with whom we habitually associate.
All friendship is a solution of the problem. Friendship and intimate
affection are not the result of information about another person even
though knowledge may further their formation. But it does so only as it
becomes an integral part of sympathy through the imagination. It is when
the desires and aims, the interests and modes of response of another
become an expansion of our own being that we understand him. We learn
to see with his eyes, hear with his ears, and their results give true
instruction, for they are built into our own structure. I find that even the
dictionary avoids defining the term "civilization." It defines civilization as
the state of being civilized and "civilized" as "being in a state of civilization." However, the verb "to civilize" is defined as "to instruct in the arts
of life and thus to raise in the scale of civilization." Instruction in the
arts of life is something other than conveying information about them. It
is a matter of communication and participation in values of life by means
of the imagination, and works of art are the most intimate and energetic
means of aiding individuals to share in the arts of living. Civilization is
uncivil because human beings are divided into non-communicating sects,
races, nations, classes and cliques.

... It is hardly enough to say that the absence of obvious organic connection of the arts with other forms of culture is explained by the complexity of modern life, by its many specializations, and by the simultaneous existence of many diverse centres of culture in different nations that exchange their products but that do not form parts of an inclusive social whole. These things are real enough, and their effect upon the status of art in relation to civilization may be readily discovered. But the significant fact is widespread disruption.

... Two forces have been injected that are distinctly late in origin and that constitute the "modern" in the present epoch. These two forces are natural science and its application in industry and commerce through machinery and the use of non-human modes of energy. In consequence, the question of the place and role of art in contemporary civilization demands notice of its relations to science and to the social consequences of machine industry. The isolation of art that now exists is not to be viewed as an isolated phenomenon. It is one manifestation of the incoherence of our civilization produced by new forces, so new that the attitudes belonging to them and the consequences issuing from them have not been incorporated and digested into integral elements of experience. ...

The fact that science tends to show that man is a part of nature has an effect that is favorable rather than unfavorable to art when its intrinsic significance is realized and when its meaning is no longer interpreted by contrast with beliefs that come to us from the past. For the closer man is brought to the physical world, the clearer it becomes that his impulsions and ideas are enacted by nature within him. Humanity in its vital operations has always acted upon this principle. Science gives this action intellectual support. The sense of relation between nature and man in some form has always been the actuating spirit of art.

Moreover, resistance and conflict have always been factors in generating art; and they are, as we have seen, a necessary part of artistic form. Neither a world wholly obdurate and sullen in the face of man nor one so congenial to his wishes that it gratifies all desires is a world in which art can arise. The fairy tales that relate situations of this sort would cease to please if they ceased to be fairy tales. Friction is as necessary to generate esthetic energy as it is to supply the energy that drives machinery. When older beliefs have lost their grip on imagination—and their hold was always there rather than upon reason—the disclosure by science of the resistance that environment offers to man will furnish new materials for fine art. Even now we owe to science a liberation of the human spirit. It has aroused a more avid curiosity, and has greatly quickened in a few at least alertness of observation with respect to things of whose existence we were not before even aware. Scientific method tends to generate a

respect for experience, and even though this new reverence is still confined to the few, it contains the promise of a new kind of experiences that
will demand expression. . . .

So far, the effect of science as far as painting, poetry, and the novel are
concerned, has been to diversify their materials and forms rather than to
create an organic synthesis. I doubt if there were at any time any large
number of persons who "saw life steadily and saw it whole." And, at the
very worst, it is something to have been freed from syntheses of the
imagination that went contrary to the grain of things. Possession of a
quickened sense of the value for esthetic experience of a multitude of
things formerly shut out, is some compensation amid the miscellany of
present objects of art. The bathing beaches, street corners, flowers and
fruits, babies and bankers of contemporary painting are after all something more than mere diffuse and disconnected objects. For they are the
fruits of a new vision. . . .

The most direct and pervasive presence of science in present civilization is found in its applications in industry. Here we find a more serious
problem regarding the relation of art to present civilization and its outlook than in the case of science itself. The divorce of useful and fine art
signifies even more than does the departure of science from the traditions of the past. The difference between them was not instituted in
modern times. It goes as far back as the Greeks when the useful arts
were carried on by slaves and "base mechanics" and shared in the low
esteem in which the latter were held. Architects, builders, sculptors,
painters, musical performers were artisans. Only those who worked in
the medium of words were esteemed artists, since their activities did not
involve the use of hands, tools and physical materials. But mass production by mechanical means has given the old separation between the
useful and fine a decidedly new turn. The split is reenforced by the
greater importance that now attaches to industry and trade in the whole
organization of society. . . .

The labor and employment problem of which we are so acutely aware
cannot be solved by mere changes in wage, hours of work and sanitary
conditions. No permanent solution is possible save in a radical social
alteration, which effects the degree and kind of participation the worker
has in the production and social disposition of the wares he produces.
Only such a change will seriously modify the content of experience into
which creation of objects made for use enters. And this modification of
the nature of experience is the finally determining element in the esthetic quality of the experience of things produced. The idea that the basic
problem can be solved merely by increase of hours of leisure is absurd.
Such an idea merely retains the old dualistic division between labor and
leisure.

The important matter is a change that will reduce the force of external pressure and will increase that of a sense of freedom and personal interest in the operations of production. Oligarchical control from the outside of the processes and the products of work is the chief force in preventing the worker from having that intimate interest in what he does and makes that is an essential prerequisite of esthetic satisfaction. There is nothing in the nature of machine production *per se* that is an insuperable obstacle in the way of workers' consciousness of the meaning of what they do and enjoyment of the satisfactions of companionship and of useful work well done. The psychological conditions resulting from private control of the labor of other men for the sake of private gain, rather than any fixed psychological or economic law, are the forces that suppress and limit esthetic quality in the experience that accompanies processes of production.

As long as art is the beauty parlor of civilization, neither art nor civilization is secure. Why is the architecture of our large cities so unworthy of a fine civilization? It is not from lack of materials nor from lack of technical capacity. And yet it is not merely slums but the apartments of the well-to-do that are esthetically repellent, because they are so destitute of imagination. Their character is determined by an economic system in which land is used—and kept out of use—for the sake of gain, because of profit derived from rental and sale. Until land is freed from this economic burden, beautiful buildings may occasionally be erected, but there is little hope for the rise of general architectural construction worthy of a noble civilization. The restriction placed on building affects indirectly a large number of allied arts, while the social forces that affect the buildings in which we subsist and wherein we do our work operate upon all the arts.

Auguste Comte said that the great problem of our time is the organization of the proletariat into the social system. The remark is even truer now than when it was made. The task is impossible of achievement by any revolution that stops short of affecting the imagination and emotions of man. The values that lead to production and intelligent enjoyment of art have to be incorporated into the system of social relationships. It seems to me that much of the discussion of proletarian art is aside from the point because it confuses the personal and deliberate intent of an artist with the place and operation of art in society. What is true is that art itself is not secure under modern conditions until the mass of men and women who do the useful work of the world have the opportunity to be free in conducting the processes of production and are richly endowed in capacity for enjoying the fruits of collective work. That the material for art should be drawn from all sources whatever and that the products of art should be accessible to all is a demand by the side of which the personal political intent of the artist is insignificant. . . .

The theories that attribute direct moral effect and intent to art fail because they do not take account of the collective civilization that is the context in which works of art are produced and enjoyed. I would not say that they tend to treat works of art as a kind of sublimated Aesop's fables. But they all tend to extract particular works, regarded as especially edifying, from their milieu and to think of the moral function of art in terms of a strictly personal relation between the selected works and a particular individual. Their whole conception of morals is so individualistic that they miss a sense of the *way* in which art exercises its humane function.

Matthew Arnold's dictum that "poetry is criticism of life" is a case in point. It suggests to the reader a moral intent on the part of the poet and a moral judgment on the part of the reader. It fails to see or at all events to state *how* poetry is a criticism of life; namely, not directly, but by disclosure, through imaginative vision addressed to imaginative experience (not to set judgment) of possibility that contrast with actual conditions. A sense of possibilities that are unrealized and that might be realized are when they are put in contrast with actual conditions, the most penetrating "criticism" of the latter that can be made. It is by a sense of possibilities opening before us that we become aware of constrictions that hem us in and of burdens that oppress.

Mr. Garrod, a follower of Matthew Arnold in more senses than one, has wittily said that what we resent in didactic poetry is not that it teaches, but that it does not teach, its incompetency. He added words to the effect that poetry teaches as friends and life teach, by being, and not by express intent. He says in another place, "Poetical values are, after all, values in a human life. You cannot mark them off from other values, as though the nature of man were built in bulkheads." I do not think that what Keats has said in one of his letters can be surpassed as to the way in which poetry acts. He asks what would be the result if every man spun from his imaginative experience "an airy Citadel" like the web the spider spins, "filling the air with a beautiful circuiting." For, he says, "man should not dispute or assert, but whisper results to his neighbour, and thus, by every germ of spirit sucking the sap from mould ethereal, every human being might become great, and Humanity instead of being a wide heath of Furze and Briars with here and there a remote Pine or Oak, would become a grand democracy of Forest Trees!"

It is by way of communication that art becomes the incomparable organ of instruction, but the way is so remote from that usually associated with the idea of education, it is a way that lifts art so far above what we are accustomed to think of as instruction, that we are repelled by any suggestion of teaching and learning on connection with art. But our revolt is in fact a reflection upon education that proceeds by methods so literal as to exclude the imagination and one not touching the desires and emotions of men. Shelley said, "The imagination is the great instrument of moral good, and poetry administers to the effect by acting upon the cause." Hence it is, he goes on to say, "a poet would do ill to embody his own conceptions of right and wrong, which are usually those of his own time and place, in his poetical creations. . . . By the assumption of this inferior office . . . he would resign participation in the cause"—the imagination. It is the lesser poets who "have frequently affected a moral aim, and the effect of their poetry is diminished in exact proportion as they compel us to advert to this purpose." But the power of imaginative projection is so great that he calls poets "the founders of civil society."

The problem of the relation of art and morals is too often treated as if the problem existed only on the side of art. It is virtually assumed that morals are satisfactory in idea if not in fact, and that the only question is whether and in what ways art should conform to a moral system already developed. But Shelley's statement goes to the heart of the matter. Imagination is the chief instrument of the good. It is more or less a commonplace to say that a person's ideas and treatment of his fellows are dependent upon his power to put himself imaginatively in their place. But the primacy of the imagination extends far beyond the scope of direct personal relationships. Except where "ideal" is used in conventional deference or as a name for a sentimental reverie, the ideal factors in every moral outlook and human loyalty are imaginative. The historic alliance of religion and art has its roots in this common quality. Hence it is that art is more moral than moralities. For the latter either are, or tend to become, consecrations of the *status quo*, reflections of custom, reenforcements of the established order. The moral prophets of humanity have always been poets even though they spoke in free verse or by parable. Uniformly, however, their vision of possibilities has soon been converted into a proclamation of facts that already exist and hardened into semipolitical institutions. Their imaginative presentation of ideals that should command thought and desire have been treated as rules of policy. Art has been the means of keeping alive the sense of purposes that outrun evidence and of meanings that transcend indurated habit.

Morals are assigned a special compartment in theory and practice because they reflect the divisions embodied in economic and political institutions. Wherever social divisions and barriers exist, practices and ideas that correspond to them fix metes and bounds, so that liberal action is placed under restraint. Creative intelligence is looked upon with distrust; the innovations that are the essence of individuality are feared, and generous impulse is put under bonds not to disturb the peace. Were art an acknowledged power in human association and not treated as the pleasuring of an idle moment or as a means of ostentatious display, and were morals understood to be identical with every aspect of value that is shared in experience, the "problem" of the relation of art and morals would not exist.

The idea and the practice of morality are saturated with conceptions that stem from praise and blame, reward and punishment. Mankind is divided into sheep and goats, the vicious and virtuous, the law-abiding and criminal, the good and bad. To be beyond good and evil is an impossibility for man, and yet as long as the good signifies only that which is lauded and rewarded, and the evil that which is currently condemned or outlawed, the ideal factors of morality are always and everywhere beyond good and evil. Because art is wholly innocent of ideas derived from praise and blame, it is looked upon with the eye of suspicion by the guardians of custom, or only the art that is itself so old and "classic" as to receive conventional praise is grudgingly admitted, provided, as with, say, the case of Shakespeare, signs of regard for conventional morality can be ingeniously extracted from his work. Yet this indifference to praise and blame because of preoccupation with imaginative experience constitutes the heart of the moral potency of art. From it proceeds the liberating and uniting power of art.

Shelley said, "The great secret of morals is love, or *a going out of our nature* and the identification of ourselves with the beautiful which exists in thought, action, or person, not our own. A man to be greatly good must imagine intensely and comprehensively." What is true of the individual is true of the whole system of morals in thought and action. While perception of the union of the possible with the actual in a work of art is itself a great good, the good does not terminate with the immediate and particular occasion in which it is had. The union that is presented in perception persists in the remaking of impulsion and thought. The first intimations of wide and large redirections of desire and purpose are of necessity imaginative. Art is a mode of prediction not found in charts and statistics, and it insinuates possibilities of human relations not to be found in rule and precept, admonition and administration.

But Art, wherein man speaks in no wise to man,
Only to mankind—Art may tell a truth
Obliquely, do the deed shall breed the thought.

EDUCATION FOR SOCIAL CHANGE

Ethical Principles Underlying Education

Apart from the thought of participation in social life the school has no end nor aim. As long as we confine ourselves to the school as an isolated institution we have no final directing ethical principles, because we have no object or ideal. But it is said the end of education may be stated in purely individual terms. For example, it is said to be the harmonious development of all the powers of the individual. Here we have no apparent reference to social life or membership, and yet it is argued we have an adequate and thoroughgoing definition of what the goal of education is. But if this definition is taken independently of social relationship we shall find that we have no standard or criterion for telling what is meant by any one of the terms concerned. We do not know what a power is; we do not know what development is; we do not know what harmony is; a power is a power with reference to the use to which it is put, the function it has to serve. There is nothing in the make-up of the human being, taken in an isolated way, which furnishes controlling ends and serves to mark out powers. If we leave out the aim supplied from social life we have nothing but the old "faculty psychology" to fall back upon to tell what is meant by power in general or what the specific powers are. The idea reduces itself to enumerating a lot of faculties like perception, memory, reasoning, etc., and then stating that each one of these powers needs to be developed. But this statement is barren and formal. It reduces training to an empty gymnastic.

Acute powers of observation and memory might be developed by studying Chinese characters; acuteness in reasoning might be got by discussion of the scholastic subtleties of the Middle Ages. The simple fact is that there is no isolated faculty of observation, or memory, or reasoning any more than there is an original faculty of blacksmithing, carpentering, or steam engineering. These faculties simply mean that particular impulses and habits have been co-ordinated and framed with reference to accomplishing certain definite kinds of work. Precisely the same thing holds of the so-called mental faculties. They are not powers in themselves, but are such only with reference to the ends to which they are put,

[First published in the *Third Yearbook of the National Herbart Society* (Chicago: The Society, 1987); reprinted in *The Early Works*, Vol. 5.]

the services which they have to perform. Hence they cannot be located nor discussed as powers on a theoretical, but only on a practical basis. We need to know the social situations with reference to which the individual will have to use ability to observe, recollect, imagine, and reason before we get any intelligent and concrete basis for telling what a training of mental powers actually means either in its general principles or in its working details. . . .

We may apply this conception of the school as a social community which reflects and organizes in typical form the fundamental principles of all community life, to both the methods and the subject-matter of instruction.

As to methods, this principle when applied means that the emphasis must be upon construction and giving out, rather than upon absorption and mere learning. We fail to recognize how essentially individualistic the latter methods are, and how unconsciously, yet certainly and effectively, they react into the child's ways of judging and of acting. Imagine forty children all engaged in reading the same books, and in preparing and reciting the same lessons day after day. Suppose that this constitutes by far the larger part of their work, and that they are continually judged from the standpoint of what they are able to take in in a study hour, and to reproduce in a recitation hour. There is next to no opportunity here for any social or moral division of labor. There is no opportunity for each child to work out something specifically his own, which he may contribute to the common stock, while he, in turn, participates in the productions of others. All are set to do exactly the same work and turn out the same results. The social spirit is not cultivated—in fact, in so far as this method gets in its work, it gradually atrophies for lack of use. It is easy to see, from the intellectual side, that one reason why reading aloud in school is as poor as it is is that the real motive for the use of language— the desire to communicate and to learn—is not utilized. The child knows perfectly well that the teacher and all his fellow pupils have exactly the same facts and ideas before them that he has; he is not giving them anything at all new. But it may be questioned whether the moral lack is not as great as the intellectual. The child is born with a natural desire to give out, to do, and that means to serve. When this tendency is not made use of, when conditions are such that other motives are substituted, the reaction against the social spirit is much larger than we have any idea of—especially when the burden of the work, week after week, and year after year, falls upon this side.

But lack of cultivation of the social spirit is not all. Positively individualistic motives and standards are inculcated. Some stimulus must be found to keep the child at his studies. At the best this will be his affection for his teacher, together with a feeling that in doing this he is not violating school rules, and thus is negatively, if not positively, contributing to the good of the school. I have nothing to say against these motives as far as they go, but they are inadequate. The relation between the piece of work to be done and affection for a third person is external, not intrinsic. It is therefore liable to break down whenever the external conditions are changed. Moreover this attachment to a particular person, while in a way social, may become so isolated and exclusive as to be positively selfish in quality. In any case, it is necessary that the child should gradually grow out of this relatively external motive, into an appreciation of the social value of what he has to do for its own sake, and because of its relations to life as a whole, not as pinned down to two or three people.

But unfortunately the motive is not always at this relative best, while it is always mixed with lower motives which are distinctly individualistic. Fear is a motive which is almost sure to enter in—not necessarily physical fear, or of punishment, but fear of losing the approbation of others; fear of failure so extreme and sensitive as to be morbid. On the other side, emulation and rivalry enter in. Just because all are doing the same work, and are judged (both in recitation and in examination, with reference to grading and to promotion) not from the standpoint of their motives or the ends which they are trying to reach, the feeling of superiority is unduly appealed to. The children are judged with reference to their capacity to present the same external set of facts and ideas. As a consequence they must be placed in the hierarchy on the basis of this purely objective standard. The weaker gradually lose their sense of capacity, and accept a position of continuous and persistent inferiority. The effect of this upon both self-respect and respect for work need not be dwelt upon. The stronger grow to glory, not in their strength, but in the fact that they are stronger. The child is prematurely launched into the region of individualistic competition, and this in a direction where competition is least applicable, viz., in intellectual and spiritual matters, whose law is cooperation and participation. . . .

I take up the discussion first from the side of content. The contention is that a study is to be considered as bringing the child to realize the social scene of action; that when thus considered it gives a criterion for the selection of material and for the judgment of value. At present, as already suggested, we have three independent values set up: one of culture, another of information, and another of discipline. In reality these refer only to three phases of social interpretation. Information is genuine or educative only in so far as it effects definite images and conceptions of material placed in social life. Discipline is genuine and educative only as it represents a reaction of the information into the individual's own powers so that he can bring them under control for social ends. Culture, if it is to be genuine and educative, and not an external polish and factitious varnish, represents the vital union of information and discipline. It designates the socialization of the individual in his whole outlook upon life and mode of dealing with it.

This abstract point may be illustrated briefly by reference to a few of the school studies. . . .

. . . History is vital or dead to the child according as it is or is not presented from the sociological standpoint. When treated simply as a record of what has passed and gone, it must be mechanical because the past, as the past, is remote. It no longer has existence and simply as past there is no motive for attending to it. The ethical value of history teaching will be measured by the extent to which it is treated as a matter of analysis of existing social relations—that is to say as affording insight into what makes up the structure and working of society.

This relation of history to comprehension of existing social forces is apparent whether we take it from the standpoint of social order or from that of social progress. Existing social structure is exceedingly complex. It is practically impossible for the child to attack it *en masse* and get any definite mental image of it. But type phases of historical development may be selected which will exhibit, as through a telescope, the essential constituents of the existing order. Greece, for example, represents what art and the growing power of individual expression stand for; Rome exhibits the political elements and determining forces of political life on a tremendous scale. Or, as these civilizations are themselves relatively complex, a study of still simpler forms of hunting, nomadic and agricultural life in the beginnings of civilization; a study of the effects of the introduction of iron, iron tools, and so forth, serves to reduce the existing complexity to its simple elements.

One reason historical teaching is usually not more effective is the fact that the student is set to acquire information in such a way that no epochs or factors stand out to his mind as typical; everything is reduced to the same dead level. The only way of securing the necessary perspective is by relating the past to the present, as if the past were a projected present in which all the elements are enlarged.

The principle of contrast is as important as that of similarity. Because the present life is so close to us, touching us at every point, we cannot get away from it to see it as it really is. Nothing stands out clearly or sharply as characteristic. In the study of past periods attention necessarily attaches itself to striking differences. Thus the child gets a locus in imagination, through which he can remove himself from the present pressure of surrounding circumstance and define it.

History is equally available as teaching the *methods* of social progress. It is commonly stated that history must be studied from the standpoint of cause and effect. The truth of this statement depends upon its interpretation. Social life is so complex and the various parts of it are so organically related to each other and to the natural environment that it is impossible to say that this or that thing is cause of some other particular thing. But what the study of history can effect is to reveal the main instruments in the way of discoveries, inventions, new modes of life, etc., which have initiated the great epochs of social advance, and it can present to the child's consciousness type illustrations of the main lines in which social progress has been made most easily and effectively and can set before him what the chief difficulties and obstructions have been. Progress is always rhythmic in its nature, and from the side of growth as well as from that of status or order it is important that the epochs which are typical should be selected. This once more can be done only in so far as it is recognized that social forces in themselves are always the same—that the same kind of influences were at work 100 and 1000 years ago that are now—and treating the particular historical epochs as affording illustration of the way in which the fundamental forces work.

Everything depends then upon history being treated from a social standpoint, as manifesting the agencies which have influenced social development, and the typical institutions in which social life has expressed itself. The culture-epoch theory, while working in the right direction, has failed to recognize the importance of treating past periods with relation to the present—that is, as affording insight into the representative factors of its structure; it has treated these periods too much as if they had some meaning or value in themselves. The way in which the biographical method is handled illustrates the same point. It is often treated in such a way as to exclude from the child's consciousness (or at least not sufficiently to emphasize) the social forces and principles involved in the association of the masses of men. It is quite true that the child is interested easily in history from the biographical standpoint; but unless the hero is treated in relation to the community life behind which he both sums up and directs, there is danger that the history will reduce itself to a mere story. When this is done moral instruction reduces itself to drawing certain lessons from the life of the particular personalities concerned, instead of having widened and deepened the child's imaginative consciousness of the social relationships, ideals, and means involved in the world in which he lives.

There is some danger, I presume, in simply presenting the illustrations without more development, but I hope it will be remembered that I am not making these points for their own sake, but with reference to the general principle that when history is taught as a mode of understanding social life it has positive ethical import. What the normal child continuously needs is not so much isolated moral lessons instilling in him the importance of truthfulness and honesty, or the beneficent results that follow from some particular act of patriotism, etc. It is the formation of habits of social imagination and conception. I mean by this it is necessary that the child should be forming the habit of interpreting the special incidents that occur and the particular situations that present themselves in terms of the whole social life. The evils of the present industrial and political situation, on the ethical side, are not due so much to actual perverseness on the part of individuals concerned, nor in mere ignorance of what constitutes the ordinary virtues (such as honesty, industry, purity, etc.) as to inability to appreciate the social environment in which we live. It is tremendously complex and confused. Only a mind trained to grasp social situations, and to reduce them to their simpler and typical elements, can get sufficient hold on the realities of this life to see what sort of action, critical and constructive, it really demands. Most people are left at the mercy of tradition, impulse, or the appeals of those who have special and class interests to serve. In relation to this highly complicated social environment, training for citizenship is formal and nominal unless it develops the power of observation, analysis, and inference with respect to what makes up a social situation and the agencies through which it is modified. Because history rightly taught is the chief instrumentality for accomplishing this, it has an ultimate ethical value.

I have been speaking so far of the school curriculum on the side of its content. I now turn to that of form; understanding by this term, as already explained, a consciousness of the instruments and methods which are necessary to the control of social movements. Studies cannot be classified into form studies and content studies. Every study has both sides. That is to say, it deals both with the actual make-up of society, and is concerned with the tools or machinery by which society maintains itself. Language and literature best illustrate the impossibility of separation. Through the ideas contained in language, the continuity of the social structure is effected. From this standpoint the study of literature is a content study. But language is also distinctly a means, a tool. It not simply has social value in itself, but is a social instrument. However, in some studies one side or the other predominates very much, and in this sense we may speak of specifically form studies. As, for example, mathematics.

My illustrative proposition at this point is that mathematics does, or does not, accomplish its full ethical purpose according as it is presented, or not presented, as such a social tool. The prevailing divorce between information and character, between knowledge and social action, stalks upon the scene here. The moment mathematical study is severed from the place which it occupies with reference to use in social life, it becomes unduly abstract, even from the purely intellectual side. It is presented as a matter of technical relations and formulæ apart from any end or use. What the study of number suffers from in elementary education is the lack of motivation. Back of this and that and the other particular bad method is the radical mistake of treating number as if it were an end in itself instead of as a means of accomplishing some end. Let the child get a consciousness of what the use of number is, of what is really is for, and half the battle is won. Now this consciousness of the use or reason implies some active end in view which is always implicitly social since it involves the production of something which may be of use to others, and which is often explicitly social.

One of the absurd things in the more advanced study of arithmetic is the extent to which the child is introduced to numerical operations which have no distinctive mathematical principles characterizing them but which represent certain general principles found in business relationships. To train the child in these operations, while paying no attention to the business realities in which they will be of use, and the conditions of social life which make these business activities necessary, is neither arithmetic nor common sense. The child is called upon to do examples in interest, partnership, banking, brokerage, and so on through a long string, and no pains are taken to see that, in connection with the arithmetic, he has any sense of the social realities involved. This part of arithmetic is essentially sociological in its nature. It ought either to be omitted entirely or else taught in connection with a study of the relevant social realities. As we now manage the study it is the old case of learning to swim apart from the water over again, with correspondingly bad results on the practical and ethical side.[1]

I am afraid one question still haunts the reader. What has all this discussion about geography, history, and number, whether from the side

1. With increasing mental maturity, and corresponding specialization which naturally accompanies it, these various instrumentalities may become ends in themselves. That is, the child may, as he ripens into the period of youth, be interested in number relations for their own sake. What was once method may become an activity in itself. The above statement is not directed against this possibility. It is simply aimed at the importance of seeing to it that the preliminary period—that in which the form or means is kept in organic relationship to real ends and values—is adequately lived through.

of content or that of form, got to do with the underlying principles of education? The very reasons which induce the reader to put this question to himself, even in a half-formed way, illustrate the very point which I am trying to make. Our conceptions of the ethical in education have been too narrow, too formal, and too pathological. We have associated the term ethical with certain special acts which are labeled virtues and set off from the mass of other acts, and still more from the habitual images and motives in the agents performing them. Moral instruction is thus associated with teaching about these particular virtues, or with instilling certain sentiments in regard to them. The ethical has been conceived in too goody-goody a way. But it is not such ethical ideas and motives as these which keep men at work in recognizing and performing their moral duty. Such teaching as this, after all is said and done, is external; it does not reach down into the depths of the character-making agency. Ultimate moral motives and forces are nothing more or less than social intelligence—the power of observing and comprehending social situations—and social power—trained capacities of control—at work in the service of social interest and aims. There is no fact which throws light upon the constitution of society, there is no power whose training adds to social resourcefulness which is not ethical in its bearing.

I sum up, then, this part of the discussion by asking your attention to the moral trinity of the school. The demand is for social intelligence, social power, and social interests. Our resources are (1) the life of the school as a social institution in itself; (2) methods of learning and of doing work; and (3) the school studies or curriculum. In so far as the school represents, in its own spirit, a genuine community life; in so far as what are called school discipline, government, order, etc., are the expressions of this inherent social spirit, in so far as the methods used are those which appeal to the active and constructive powers, permitting the child to give out, and thus to serve; in so far as the curriculum is so selected and organized as to provide the material for affording the child a consciousness of the world in which he has to play a part, and the relations he has to meet; in so far as these ends are met, the school is organized on an ethical basis. So far as general principles are concerned, all the basic ethical requirements are met. The rest remains between the individual teacher and the individual child.

II.

I pass over now to the other side of the discussion—the psychological. We have so far been concerned with the principle that the end and standard of the school work is to be found in its functional relation to social life. We have endeavored to apply this principle to some of the typical features of the school in order to give an illustration of what is meant by this statement. We now recur to the counterpart principle: These ends and aims are to be realized in the child as an individual, and by the child as an individual. The social values are abstract until they are taken up and manifested in the life of the individual pupils. We have to ask, therefore, what they mean when translated over into terms of individual conduct. These values are not only to be manifested in individual conduct, but they are to be worked out by individual effort and energy. We have to consider the child as an agent or doer—the methods by which he can reproduce in his own life the constituent values of social life. . . .

I propose, then, to give a brief statement of the nature of character from this point of view. In general, character means power of social agency, organized capacity of social functioning. It means, as already suggested, social insight or intelligence, social executive power, and social interest or responsiveness. Stated in psychological terms, it means that there must be a training of the primary impulses and instincts, which organizes them into habits which are reliable means of action.

(1) Force, efficiency in execution, or overt action, is the necessary constituent of character. In our moral books and lectures we may lay all the stress upon good intentions, etc. But we know practically that the kind of character we hope to build up through our education is one which not only has good intentions, but which insists upon carrying them out. Any other character is wishy-washy; it is goody, not good. The individual must have the power to stand up and count for something in the actual conflicts of life. He must have initiative, insistence, persistence, courage and industry. He must, in a word, have all that goes under a term, "force of character." Undoubtedly, individuals differ greatly in their native endowment in this respect. None the less, each has a certain primary equipment of impulse, of tendency forward, of innate urgency to do. The problem of education on this side is that of discovering what this native fund of power is, and then of utilizing it in such a way (affording conditions which both stimulate and control) as to organize it into definite conserved modes of action—habits.

(2) But something more is required than sheer force. Sheer force may be brutal; it may override the interests of others. Even when aiming at right ends it may go at them in such a way as to violate the rights of others. More than this, in sheer force there is no guarantee for the right end itself. It may be directed towards mistaken ends, and result in posi-

tive mischief and destruction. Power, as already suggested, must be directed. It must be organized along certain channels of output or expression in such a way as to be attached to the valuable ends.

This involves training on both the intellectual and emotional side. On the intellectual side we must have judgment—what is ordinarily called good sense. The difference between mere knowledge, or information, and judgment is that the former is simply held, not used; judgment is ideas directed with reference to the accomplishment of ends. Good judgment is a sense of respective or proportionate values. The one who has judgment is the one who has ability to size up a situation. He is the one who can grasp the scene or situation before him, ignoring what is irrelevant, or what for the time being is unimportant, and can seize upon the factors which demand attention, and grade them according to their respective claims. Mere knowledge of what the right is in the abstract, mere intentions of following the right in general, however praiseworthy in themselves, are never a substitute for this power of trained judgment. Action is always in the concrete. It is definite and individualized. Except, therefore, as it is backed and controlled by a knowledge of the actual concrete factors in the situation demanding action, it must be relatively futile and waste.

(3) But the consciousness of end must be more than merely intellectual. We can imagine a person with most excellent judgment, who yet does not act upon his judgment. There must not only be force to insure effort in execution against obstacles, but there must also be a delicate personal responsiveness—there must be an emotional reaction. Indeed good judgment is impossible without this susceptibility. Unless there is a prompt and almost instinctive sensitiveness to the conditions about one, to the ends and interests of others, the intellectual side of judgment will not have its proper material to work upon. Just as the material of objects of knowledge is related to the senses, so the material of ethical knowledge is related to emotional responsiveness. It is difficult to put this quality into words, but we all know the difference between the character which is somewhat hard and formal, and that which is sympathetic, flexible, and open. In the abstract the former may be as sincerely devoted to moral ideas as the latter, but as a practical matter we prefer to live with the latter, and we count upon it to accomplish more in the end by tact, by instinctive recognition of the claims of others, by skill in adjusting, than the former can accomplish by mere attachment to rules and principles which are intellectually justified.

We get here, then, the ethical standard upon the psychological side, by which to test the work of the school. (*a*) Does the school as a system, at present, attach sufficient importance to the spontaneous instincts and impulses? Does it afford sufficient opportunity for these to assert themselves and work out their own results? Omitting quantitative considerations, can we even say that the school in principle attaches itself, at present, to the active constructive powers rather than to processes of absorption and learning, acquiring information? Does not our talk about self-activity largely render itself meaningless because the self-activity we have in mind is purely intellectual, out of relation to the impulses of the child which work through hand and eye?

Just in so far as the present school methods fail to meet the test of these questions we must not be surprised if the ethical results attained are unsatisfactory. We cannot secure the development of positive force of character unless we are willing to pay the price psychologically required. We cannot smother and repress the child's powers, or gradually abort them (from failure to permit sufficient opportunity for exercise), and then expect to get a character with initiative and consecutive industry. I am aware of the importance attaching to inhibition, but mere inhibition is valueless. The only restraint, the only holding-in that is of any worth is that which comes through holding all the powers concentrated in devotion to a positive end. The end cannot be attained excepting as the instinct and impulses are kept from discharging at random and from running off on side tracks. In keeping the powers at work upon their relevant ends, there is sufficient opportunity for genuine inhibition. To say that inhibition is higher than power of direction, morally, is like saying that death is worth more than life, negation worth more than affirmation, sacrifice worth more than service. Morally educative inhibition is one of the factors of the power of direction.

(*b*) We must also test our school work as to whether it affords the conditions psychologically necessary for the formation of good judgment. Judgment as the sense of relative values involves ability to select, to discriminate, by reference to a standard. Acquiring information can therefore never develop the power of judgment. Whatever development the child gets is in spite of, not because of, those methods of instruction which emphasize simple learning. The test comes only when the information acquired has to be put to use. Will it do what we expect of it? I have heard an educator of large experience say that in her judgment the greatest defect of instruction today, on the intellectual side, is found in the fact that children leave school without a mental perspective. Facts seem to them all of the same importance. There is no foreground nor background. There is no instinctive habit of sorting out our facts upon any scale of worth, and of grading them accordingly. This may be an exaggerated statement, but in so far as there is any truth in it, it points to moral evils as serious as the intellectual ones.

The child cannot get power of judgment excepting as he is continually exercised in forming and testing judgment. He must have an opportunity to select for himself, and than to attempt to put his own selections into execution that he may submit them to the only final test, that of action. Only thus can he learn to discriminate that which promises success from that which promises failure; only thus can he form the habit of continually relating his otherwise isolated ideas to the conditions which determine their value. Does the school, as a system, afford, at present, sufficient opportunity for this sort of experimentation? Excepting in so far as the emphasis of the school work is upon the doing side, upon construction, upon active investigation, it cannot meet the psychological conditions necessary for the judgment which is an integral factor of good character.

(c) I shall be brief with respect to the other point, the need of susceptibility and responsiveness. The informal, social side of education, the æsthetic environment and influences, are all-important here. In so far as all the work is laid out in regular and formulated ways, in so far as there are lacking opportunities for casual and free social intercourse between the pupils, and between the pupils and the teacher, this side of the child's nature is either being starved or else left to find haphazard expression along more or less secret channels. When the school system under plea of the practical (meaning by the practical the narrowly utilitarian) confines the child to the three R's and the formal studies connected with them, and shuts him out from the vital sources of literature and history, and deprives him of his right to contact with what is best in architecture, music, sculpture and picture, it is hopeless to expect any definite results with respect to the training of this integral element in character.

What we need in education more than anything else is a genuine, not merely nominal faith in the existence of moral principles which are capable of effective application. We believe that, so far as the mass of children are concerned, if we keep at them long enough we can teach reading and writing and figuring. We are practically, even if unconsciously, skeptical as to the possibility of anything like the same sort of assurance on the moral side. We believe in moral laws and rules, to be sure, but they are in the air. They are something set off by themselves. They are so *very* "moral" that there is no working contact between them and the average affairs of everyday life. What we need is to have these moral principles brought down to the ground through their statement in social and in psychological terms. We need to see that moral principles are not arbitrary, that they are not merely transcendental; that the term "moral" does not designate a special region or portion of life. We need to translate the moral into the actual conditions and working forces of our community life, and into the impulses and habits which make up the doing of the individual.

All the rest is mint, anise, and cummin. The one thing needful is that we recognize that moral principles are real in the same sense in which other forces are real; that they are inherent in community life, and in the running machinery of the individual. If we can secure a genuine faith in this fact, we shall have secured the only condition which is finally necessary in order to get from our educational system all the effectiveness there is in it. The teacher who operates in this faith will find every subject, every method of instruction, every incident of school life pregnant with ethical life.

The Democratic
Conception in Education

Every expansive era in the history of mankind has coincided with the operation of factors which have tended to eliminate distance between peoples and classes previously hemmed off from one another. Even the alleged benefits of war, so far as more than alleged, spring from the fact that conflict of peoples at least enforces intercourse between them and thus accidentally enables them to learn from one another, and thereby to expand their horizons. Travels, economic and commercial tendencies, have at present gone far to break down external barriers; to bring peoples and classes into closer and more perceptible connection with one another. It remains for the most part to secure the intellectual and emotional significance of this physical annihilation of space.

2. *The Democratic Ideal.*—The two elements in our criterion both point to democracy. The first signifies not only more numerous and more varied points of shared common interest, but greater reliance upon the recognition of mutual interests as a factor in social control. The second means not only freer interaction between social groups (once isolated so far as intention could keep up a separation) but change in social habit—its continuous readjustment through meeting the new situations produced by varied intercourse. And these two traits are precisely what characterize the democratically constituted society.

Upon the educational side, we note first that the realization of a form of social life in which interests are mutually interpenetrating, and where progress, or readjustment, is an important consideration, makes a democratic community more interested than other communities have cause to be in deliberate and systematic education. The devotion of democracy to education is a familiar fact. The superficial explanation is that a government resting upon popular suffrage cannot be successful unless those who elect and who obey their governors are educated. Since a democratic society repudiates the principle of external authority, it must find a substitute in voluntary disposition and interest; these can be created only by education. But there is a deeper explanation. A democracy is more than a form of government; it is primarily a mode of associated living, of conjoint communicated experience. The extension in space of the number of

[From *Democracy and Education* (New York: The Macmillan Company, 1916); reprinted in *The Middle Works*, Vol. 9.]

individuals who participate in an interest so that each has to refer his own action to that of others, and to consider the action of others to give point and direction to his own, is equivalent to the breaking down of those barriers of class, race, and national territory which kept men from perceiving the full import of their activity. These more numerous and more varied points of contact denote a greater diversity of stimuli to which an individual has to respond; they consequently put a premium on variation in his action. They secure a liberation of powers which remain suppressed as long as the incitations to action are partial, as they must be in a group which in its exclusiveness shuts out many interests.

The widening of the area of shared concerns, and the liberation of a greater diversity of personal capacities which characterize a democracy, are not of course the product of deliberation and conscious effort. On the contrary, they were caused by the development of modes of manufacture and commerce, travel, migration, and intercommunication which flowed from the command of science over natural energy. But after greater individualization on one hand, and a broader community of interest on the other have come into existence, it is a matter of deliberate effort to sustain and extend them. Obviously a society to which stratification into separate classes would be fatal, must see to it that intellectual opportunities are accessible to all on equable and easy terms. A society marked off into classes need be specially attentive only to the education of its ruling elements. A society which is mobile, which is full of channels for the distribution of a change occurring anywhere, must see to it that its members are educated to personal initiative and adaptability. Otherwise, they will be overwhelmed by the changes in which they are caught and whose significance or connection they do not perceive. The result will be a confusion in which a few will appropriate to themselves the results of the blind and externally directed activities of others.

3. *The Platonic Educational Philosophy.*—Subsequent chapters will be devoted to making explicit the implications of the democratic ideas in education. In the remaining portions of this chapter, we shall consider the educational theories which have been evolved in three epochs when the social import of education was especially conspicuous. The first one to be considered is that of Plato. No one could better express than did he the fact that a society is stably organized when each individual is doing that for which he has aptitude by nature in such a way as to be useful to others (or to contribute to the whole to which he belongs); and that it is the business of education to discover these aptitudes and progressively to train them for social use. Much which has been said so far is borrowed from what Plato first consciously taught the world. But conditions which he could not intellectually control led him to restrict these ideas in their

application. He never got any conception of the indefinite plurality of activities which may characterize an individual and a social group, and consequently limited his view to a limited number of *classes* of capacities and of social arrangements.

Plato's starting point is that the organization of society depends ultimately upon knowledge of the end of existence. If we do not know its end, we shall be at the mercy of accident and caprice. Unless we know the end, the good, we shall have no criterion for rationally deciding what the possibilities are which should be promoted, nor how social arrangements are to be ordered. We shall have no conception of the proper limits and distribution of activities—what he called justice—as a trait of both individual and social organization. But how is the knowledge of the final and permanent good to be achieved? In dealing with this question we come upon the seemingly insuperable obstacle that such knowledge is not possible save in a just and harmonious social order. Everywhere else the mind is distracted and misled by false valuations and false perspectives. A disorganized and factional society sets up a number of different models and standards. Under such conditions it is impossible for the individual to attain consistency of mind. Only a complete whole is fully self-consistent. A society which rests upon the supremacy of some factor over another irrespective of its rational or proportionate claims, inevitably leads thought astray. It puts a premium on certain things and slurs over others, and creates a mind whose seeming unity is forced and distorted. Education proceeds ultimately from the patterns furnished by institutions, customs, and laws. Only in a just state will these be such as to give the right education; and only those who have rightly trained minds will be able to recognize the end, and ordering principle of things. We seem to be caught in a hopeless circle. However, Plato suggested a way out. A few men, philosophers or lovers of wisdom—or truth—may by study learn at least in outline the proper patterns of true existence. If a powerful ruler should form a state after these patterns, then its regulations could be preserved. An education could be given which would sift individuals, discovering what they were good for, and supplying a method of assigning each to the work in life for which his nature fits him. Each doing his own part, and never transgressing, the order and unity of the whole would be maintained.

It would be impossible to find in any scheme of philosophic thought a more adequate recognition on one hand of the educational significance of social arrangements and, on the other, of the dependence of those arrangements upon the means used to educate the young. It would be impossible to find a deeper sense of the function of education in discovering and developing personal capacities, and training them so that they would connect with the activities of others. Yet the society in which the theory was propounded was so undemocratic that Plato could not work out a solution for the problem whose terms he clearly saw.

While he affirmed with emphasis that the place of the individual in society should not be determined by birth or wealth or any conventional status, but by his own nature as discovered in the process of education, he had no perception of the uniqueness of individuals. For him they fall by nature into classes, and into a very small number classes at that. Consequently the testing and sifting function of education only shows to which one of three classes an individual belongs. There being no recognition that each individual constitutes his own class, there could be no recognition of the infinite diversity of active tendencies and combinations of tendencies of which an individual is capable. There were only three types of faculties or powers in the individual's constitution. Hence education would soon reach a static limit in each class, for only diversity makes change and progress.

In some individuals, apetites naturally dominate; they are assigned to the laboring and trading class, which expresses and supplies human wants. Others reveal, upon education, that over and above appetites, they have a generous, outgoing, assertively courageous disposition. They become the citizen-subjects of the state; its defenders in war; its internal guardians in peace. But their limit is fixed by their lack of reason, which is a capacity to grasp the universal. Those who possess this are capable of the highest kind of education, and become in time the legislators of the state—for laws are the universals which control the particulars of experience. Thus it is not true that in intent, Plato subordinated the individual to the social whole. But it is true that lacking the perception of the uniqueness of every individual, his incommensurability with others, and consequently not recognizing that a society might change and yet be stable, his doctrine of limited powers and classes came in net effect to the idea of the subordination of individuality.

We cannot better Plato's conviction that an individual is happy and society well organized when each individual engages in those activities for which he has a natural equipment, nor his conviction that it is the primary office of education to discover this equipment to its possessor and train him for its effective use. But progress in knowledge has made us aware of the superficiality of Plato's lumping of individuals and their original powers into a few sharply marked-off classes; it has taught us that original capacities are indefinitely numerous and variable. It is but the other side of this fact to say that in the degree in which society has become democratic, social organization means utilization of the specific and variable qualities of individuals, not stratification by classes. Although his educational philosophy was revolutionary, it was none the less in bondage to static ideals. He thought that change or alteration was evidence of lawless flux; that true reality was unchangeable. Hence while he would radically change the existing state of society, his aim was to construct a state in which change would subsequently have no place. The final end of life is fixed; given a state framed with this end in view, not even minor details are to be altered. Though they might not be inherently important, yet if permitted they would inure the minds of men to the idea of change, and hence be dissolving and anarchic. The breakdown of his philosophy is made apparent in the fact that he could not trust to gradual improvements in education to bring about a better society which should then improve education, and so on indefinitely. Correct education could not come into existence until an ideal state existed, and after that education would be devoted simply to its conservation. For the existence of this state he was obliged to trust to some happy accident by which philosophic wisdom should happen to coincide with possession of ruling power in the state.

4. *The "Individualistic" Ideal of the Eighteenth Century.*—In the eighteenth-century philosophy we find ourselves in a very different circle of ideas. "Nature" still means something antithetical to existing social organization; Plato exercised a great influence upon Rousseau. But the voice of nature now speaks for the diversity of individual talent and for the need of free development of individuality in all its variety. Education in accord with nature furnishes the goal and the method of instruction and discipline. Moreover, the native or original endowment was conceived, in extreme cases, as nonsocial or even as antisocial. Social arrangements were thought of as mere external expedients by which these nonsocial individuals might secure a greater amount of private happiness for themselves.

Nevertheless, these statements convey only an inadequate idea of the true significance of the movement. In reality its chief interest was in progress and in social progress. The seeming antisocial philosophy was a somewhat transparent mask for an impetus toward a wider and freer society—towards cosmopolitanism. The positive ideal was humanity. In membership in humanity, as distinct from a state, man's capacities would be liberated; while in existing political organizations his powers were hampered and distorted to meet the requirements and selfish interests of the rulers of the state. The doctrine of extreme individualism was but the counterpart, the obverse, of ideals of the indefinite perfectibility of man and of a social organization having a scope as wide as humanity. The emancipated individual was to become the organ and agent of a comprehensive and progressive society.

The heralds of this gospel were acutely conscious of the evils of the social estate in which they found themselves. They attributed these evils to the limitations imposed upon the free powers of man. Such limitation was both distorting and corrupting. Their impassioned devotion to emancipation of life from external restrictions which operated to the exclusive advantage of the class to whom a past feudal system consigned power, found intellectual formulation in a worship of nature. To give "nature" full swing was to replace an artificial, corrupt, and inequitable social order by a new and better kingdom of humanity. Unrestrained faith in Nature as both a model and a working power was strengthened by the advances of natural science. Inquiry freed from prejudice and artificial restraints of church and state had revealed that the world is a scene of law. The Newtonian solar system, which expressed the reign of natural law, was a scene of wonderful harmony, where every force balanced with every other. Natural law would accomplish the same result in human relations, if men would only get rid of the artificial man-imposed coercive restrictions.

Education in accord with nature was thought to be the first step in insuring this more social society. It was plainly seen that economic and political limitations were ultimately dependent upon limitations of thought and feeling. The first step in freeing men from external chains was to emancipate them from the internal chains of false beliefs and ideals. What was called social life, existing institutions, were too false and corrupt to be entrusted with this work. How could it be expected to undertake it when the undertaking meant its own destruction? "Nature" must then be the power to which the enterprise was to be left. Even the extreme sensationalistic theory of knowledge which was current derived itself from this conception. To insist that mind is originally passive and empty was one way of glorifying the possibilities of education. If the mind was a wax tablet to be written upon by objects, there were no limits to the possibility of education by means of the natural environment. And since the natural world of objects is a scene of harmonious "truth," this education would infallibly produce minds filled with the truth.

5. *Education as National and as Social.*—As soon as the first enthusiasm for freedom waned, the weakness of the theory upon the constructive side became obvious. Merely to leave everything to nature was, after all, but to negate the very idea of education; it was to trust to the accidents of circumstance. Not only was some method required but also some positive organ, some administrative agency for carrying on the process of instruction. The "complete and harmonious development of all powers," having as its social counterpart an enlightened and progressive humanity, required definite organization for its realization. Pri-

vate individuals here and there could proclaim the gospel; they could not execute the work. A Pestalozzi could try experiments and exhort phil-anthropically inclined persons having wealth and power to follow his example. But even Pestalozzi saw that any effective pursuit of the new education ideal required the support of the state. The realization of the new education destined to produce a new society was, after all, dependent upon the activities of existing states. The movement for the democratic idea inevitably became a movement for publicly conducted and administered schools.

So far as Europe was concerned, the historic situation identified the movement for a state-supported education with the nationalistic movement in political life—a fact of incalculable significance for subsequent movements. Under the influence of German thought in particular, education became a civic function and the civic function was identified with the realization of the ideal of the national state. The "state" was substituted for humanity; cosmopolitanism gave way to nationalism. To form the citizen, not the "man," became the aim of education.[2] The historic situation to which reference is made is the after-effects of the Napoleonic conquests, especially in Germany. The German states felt (and subsequent events demonstrate the correctness of the belief) that systematic attention to education was the best means of recovering and maintaining their political integrity and power. Externally they were weak and divided. Under the leadership of Prussian statesmen they made this condition a stimulus to the development of an extensive and thoroughly grounded system of public education.

This change in practice necessarily brought about a change in theory. The individualistic theory receded into the background. The state furnished not only the instrumentalities of public education but also its goal. When the actual practice was such that the school system, from the elementary grades through the university faculties, supplied the patriotic citizen and soldier and the future state official and administrator and furnished the means for military, industrial, and political defense and expansion, it was impossible for theory not to emphasize the aim of social efficiency. And with the immense importance attached to the nationalistic state, surrounded by other competing and more or less hostile states,

2. There is a much neglected strain in Rousseau tending intellectually in this direction. He opposed the existing state of affairs on the ground that it formed *neither* the citizen nor the man. Under existing conditions, he preferred to try for the latter rather than for the former. But there are many sayings of his which point to the formation of the citizen as ideally the higher, and which indicate that his own endeavor, as embodied in the *Émile,* was simply the best makeshift the corruption of the times permitted him to sketch.

it was equally impossible to interpret social efficiency in terms of a vague cosmopolitan humanitarianism. Since the maintenance of a particular national sovereignty required subordination of individuals to the superior interests of the state both in military defense and in struggles for international supremacy in commerce, social efficiency was understood to imply a like subordination. The educational process was taken to be one of disciplinary training rather than of personal development. Since, however, the ideal of culture as complete development of personality persisted, educational philosophy attempted a reconciliation of the two ideas. The reconciliation took the form of the conception of the "organic" character of the state. The individual in his isolation is nothing; only in and through an absorption of the aims and meaning of organized institutions does he attain true personality. What appears to be his subordination to political authority and the demand for sacrifice of himself to the commands of his superiors is in reality but making his own the objective reason manifested in the state—the only way in which he can become truly rational. The notion of development which we have seen to be characteristic of institutional idealism (as in the Hegelian philosophy) was just such a deliberate effort to combine the two ideas of complete realization of personality and thoroughgoing "disciplinary" subordination to existing institutions.

The extent of the transformation of educational philsophy which occurred in Germany in the generation occupied by the struggle against Napoleon for national independence, may be gathered from Kant, who well expresses the earlier individual-cosmopolitan ideal. In his treatise on Pedagogics, consisting of lectures given in the later years of the eighteenth century, he defines education as the process by which man becomes man. Mankind begins its history submerged in nature—not as Man who is a creature of reason, while nature furnishes only instinct and appetite. Nature offers simply the germs which education is to develop and perfect. The peculiarity of truly human life is that man has to create himself by his own voluntary efforts; he has to make himself a truly moral, rational, and free being. This creative effort is carried on by the educational activities of slow generations. Its acceleration depends upon men consciously striving to educate their successors not for the existing state of affairs but so as to make possible a future better humanity. But there is the great difficulty. Each generation is inclined to educate its young so as to get along in the present world instead of with a view to the proper end of education: the promotion of the best possible realization of humanity as humanity. Parents educate their children so that they may get on; princes educate their subjects as instruments of their own purposes.

Who, then shall conduct education so that humanity may improve? We must depend upon the efforts of enlightened men in their private capacity. "All culture begins with private men and spreads outward from them. Simply through the efforts of persons of enlarged inclinations, who are capable of grasping the ideal of a future better condition, is the gradual approximation of human nature to its end possible. . . . Rulers are simply interested in such training as will make their subjects better tools for their own intentions." Even the subsidy by rulers of privately conducted schools must be carefully safeguarded. For the rulers' interest in the welfare of their own nation instead of in what is best for humanity, will make them, if they give money for the schools, wish to draw their plans. We have in this view an express statement of the points characteristic of the eighteenth-century individualistic cosmopolitanism. The full development of private personality is identified with the aims of humanity as a whole and with the idea of progress. In addition we have an explicit fear of the hampering influence of a state-conducted and state-regulated education upon the attainment of these ideas. But in less than two decades after this time, Kant's philosophic successors, Fichte and Hegel, elaborated the idea that the chief function of the state is educational; that in particular the regeneration of Germany is to be accomplished by an education carried on in the interests of the state, and that the private individual is of necessity an egoistic, irrational being, enslaved to his appetites and to circumstances unless he submits voluntarily to the educative discipline of state institutions and laws. In this spirit, Germany was the first country to undertake a public, universal, and compulsory system of education extending from the primary school through the university, and to submit to jealous state regulation and supervision all private educational enterprises.

Two results should stand out from this brief historical survey. The first is that such terms as the individual and the social conceptions of education are quite meaningless taken at large, or apart from their context. Plato had the ideal of an education which should equate individual realization and social coherency and stability. His situation forced his ideal into the notion of a society organized in stratified classes, losing the individual in the class. The eighteenth-century educational philosophy was highly individualistic in form, but this form was inspired by a noble and generous social ideal: that of a society organized to include humanity, and providing for the indefinite perfectibility of mankind. The idealistic philosophy of Germany in the early nineteenth century endeavored again to equate the ideals of a free and complete development of cultured personality with social discipline and political subordination. It made the national state an intermediary between the realization of private personality on one side and of humanity on the other. Consequently, it is equally possible to state its animating principle with equal truth either in

the classic terms of "harmonious development of all the powers of personality" or in the more recent terminology of "social efficiency." All this
reenforces the statement which opens this chapter: The conception of
education as a social process and function has no definite meaning until
we define the kind of society we have in mind.

These considerations pave the way for our second conclusion. One of
the fundamental problems of education in and for a democratic society is
set by the conflict of a nationalistic and a wider social aim. The earlier
cosmopolitan and "humanitarian" conception suffered both from vagueness and from lack of definite organs of execution and agencies of administration. In Europe, in the Continental states particularly, the new
idea of the importance of education for human welfare and progress was
captured by national interests and harnessed to do a work whose social
aim was definitely narrow and exclusive. The social aim of education and
its national aim were identified, and the result was a marked obscuring of
the meaning of a social aim.

This confusion corresponds to the existing situation of human intercourse. On the one hand, science, commerce, and art transcend national
boundaries. They are largely international in quality and method. They
involve interdependencies and cooperation among the peoples inhabiting
different countries. At the same time, the idea of national sovereignty has
never been as accentuated in politics as it is at the present time. Each
nation lives in a state of suppressed hostility and incipient war with its
neighbors. Each is supposed to be the supreme judge of its own interests,
and it is assumed as matter of course that each has interests which are
exclusively its own. To question this is to question the very idea of
national sovereignty which is assumed to be basic to political practice and
political science. This contradiction (for it is nothing less) between the
wider sphere of associated and mutually helpful social life and the narrower sphere of exclusive and hence potentially hostile pursuits and
purposes, exacts of educational theory a clearer conception of the meaning of "social" as a function and test of education than has yet been
attained.

Is it possible for an educational system to be conducted by a national
state and yet the full social ends of the educative process not be restricted, constrained, and corrupted? Internally, the question has to face
the tendencies, due to present economic conditions, which split society
into classes some of which are made merely tools for the higher culture
of others. Externally, the question is concerned with the reconciliation of
national loyalty, of patriotism, with superior devotion to the things which
unite men in common ends, irrespective of national political boundaries.
Neither phase of the problem can be worked out by merely negative

means. It is not enough to see to it that education is not actively used as an instrument to make easier the exploitation of one class by another. School facilities must be secured of such amplitude and efficiency as will in fact and not simply in name discount the effects of economic inequalities, and secure to all the wards of the nation equality of equipment for their future careers. Accomplishment of this end demands not only adequate administrative provision of school facilities, and such supplementation of family resources as will enable youth to take advantage of them, but also such modification of traditional ideals of culture, traditional subjects of study and traditional methods of teaching and discipline as will retain all the youth under educational influences until they are equipped to be masters of their own economic and social careers. The ideal may seem remote of execution, but the democratic ideal of education is a farcical yet tragic delusion except as the ideal more and more dominates our public system of education.

The same principle has application on the side of considerations which concern the relations of one nation to another. It is not enough to teach the horrors of war and to avoid everything which would stimulate international jealousy and animosity. The emphasis must be put upon whatever binds people together in cooperative human pursuits and results, apart from geographical limitations. The secondary and provisional character of national sovereignty in respect to the fuller, freer, and more fruitful association and intercourse of all human beings with one another must be instilled as a working disposition of mind. If these applications seem to be remote from a consideration of the philosophy of education, the impression shows that the meaning of the idea of education previously developed has not been adequately grasped. This conclusion is bound up with the very idea of education as a freeing of individual capacity in a progressive growth directed to social aims. Otherwise a democratic criterion of education can only be inconsistently applied. . . .

The Need of an Industrial Education in an Industrial Democracy

The need for industrial education may be approached from many standpoints. Industrial education may be treated as an indispensable factor in material prosperity, or as a factor in promoting the ability of a nation in the competitive race for commercial supremacy among nations— a point of view from which the example of Germany is urged. Or it may be regarded from the standpoint of its effect upon the contentment of the workers, or as a means of providing a more stable and efficient set of employees, and reducing the waste now found in most manufacturing enterprises. All of these things have their importance. But they all look at education as an instrument for external ends, and they pass lightly over that part of the subject represented in our title by the words, "education in an industrial democracy." The standpoint from which we are to approach the matter is, in short, that of the demands laid upon education by the need of fostering democracy in a country largely industrial, and where the need is recognized of making the spirit of democracy permeate industry.

Hence, a few words about democracy itself seem to be called for. Democracy has its political aspect. Probably this is the first aspect to present itself to view. Politically, democracy means a form of government which does not esteem the well-being of one individual or class above that of another; a system of laws and administration which ranks the happiness and interests of all as upon the same plane, and before whose law and administration all individuals are alike, or equal. But experience has shown that such a state of affairs is not realizable save where all interests have an opportunity to be heard, to make themselves felt, to take a hand in shaping policies. Consequently, universal suffrage, direct participation in choice of rulers, is an essential part of political democracy.

But political democracy is not the whole of democracy. On the contrary, experience has proved that it cannot stand in isolation. It can be effectively maintained only where democracy is social—where, if you please, it is moral. A social democracy signifies, most obviously, a state of

[First published in *Manual Training and Vocational Education* 17 (1916); reprinted in *The Middle Works*, Vol. 10.]

social life where there is a wide and varied distribution of opportunities; where there is social mobility or scope for change of position and station; where there is free circulation of experiences and ideas, making for a wide recognition of common interests and purposes, and where utility of social and political organization to its members is so obvious as to enlist their warm and constant support in its behalf. Without ease in change, society gets stratified into classes, and these classes prevent anything like fair and even distribution of opportunity for all. The stratified classes become fossilized, and a feudal society comes into existence. Accident, rather than capacity and training, determines career, reward, and repute. Since democracies forbid, by their very nature, highly centralized governments working by coercion, they depend upon shared interests and experiences for their unity, and upon personal appreciation of the value of institutions for stability and defense.

Such qualities as these, such qualities as insistence upon widespread opportunity, free exchange of ideas and experiences, and extensive realization of the purposes which hold men together, are intellectual and emotional traits. The importance of such qualities is the reason why we venture to call a social democracy a moral democracy. And they are traits which do not grow spontaneously on bushes. They have to be planted and nurtured. They are dependent upon education. It is no accident that all democracies have put a high estimate upon education; that schooling has been their first care and enduring charge. Only through education can equality of opportunity be anything more than a phrase. Accidental inequalities of birth, wealth, and learning are always tending to restrict the opportunities of some as compared with those of others. Only free and continued education can counteract those forces which are always at work to restore, in however changed a form, feudal oligarchy. Democracy has to be born anew every generation, and education is its midwife. Moreover, it is only education which can guarantee widespread community of interest and aim. In a complex society, ability to understand and sympathize with the operations and lot of others is a condition of common purpose which only education can procure. The external differences of pursuit and experience are so very great in our complicated industrial civilization, that men will not see across and through the walls which separate them, unless they have been trained to do so. And without this lively and ardent sense of common life, it is hopeless to secure in individuals that loyalty to the organized group which needs to be an animating motive of conduct.

To recall these generalities, these commonplaces, would be idle were it not that there is a tendency to drop them from view when the topic of industrial education is under consideration. Its purpose is often thought to be so much narrower, so much more practical and technical, than that of other established modes of education, that these features may be—nay, must be—left out of account. But the contrary is the case. Just because of the part played by industry in modern life, an education which has to do with preparation for it must bear these considerations in mind more than other forms, if democracy is to remain an actuality. Just these things provide the controlling considerations for deciding the curricula, methods, and administration of a system of industrial education.

There are many phases of industry, as that is at present carried on, which are unfavorable to a genuine democracy, just as, on the other hand, the development of modern industrial and commercial methods has been a chief factor in calling political democracy into existence and endowing it with social aspirations. There are extreme divisions of work between the skilled and unskilled, and also between the most skilled workers on the technical side, whether inventors or doers, and the managers on the fiscal and marketing side. These tend to segregate men and women into exclusive classes. The difference between those who can barely maintain a low standard of living and those who are relieved by circumstances from any responsible thought for expenditure, and hence give themselves up to display and idleness, has never been so large or so overtly conspicuous as it is today. Older divisions of master and subject class tend to reinstate themselves in a subtle form.

Machine industry, moreover, tends to reduce great masses of men to a level where their work becomes mechanical and servile. Work loses its intellectual and esthetic cast and becomes a mere necessity to procure the pay which buys daily support. The machine operator engaged in manipulation of a machine becomes identified with the monotonous movements of the monster he tends. As long as he has to do new things, he learns. The moment he has mastered his unchanging work it masters him; its habits absorb and swallow his. Employers whose methods have bred lack of initiative, and have practically forbidden workers to think, then complain because men can not be found for places of greater responsibility. But the evils are far from being confined to the laboring class. When social responsibilities have at most to do with the expenditure of wealth, not with earning it, when business is pursued not as an exercise in social cooperation but as a means to personal power, the mind is so hardened and restricted that democracy becomes a mere name.

To recall such dangers is to recognize some of the offices thrust upon industrial education in a democracy. To counteract the soulless monotony of machine industry, a premium must be put upon initiative, intellectual independence, and inventiveness. Hence schooling must not model itself upon the automatic repetitiousness of machines, whether in the name of the false gods of practical skill or of discipline. Personal control of power, strong discontent with whatever subordinates mental capacity to merely external regulation, must be made primary. The imagination must be so stored that in the inevitable monotonous stretches of work, it may have worthy material of art and literature and science upon which to feed, instead of being frittered away upon undisciplined dreamings and sensual fancies. Since new inventions and applications of science are actively remaking technical and technological methods of industry, the desire for immediate results and immediate efficiency must be held in check so as to secure powers which will enable individuals to adapt themselves to inevitable change,—so that they will not become helpless burdens on society when the methods in which they have been trained pass away. Moreover, since the worker is to be an integral part of a self-managing society, pains must be taken at every turn to see that instead of being prepared for a special, exclusive, practical service, as a hide might be prepared for a shoemaker, he is educated into ability to recognize and apply his own abilities—is given self-command, intellectual as well as moral. . . .

Can Education Share
in Social Reconstruction?

That upon the whole the schools have been educating for something called the *status quo* can hardly be doubted by observing persons. The fallacy in this attempt should be equally evident. There is no *status quo*—except in the literal sense in which Andy explained the phrase to Amos: a name for the "mess we are in." It is not difficult, however, to define that which is called the "*status quo*"; the difficulty is that the movement of actual events has little connection with the name by which it is called.

For the alleged *status quo* is summed up in the phrase "rugged individualism." The assumption is—or was—that we are living in a free economic society in which every individual has an equal chance to exercise his initiative and his other abilities, and that the legal and political order is designed and calculated to further this equal liberty on the part of all individuals. No grosser myth ever received general currency. Economic freedom has been either non-existent or precarious for large masses of the population. Because of its absence and its tenuousness for the majority, political and cultural freedom has been sapped; the legally constituted order has supported the ideal of *beati possidentes*.

There is no need here to review the historic change from a simple agrarian order, in which the idea of equal opportunity contained a large measure of truth, to a complex industrial order with highly concentrated economic and political control. The point is that the earlier idea and theory persisted after it had lost all relevance to actual facts, and was then used to justify and strengthen the very situation that had undermined it in practice. What then is the real *status quo*? Is it the condition of free individuality postulated by the ruling theoretical philosophy, or is it the increasing encroachment of the power of a privileged minority, a power exercised over the liberties of the mass without corresponding responsibility?

It would not be difficult to make out a case for a positive and sweeping answer in favor of the latter alternative. Let me quote, as far as schools are concerned, from Roger Baldwin. "On the whole, it may be said without question that the public schools have been handed over to the keeping of the militant defenders of the *status quo*—the Daughters of the

[First published in *Social Frontier* 1 (October 1934); reprinted in *The Later Works*, Vol. 9.]

American Revolution, the American Legion, the Fundamentalists, the Ku Klux Klan, and the War Department. Look at the twelve year record! Compulsory patriotic rites and flag saluting by law in most states; compulsory reading of the Protestant Bible in eighteen states, contrary to the provision for the separation of church and state; compulsory teaching of the Constitution by prescribed routine; making a crime of the teaching of evolution in three states; special oaths of loyalty not required of other public servants in ten states; loyalty oaths required of students as a condition of graduation in many cities; history textbooks revised under pressure to conform to prejudice; restriction or ban on teachers' unions affiliated with the labor movement; laws protecting tenure beaten or emasculated; compulsory military training in both high schools and colleges, with inevitable pressure on students and teachers by the military mind." To these forms of outward and overt pressure may be added—as indeed Mr. Baldwin does add—more powerful, because more subtle and unformulated, pressures that act constantly upon teachers and students.

It might seem then that, judged by the present situation, *limitation* upon the efforts of teachers to promote a new social order—in which the ideal of freedom and equality of individuals will be a fact and not a fiction—tremendously outweighs the element of *possibility* of their doing so. Such is not the case, however, great as are the immediate odds against effort to realize the possibility. The reason is that the actual *status quo* is in a state of flux; there *is* no *status quo*, if by that term is meant something stable and constant. The last forty years have seen in every industrialized society all over the world a steady movement in the direction of social control of economic forces. Pressure for this control of capital—or if you please for its "regimentation"—is exercised both through political agencies and voluntary organizations. Laissez faire has been dying of strangulation. Mr. Hoover, who gave currency to the phrase "rugged individualism" while President, acted repeatedly and often on a fairly large scale for governmental intervention and regulation of economic forces. The list of interferences with genuine educational freedom that has been cited is itself a sign of an effort, and often a conscious one, to stem a tide that is running in the opposite direction—that is, toward a collectivism that is hostile to the idea of unrestricted action on the part of those individuals who are possessed of economic and political power because of control of capital.

I hope the bearing of these remarks upon the theme of the limitations and the possibilities of educational effort for establishing a new social order is fairly evident. Teachers and administrators often say they must "conform to conditions" rather than do what they would personally prefer to do. The proposition might be sound if conditions were fixed or even reasonably stable. But they are not. They are highly unstable; social conditions are running in different, often opposed directions. Because of this fact the educator in respect to the relation of educational work to present and future society is constantly compelled to make a choice. With what phase and direction of social forces will he throw in his energies? The chief evil is that the choice is so often made unconsciously by accommodation to the exigencies of immediate pressure and of estimate of probability of success in carrying out egoistic ambitions.

I do not think, accordingly, that the schools can in any literal sense be the builders of a new social order. But the schools will surely, as a matter of fact and not of ideal, *share* in the building of the social order of the future according as they ally themselves with this or that movement of existing social forces. This fact is inevitable. The schools of America have furthered the present social drift and chaos by their emphasis upon an economic form of success which is intrinsically pecuniary and egoistic. They will of necessity, and again not as a matter of theory, take an active part in determining the social order—or disorder—of the future, according as teachers and administrators align themselves with the older so-called "individualistic" ideals—which in fact are fatal to individuality for the many—or with the newer forces making for social control of economic forces. The plea that teachers must passively accommodate themselves to existing conditions is but one way—and a cowardly way— of making a choice in favor of the old and the chaotic.

If the teacher's choice is to throw himself in with the forces and conditions that are making for change in the direction of social control of capitalism—economic and political—there will hardly be a moment of the day when he will not have the opportunity to make his choice good in action. If the choice is conscious and intelligent, he will find that it affects the details of school administration and discipline, of methods of teaching, of selection and emphasis in subject-matter. The educator is, even now, I repeat, making this choice, but too often is making it blindly and unintelligently. If he or she is genuinely committed to alliance with present forces that tend to develop a social order which will, through collective control and ownership, make possible a genuine and needed "rugged individualism" (in the sense of individuality) for all members of the community, the teacher will, moreover, not be content with generalities about the desired future order. The task is to translate the desired ideal over into the conduct of the detail of the school in administration, instruction, and subject-matter. Here, it seems to me, is the great present need and responsibility of those who think the schools should consciously be partners in the construction of a changed society. The challenge to teachers must be issued and in clear tones. But the challenge is merely a beginning. What does it mean in the particulars of work in the school and on the playground? An answer to this question and not more general commitment to social theory and slogans is the pressing demand.

In spite of the lethargy and timidity of all too many teachers, I believe there are enough teachers who will respond to the great task of making schools active and militant participants in creation of a new social order, provided they are shown not merely the general end in view but also the means of its accomplishment. Dr. Kandel, at the close of a somewhat scornful article as to the part of the schools in this task of social reconstruction, says of society in general: "It would welcome help from any direction to correct the existing abuses and make it true to itself; beyond that it would not permit the schools to go. If the teaching body, whose duty it is to define and interpret society's culture and ideal to the oncoming generation, undertook this much it would still be faced with a formidable task; it may lay the basis for a new social order, but society and not the teaching body will determine its particulars."

There are, in this statement, many words and phrases that I am tempted to underscore: correction of *abuses*; the *duty* of the teacher; the *basis* for a new social order; leaving *particulars* to society. But I content myself with asking what more can any educator, however "radical," want? Abuses cannot be corrected by merely negative means; they can be eliminated only by substitution of just and humane conditions. Laying the *basis*, intellectual and moral, for a new social order is a sufficiently novel and inspiring ideal to arouse a new spirit in the teaching profession and to give direction to radically changed effort. Those who hold such an ideal are false to what they profess in words when they line up with reactionaries by ridicule of those who would make the profession a reality. That task may well be left to educational fascists.

How Much Freedom
in New Schools?

It is not easy to take stock of the achievements of progressive schools in the last decade: these schools are too diverse both in aims and in mode of conduct. In one respect, this is as it should be: it indicates that there is no cut-and-dried program to follow, that schools are free to grow along the lines of special needs and conditions and so to express the variant ideas of innovating leaders. But there is more than is suggested by these considerations in the existing diversity. It testifies also to the fact that the underlying motivation is so largely a reaction against the traditional school that the watchwords of the progressive movement are capable of being translated into inconsistent practices.

The negative aspect of progressive education results from the conditions of its origin. Progressive schools are usually initiated by parents who are dissatisfied with existing schools and find teachers who agree with them. Often they express discontent with traditional education or locally available schools without embodying any well thought-out policies and aims. They are symptoms of reaction against formalism and mass regimentation; they are manifestations of a desire for an education at once freer and richer. In extreme cases they represent enthusiasm much more than understanding.

Their common creed is the belief in freedom, in esthetic enjoyment and artistic expression, in opportunity for individual development, and in learning through activity rather than by passive absorption. Such aims give progressive schools a certain community of spirit and atmosphere. But they do not determine any common procedure in discipline or instruction; they do not fix the subject matter to be taught; they do not decide whether the emphasis shall be upon science, history, the fine arts, different modes of industrial art, or social issues and questions. Hence the diversity of the progressive schools, and hence the great difficulty in appraising them. Adverse criticisms may be readily and often effectively answered on the ground that they do not apply to specific schools. . . .

That there was need for the reaction, indeed for a revolt, seems to me unquestionable. The evils of the traditional, conventional school room, its almost complete isolation from actual life, and the deadly depression

[First published in *New Republic* 63 (9 July 1930); reprinted in *The Later Works*, Vol. 5.]

of mind which the weight of formal material caused, all cried out for reform. But rebellion against formal studies and lessons can be effectively completed only through the development of a new subject matter, as well organized as was the old—indeed, better organized in any vital sense of the word organization—but having an intimate and developing relation to the experience of those in school. The relative failure to accomplish this result indicates the one-sidedness of the idea of the "child-centered" school.

I do not mean, of course, that education does not centre in the pupil. It obviously takes its start with him and terminates in him. But the child is not something isolated; he does not live inside himself, but in a world of nature and man. His experience is not complete in his impulses and emotions; these must reach out into a world of objects and persons. And until an experience has become relatively mature, the impulses do not even know what they are reaching out toward and for; they are blind and inchoate. To fail to assure them guidance and direction is not merely to permit them to operate in a blind and spasmodic fashion, but it promotes the formation of *habits* of immature, undeveloped and egoistic activity. Guidance and direction mean that the impulses and desires take effect through material that is impersonal and objective. And this subject matter can be provided in a way which will obtain ordered and consecutive development of experience only by means of the thoughtful selection and organization of material by those having the broadest experience—those who treat impulses and inchoate desires and plans as potentialities of growth through interaction and not as finalities.

To be truly self-centered is not to be centered in one's feelings and desires. Such a centre means dissipation, and the ultimate destruction of any centre whatever. Nor does it mean to be egoistically bent on the fulfillment of personal wishes and ambitions. It means rather to have a rich field of social and natural relations, which are at first external to the self, but now incorporated into personal experience so that they give it weight, balance and order. In some progressive schools the fear of adult imposition has become a veritable phobia. When the fear is analyzed, it means simply a preference for an immature and undeveloped experience over a ripened and thoughtful one; it erects into a standard something which by its nature provides no steady measure or tested criterion. In some recent articles in the *New Republic* I have argued that an adult cannot attain an integrated personality except by incorporating into himself the realities of the life-situations in which he finds himself. This operation is certainly even more necessary for the young; what is called "subject matter" represents simply the selected and organized material that is relevant to such incorporation at any given time. The neglect of it means arrest of growth at an immature level and ultimate disintegration of selfhood.

It is, of course, difficult to use words that are not open to misapprehension. There may be those who think that I am making a plea for return to some kind of adult imposition, or at least to ready-made and rather rigidly predetermined topics and sequences of study. But in fact many of the current interpretations of the child-centered school, of pupil initiative and pupil-purposing and planning, suffer from exactly the same fallacy as the adult-imposition method of the traditional school—only in an inverted form. That is, they are still obsessed by the personal factor; they conceive of no alternative to adult dictation save child dictation. What is wanted is to get away from every mode of personal dictation and merely personal control. When the emphasis falls upon having experiences that are educationally worth while, the centre of gravity shifts from the personal factor, and is found within the developing experience in which pupils and teachers alike participate. The teacher, because of greater maturity and wider knowledge, is the natural leader in the shared activity, and is naturally accepted as such. The fundamental thing is to find the types of experience that are worth having, not merely for the moment, but because of what they lead to—the questions they raise, the problems they create, the demands for new information they suggest, the activities they invoke, the larger and expanding fields into which they continuously open.

In criticizing the progressive schools, as I have indicated already, it is difficult to make sweeping generalizations. But some of these schools indulge pupils in unrestrained freedom of action and speech, of manners and lack of manners. Schools farthest to the left (and there are many parents who share the fallacy) carry the thing they call freedom nearly to the point of anarchy. This license, however—this outer freedom in action—is but an included part of the larger question just touched upon. When there is genuine control and direction of experiences that are intrinsically worth while by objective subject matter, excessive liberty of outward action will also be naturally regulated. Ultimately it is the absence of intellectual control through significant subject matter which stimulates the deplorable egotism, cockiness, impertinence and disregard for the rights of others apparently considered by some persons to be the inevitable accompaniment, if not the essence, of freedom.

The fact that even the most extreme of the progressive schools do obtain for their pupils a degree of mental independence and power which stands them in good stead when they go to schools where formal methods prevail, is evidence of what might be done if the emphasis were put upon the rational freedom which is the fruit of objective knowledge and understanding. And thus we are brought to the nub of the matter. To conduct a progressive school is much more difficult than to conduct a formal one. Standards, materials, methods are already at hand for the latter; the teacher needs only to follow and conform. Upon the whole, it is not surprising that, in history, science, the arts and other school "studies," there is still a lack of subject matter which has been organized upon the basis of connection with the pupils' own growth in insight and power. The time-span of progressive schools has been too short to permit very much to be accomplished. What may rightfully be demanded, however, is that the progressive schools recognize their responsibility for accomplishing this task, so as not to be content with casual improvisation and living intellectually from hand to mouth.

Again one needs to guard against misunderstanding. There is no single body of subject matter which can be worked out, even in the course of years, which will be applicable all over the country. I am not arguing for any such outcome; I know of nothing that would so completely kill progressive schools and turn them into another kind of formal schools, differentiated only by having another set of conventions. Even in the same school, what will work with one group of children will not "take" with another group of the same age. Full recognition of the fact that subject matter must be always changing with locality, with the situation and with the particular type of children is, however, quite consistent with equal recognition of the fact that it is possible to work out varied bodies of consecutive subject matter upon which teachers may draw, each in his own way, in conducting his own work. The older type of education could draw upon a body of information, of subject matter and skills which was arranged from the adult standpoint. Progressive education must have a much larger, more expansive and adaptable body of materials and activities, developed through constant study of the conditions and methods favorable to the consecutive development of power and understanding. The weakness of existing progressive education is due to the meagre knowledge which anyone has regarding the conditions and laws of continuity which govern the development of mental power. To this extent its defects are inevitable and are not to be complained of. But if progressive schools become complacent with existing accomplishments, unaware of the slight foundation of knowledge upon which they rest, and careless regarding the amount of study of the laws of growth that remains to be done, a reaction against them is sure to take place. . . .

There is an intrinsic connection between choice as freedom and power of action as freedom. A choice which intelligently manifests individuality enlarges the range of action, and this enlargement in turn confers upon our desires greater insight and foresight, and makes choice more intelligent. There is a circle, but an enlarging circle, or, if you please, a widening spiral. This statement is of course only a formula. We may perhaps supply it with meaning by first considering the matter negatively. Take for example an act following from a blind preference, from an impulse not reflected upon. It will be a matter of luck if the resulting action does not get the one who acts into conflict with surrounding conditions. Conditions go against the realization of his preference; they cut across it, obstruct it, deflect its course, get him into new and perhaps more serious entanglements. Luck may be on his side. Circumstances may happen to be propitious or he may be endowed with native force that enables him to brush aside obstructions and sweep away resistances. He thus gets a certain freedom, judged from the side of power-to-do. But this result is a matter of favor, of grace, of luck; it is not due to anything in himself. Sooner or later he is likely to find his deeds at odds with conditions; an accidental success may only reinforce a foolhardy impulsiveness that renders a man's future subjection the more probable. Enduringly lucky persons are exceptions.

Suppose, on the other hand, our hero's act exhibits a choice expressing a preference formed after consideration of consequences, an intelligent preference. Consequences depend upon an interaction of what he starts to perform with his environment, so he must take the latter into account. No one can foresee all consequences because no one can be aware of all the conditions that enter into their production. Every person builds better or worse than he knows. Good fortune or the favorable cooperation of environment is still necessary. Even with his best thought, a man's proposed course of action may be defeated. But in as far as his act is truly a manifestation of intelligent choice, he learns something:—as in a scien-

[First published in *Freedom in the Modern World*, ed. Horace M. Kallen (New York: Coward-McCann, 1928); reprinted in *The Later Works*, Vol. 3.]

tific experiment an inquirer may learn through his experimentation, his intelligently directed action, quite as much or even more from a failure than from a success. He finds out at least a little as to what was the matter with his prior choice. He can choose better and *do* better next time; "better choice" meaning a more reflective one, and "better doing" meaning one better coordinated with the conditions that are involved in realizing his purpose. Such control or power is never complete; luck or fortune, the propitious support of circumstances not foreseeable is always involved. But at least such a person forms the habit of choosing and acting with conscious regard to the grain of circumstance, the run of affairs. And what is more to the point, such a man becomes able to turn frustration and failure to account in his further choices and purposes. Everything insofar serves his purpose—to be an intelligent human being. This gain in power or freedom can be nullified by no amount of external defeats.

In a phrase just used, it was implied that intelligent choice may operate on different levels or in different areas. A man may, so to speak, specialize in intelligent choices in the region of economic or political affairs; he may be shrewd, politic, within the limit of these conditions, and insofar attain power in action or be free. Moralists have always held that such success is not success, such power not power, such freedom not freedom, in the ultimate sense.

One does not need to enter upon hortatory moralization in order to employ this contention of the great moral teachers for the sake of eliciting two points. The first is that there are various areas of freedom, because there is a plural diversity of conditions in our environment, and choice, intelligent choice, may select the special area formed by one special set of conditions—familial and domestic, industrial, pecuniary, political, charitable, scientific, ecclesiastic, artistic, etc. I do not mean of course that these areas are sharply delimited or that there is not something artificial in their segregation. But within limits, conditions are such that specialized types of choice and kinds of power or freedom develop. The second (and this is the one emphasized by moral teachers in drawing a line between true and false power and freedom), is that there *may* be—these moral idealists insist there *is*—one area in which freedom and power are always attainable by any one, no matter how much he may be blocked in other fields. This of course is the area they call *moral* in a distinctive sense. To put it roughly but more concretely: Any one can be kind, helpful to others, just and temperate in his choices, and insofar be sure of achievement and power in action. It would take more rashness than I possess to assert that there is not an observation of reality in this insight of the great teachers of the race. But without taking up that point, one may venture with confidence upon a hypothetical statement. If and inasfar as this idea is correct, there is one way in which the force of fortunate circumstance and lucky original endowment is reduced in comparison with the force of the factor supplied by personal individuality itself. Success, power, freedom in *special* fields is in a maximum degree relatively at the mercy of external conditions. But against kindness and justice there is no law: that is, no counteracting grain of things nor run of affairs. With respect to such choices, there may be freedom and power, no matter what the frustrations and failures in other modes of action. Such is the virtual claim of moral prophets.

An illustration drawn from the denial of the idea that there is an intimate connection of the two modes of freedom, namely, intelligent choice and power in action, may aid in clearing up the idea. The attitude and acts of other persons is of course one of the most important parts of the conditions involved in bringing the manifestation of preference to impotency or to power in action. Take the case of a child in a family where the environment formed by others is such as to humor all his choices. It is made easy for him to do what he pleases. He meets a minimum of resistance; upon the whole others cooperate with him in bringing his preferences to fulfillment. Within this region he seems to have free power of action. By description he is unimpeded, even aided. But it is obvious that as far as he is concerned, this is a matter of luck. He is "free" merely because his surrounding conditions happen to be of the kind they are, a mere happening or accident as far as his make-up and his preferences are concerned. It is evident in such a case that there is *no growth* in the intelligent exercise of preferences. There is rather a conversion of blind impulse into regular habits. Hence his attained freedom is such only in appearance: it disappears as he moves into other social conditions.

Now consider the opposite case. A child is balked, inhibited, interfered with and nagged pretty continuously in the manifestation of his spontaneous preferences. He is constantly "disciplined" by circumstances adverse to his preferences—as discipline is not infrequently conceived. Does it follow then that he develops in "inner" freedom, in thoughtful preference and purpose? The question answers itself. Rather is some pathological condition the outcome. "Discipline" is indeed necessary as a preliminary to any freedom that is more than unrestrained outward power. But our dominant conception of discipline is a travesty; there is only one genuine discipline, namely, that which takes effect in producing habits of observation and judgment that ensure intelligent desires. In short, while men do not think about and gain freedom in conduct unless they run during action against conditions that resist their original impulses, the secret of education consists in having that blend of check and favor which influences thought and foresight, and that takes effect in outward action through this modification of disposition and outlook.

I have borrowed the illustration from the life of a child at home or in school, because the problem is familiar and easily recognizable in those settings. But there is no difference when we consider the adult in industrial, political and ecclesiastic life. When social conditions are such as to prepare a prosperous career for a man's spontaneous preferences in advance, when things are made easy by institutions and by habits of admiration and approval, there is precisely the same kind of outward freedom, of relatively unimpeded action, as in the case of the spoiled child. But there is hardly more of freedom on the side of varied and flexible capacity of choice; preferences are restricted to the one line laid down, and in the end the individual becomes the slave of his successes. Others, vastly more in number, are in the state of the "disciplined" child. There is hard sledding for their spontaneous preferences; the grain of the environment, especially of existing economic arrangements, runs against them. But the check, the inhibition to the immediate operation of their native preferences no more confers on them the quality of intelligent choice than it does with the child who never gets a fair chance to try himself out. There is only a crushing that results in apathy and indifference; a deflection into evasion and deceit; a compensatory over-responsiveness to such occasions as permit untrained preferences to run riot—and all the other consequences which the literature of mental and moral pathology has made familiar.

I hope these illustrations may at least have rendered reasonably clear what is intended by our formula; by the idea that freedom consists in a trend of conduct that causes choices to be more diversified and flexible, more plastic and more cognizant of their own meaning, while it enlarges their range of unimpeded operation. There is an important implication in this idea of freedom. The orthodox theory of freedom of the will and the classic theory of Liberalism both define freedom on the basis of something antecedently given, something already possessed. Unlike in contents as are the imputation of unmotivated liberty of choice and of natural rights and native wants, the two ideas have an important element in common. They both seek for freedom in something already there, given in advance. Our idea compels us on the other hand to seek for freedom in something which comes to be, in a certain kind of growth; in consequences, rather than in antecedents. We are free not because of what we statically are, but insofar as we are becoming different from what we have been. Reference to another philosophy of freedom, that of Immanuel Kant, who is placed chronologically in the generation preceding that of Hegel and institutional idealism, may aid in developing this idea. If we ignore the cumbrous technicalities of Kant, we may take him as one who was impressed by the rise of natural science and the role played in science by the idea of causation, this being defined as a necessary, universal or invariant connection of phenomena. Kant saw that in all consistency this principle applies to human phenomena as well as to physical; it is a law of all phenomena. Such a chain of linked phenomena left no room for freedom. But Kant believed in duty and duty postulates freedom. Hence in his moral being, man is not a phenomenon but a member of a realm of noumena to which as things-in-themselves free causality may be ascribed. It is with the problem rather than the solution we are concerned. How one and the same act can be, naturalistically speaking, causally determined while transcendentally speaking it is free from any such determination is so high a mystery that I shall pass it by.

But the *problem* as Kant stated it has the form in which it weighs most heavily on contemporary consciousness. The idea of a reign of law, of the inclusion of all events under law, has become almost omnipresent. No freedom seems to be left save by alleging that man is somehow supranatural in his make-up—an idea of which Kant's noumenal and transcendental man is hardly more than a translation into a more impressive phraseology.

This way of stating the problem of freedom makes overt, explicit, the assumption that either freedom is something antecedently possessed or else it is nothing at all. The idea is so current that it seems hopeless to question its value. But suppose that the origin of every thought I have had and every word I have uttered is in some sense causally determined, so that if anybody knew enough he could explain the origin of each thought and each word just as the scientific inquirer ideally hopes to explain what happens physically. Suppose also—the argument is hypothetical and so imagination may be permitted to run riot—that my words had the effect of rendering the future choices of some one of my hearers more thoughtful; more cognizant of possible alternatives, and thereby rendering his future choices more varied, flexible and apt. Would the fact of antecedent causality deprive those future preferences of their actual quality? Would it take away their reality and that of their operation in producing their distinctive effects? There is no superstition more benumbing, I think, than the current notion that things are not what they are, and do not do what they are seen to do, because these things have themselves come into being in a causal way. Water is what it *does* rather than what it is caused by. The same is true of the fact of intelligent choice. A philosophy which looks for freedom in antecedents and one which looks for it in consequences, in a developing course of action, in becoming rather than in static being, will have very different notions about it.

Yet we cannot separate power to become from consideration of what already and antecedently is. Capacity to become different, even though we define freedom by it, must be a present capacity, something in some sense present. At this point of the inquiry, the fact that all existences whatever possess selectivity in action recurs with new import. It may sound absurd to speak of electrons and atoms exhibiting preference, still more perhaps to attribute bias to them. But the absurdity is wholly a matter of the words used. The essential point is that they have a certain opaque and irreducible individuality which shows itself in what they do; in the fact that they behave in certain ways and not in others. In the description of causal sequences, we still have to start with and from existences, things that are individually and uniquely just what they are. The fact that we can state changes which occur by certain uniformities and regularities does not eliminate this original element of individuality, of preference and bias. On the contrary, the statement of laws presupposes just this capacity. We cannot escape this fact by an attempt to treat each thing as an effect of other things. That merely pushes individuality back into those other things. Since we have to admit individuality no matter how far we carry the chase, we might as well forego the labor and start with the unescapable fact.

In short, anything that is has something unique in itself, and this unique something enters into what it does. Science does not concern itself with the individualities of things. It is concerned with their *relations*. A law or statement of uniformity like that of the so-called causal sequence tells us nothing about a thing inherently; it tells us only about an invariant relation sustained in behavior of that thing with that of other things. That this fact implies contingency as an ultimate and irreducible trait of existence is something too complicated to go into here. But evidence could be stated from many contemporary philosophers of science, not writing with any thought of freedom in mind, but simply as interpreters of the methods and conclusions of science, to the effect that the laws leave out of account the inner being of things, and deal only with their relations with other things. Indeed, if this were the place and if I only knew enough, it could be shown, I think, that the great change now going on in the physical sciences, is connected with this idea. Older formulas were in effect guilty of confusion. They took knowledge of the relations that things bear to one another as if it were knowledge of the things themselves. Many of the corrections that are now being introduced into physical theories are due to recognition of this confusion.

The point needs an elaboration that cannot here be given if its full import for the idea and fact of freedom is to be clearly perceived. But the connection is there and its general nature may be seen. The fact that all things show bias, preference or selectivity of reaction, while not itself freedom, is an indispensable condition of any human freedom. The present tendency among scientific men is to think of laws as statistical in nature—that is, as statements of an "average" found in the behavior of an enormous number of things, no two of which are exactly alike. If this line of thought be followed out, it implies that the existence of laws or uniformities and regularities among natural phenomena, human acts included, does not in the least exclude the item of choice as a distinctive fact having its own distinctive consequences. No law does away with individuality of existence, having its own particular way of operating; for a law is concerned with relations and hence presupposes the being and operation of individuals. If choice is found to be a distinctive act, having distinctive consequences, then no appeal to the authority of scientific law can militate in any way against its reality. The problem reduces itself to one of fact. Just what *is* intelligent choice and just what does it effect in human life? I cannot ask you to retraverse the ground already gone over. But I do claim that the considerations already adduced reveal that what men actually cherish under the name of freedom is that power of varied and flexible growth, of change of disposition and character, that springs from intelligent choice, so there is a sound basis for the common-sense practical belief in freedom, although theories in justification of this belief have often taken an erroneous and even absurd form.

We may indeed go further than we have gone. Not only is the presence of uniform relations of change no bar to the reality of freedom, but these are, *when known*, aids to the development of that freedom. Take the suppositious case already mentioned. That my ideas have causes signifies that their *rise*, their *origin* (not their nature), is a change connected with other changes. If I only knew the connection, my power over obtaining the ideas I want would be that much increased. The same thing holds good of any effect my idea may have upon the ideas and choices of some one else. Knowledge of the conditions under which a choice *arises* is the same as potential ability to guide the formation of choices intelligently. This does not eliminate the distinctive quality of choice; choice is still choice. But it is now an intelligent choice instead of a dumb and stupid one, and thereby the probability of its leading to freedom in unimpeded action is increased.

This fact explains the strategic position occupied in our social and political life by the issue of freedom of thought and freedom of speech. It is unnecessary to dwell by way of either laudation or exhortation upon the importance of this freedom. If the position already taken—namely, that freedom resides in the development of preferences into intelligent choices—is sound, there is an explanation of the central character of this particular sort of freedom. It has been assumed, in accord with the whole theory of Liberalism, that all that is necessary to secure freedom of thought and expression, is removal of external impediments: take away artificial obstructions and thought will operate. This notion involves all the errors of individualistic psychology. Thought is taken to be a native capacity or faculty; all it needs to operate is an outer chance. Thinking, however, is the most difficult occupation in which man engages. If the other arts have to be acquired through ordered apprenticeship, the power to think requires even more conscious and consecutive attention. No more than any other art is it developed internally. It requires favorable objective conditions, just as the art of painting requires paint, brushes and canvas. The most important problem in freedom of thinking is whether social conditions obstruct the development of judgment and insight or effectively promote it. We take for granted the necessity of special opportunity and prolonged education to secure ability to think in a special calling, like mathematics. But we appear to assume that ability to think effectively in social, political and moral matters is a gift of God, and that the gift operates by a kind of spontaneous combustion. Few would perhaps defend this doctrine thus boldly stated; but upon the whole we act as if that were true. Even our deliberate education, our schools are conducted so as to indoctrinate certain beliefs rather than to promote habits of thought. If that is true of them, what is not true of the other social institutions as to their effect upon thought?

This state of things accounts, to my mind, for the current indifference to what is the very heart of actual freedom: freedom of thought. It is considered to be enough to have certain legal guarantees of its possibility. Encroachment upon even the nominal legal guarantees appears to arouse less and less resentment. Indeed, since the mere absence of legal restrictions may take effect only in stimulating the expression of half-baked and foolish ideas, and since the effect of their expression may be idle or harmful, popular sentiment seems to be growing less and less adverse to the exercise of even overt censorships. A genuine energetic interest in the cause of human freedom will manifest itself in a jealous and unremitting care for the influence of social institutions upon the attitudes of curiosity, inquiry, weighing and testing of evidence. I shall begin to believe that we care more for freedom than we do for imposing our own beliefs upon others in order to subject them to our will, when I see that the main purpose of our schools and other institutions is to develop powers of unremitting and discriminating observation and judgment.

The other point is similar. It has often been assumed that freedom of speech, oral and written, is independent of freedom of thought, and that you cannot take the latter away in any case, since it goes on inside of minds where it cannot be got at. No idea could be more mistaken. Expression of ideas in communication is one of the indispensable conditions of the awakening of thought not only in others, but in ourselves. If ideas when aroused cannot be communicated they either fade away or become warped and morbid. The open air of public discussion and communication is an indispensable condition of the birth of ideas and knowledge and of other growth into health and vigor.

I sum up by saying that the possibility of freedom is deeply grounded in our very beings. It is one with our individuality, our being uniquely what we are and not imitators and parasites of others. But like all other possibilities, this possibility has to be actualized; and, like all others, it can only be actualized through interaction with objective conditions. The question of political and economic freedom is not an addendum or afterthought, much less a deviation or excrescence, in the problem of personal freedom. For the conditions that form political and economic liberty are required in order to realize the potentiality of freedom each of us carries with him in his very structure. Constant and uniform relations in change and a knowledge of them in "laws," are not a hindrance to freedom, but a necessary factor in coming to be effectively that which we have the capacity to grow into. Social conditions interact with the preferences of an individual (that *are* his individuality) in a way favorable to actualizing freedom only when they develop intelligence, not abstract knowledge and abstract thought, but power of vision and reflection. For these take effect in making preference, desire and purpose more flexible, alert, and resolute. Freedom has too long been thought of as an indeterminate power operating in a closed and ended world. In its reality, freedom is a resolute will operating in a world in some respects indeterminate, because open and moving toward a new future.

Renascent Liberalism

I begin with an example of what is really involved in the issue. Why is it, apart from our tradition of violence, that liberty of expression is tolerated and even lauded when social affairs seem to be going in a quiet fashion, and yet is so readily destroyed whenever matters grow critical? The general answer, of course, is that at bottom social institutions have habituated us to the use of force in some veiled form. But a part of the answer is found in our ingrained habit of regarding intelligence as an individual possession and its exercise as an individual right. It is false that freedom of inquiry and of expression are not modes of action. They are exceedingly potent modes of action. The reactionary grasps this fact, in practice if not in express idea, more quickly than the liberal, who is too much given to holding that this freedom is innocent of consequences, as well as being a merely individual right. The result is that this liberty is tolerated as long as it does not seem to menace in any way the *status quo* of society. When it does, every effort is put forth to identify the established order with the public good. When this identification is established, it follows that any merely individual right must yield to the general welfare. As long as freedom of thought and speech is claimed as a merely individual right, it will give way, as do other merely personal claims, when it is, or is successfully represented to be, in opposition to the general welfare. . . .

Liberalism has to assume the responsibility for making it clear that intelligence is a social asset and is clothed with a function as public as is its origin, in the concrete, in social cooperation. It was Comte who, in reaction against the purely individualistic ideas that seemed to him to underlie the French Revolution, said that in mathematics, physics and astronomy there is no right of private conscience. If we remove the statement from the context of actual scientific procedure, it is dangerous because it is false. The individual inquirer has not only the right but the duty to criticize the ideas, theories and "laws" that are current in science. But if we take the statement in the context of scientific method, it indicates that he carries on this criticism in virtue of a socially generated body of knowledge and by means of methods that are not of private origin and possession. He uses a method that retains public validity even when innovations are introduced in its use and application. . . .

[From *Liberalism and Social Action* (New York: G. P. Putnam's Sons, 1935); reprinted in *The Later Works*, Vol. 11.]

. . . I wish to say something about the operation of intelligence in our present political institutions, as exemplified by current practices of democratic government. I would not minimize the advance scored in substitution of methods of discussion and conference for the method of arbitrary rule. But the better is too often the enemy of the still better. Discussion, as the manifestation of intelligence in political life, stimulates publicity; by its means sore spots are brought to light that would otherwise remain hidden. It affords opportunity for promulgation of new ideas. Compared with despotic rule, it is an invitation to individuals to concern themselves with public affairs. But discussion and dialectic, however indispensable they are to the elaboration of ideas and policies after ideas are once put forth, are weak reeds to depend upon for systematic origination of comprehensive plans, the plans that are required if the problem of social organization is to be met. There was a time when discussion, the comparison of ideas already current so as to purify and clarify them, was thought to be sufficient in discovery of the structure and laws of physical nature. In the latter field, the method was displaced by that of experimental observation guided by comprehensive working hypotheses, and using all the resources made available by mathematics.

But we still depend upon the method of discussion, with only incidental scientific control, in politics. Our system of popular suffrage, immensely valuable as it is in comparison with what preceded it, exhibits the idea that intelligence is an individualistic possession, at best enlarged by public discussion. Existing political practice, with its complete ignoring of occupational groups and the organized knowledge and purposes that are involved in the existence of such groups, manifests a dependence upon a summation of individuals quantitatively, similar to Bentham's purely quantitative formula of the greatest sum of pleasures of the greatest possible number. The formation of parties or, as the eighteenth-century writers called them, factions, and the system of party government is the practically necessary counterweight to a numerical and atomistic individualism. The idea that the conflict of parties will, by means of public discussion, bring out necessary public truths is a kind of political watered-down version of the Hegelian dialectic, with its synthesis arrived at by a union of antithetical conceptions. The method has nothing in common with the procedure of organized cooperative inquiry which has won the triumphs of science in the field of physical nature.

Intelligence in politics when it is identified with discussion means reliance upon symbols. The invention of language is probably the greatest single invention achieved by humanity. The development of political forms that promote the use of symbols in place of arbitrary power was another great invention. The nineteenth-century establishment of parliamentary institutions, written constitutions and the suffrage as means of political rule, is a tribute to the power of symbols. But symbols are significant only in connection with realities behind them. No intelligent observer can deny, I think, that they are often used in party politics as a substitute for realities instead of as means of contact with them. Popular literacy, in connection with the telegraph, cheap postage and the printing press, has enormously multiplied the number of those influenced. That which we term education has done a good deal to generate habits that put symbols in the place of realities. The forms of popular government make necessary the elaborate use of words to influence political action. "Propaganda" is the inevitable consequence of the combination of these influences and it extends to every area of life. Words not only take the place of realities but are themselves debauched. Decline in the prestige of suffrage and of parliamentary government are intimately associated with the belief, manifest in practice even if not expressed in words, that intelligence is an individual possession to be reached by means of verbal persuasion.

This fact suggests, by way of contrast, the genuine meaning of intelligence in connection with public opinion, sentiment and action. The crisis in democracy demands the substitution of the intelligence that is exemplified in scientific procedure for the kind of intelligence that is now accepted. The need for this change is not exhausted in the demand for greater honesty and impartiality, even though these qualities be now corrupted by discussion carried on mainly for purposes of party supremacy and for imposition of some special but concealed interest. These qualities need to be restored. But the need goes further. The social use of intelligence would remain deficient even if these moral traits were exalted, and yet intelligence continued to be identified simply with discussion and persuasion, necessary as are these things. Approximation to use of scientific method in investigation and of the engineering mind in the invention and projection of far-reaching social plans is demanded. The habit of considering social realities in terms of cause and effect and social policies in terms of means and consequences is still inchoate. The contrast between the state of intelligence in politics and in the physical control of nature is to be taken literally. What has happened in this latter is the outstanding demonstration of the meaning of organized intelligence. The combined effect of science and technology has released more productive energies in a bare hundred years than stands to the credit of prior human history in its entirety. Productively it has multiplied nine million times in the last generation alone. The prophetic vision of

Francis Bacon of subjugation of the energies of nature through change in methods of inquiry has well-nigh been realized. The stationary engine, the locomotive, the dynamo, the motor car, turbine, telegraph, telephone, radio and moving picture are not the products of either isolated individual minds nor of the particular economic régime called capitalism. They are the fruit of methods that first penetrated to the working causalities of nature and then utilized the resulting knowledge in bold imaginative ventures of invention and construction.

We hear a great deal in these days about class conflict. The past history of man is held up to us as almost exclusively a record of struggles between classes, ending in the victory of a class that had been oppressed and the transfer of power to it. It is difficult to avoid reading the past in terms of the contemporary scene. Indeed, fundamentally it is impossible to avoid this course. With a certain proviso, it is highly important that we are compelled to follow this path. For the past as past is gone, save for esthetic enjoyment and refreshment, while the present is with us. Knowledge of the past is significant only as it deepens and extends our understanding of the present. Yet there is a proviso. We must grasp the things that are most important in the present when we turn to the past and not allow ourselves to be misled by secondary phenomena no matter how intense and immediately urgent they are. Viewed from this standpoint, the rise of scientific method and of technology based upon it is the genuinely active force in producing the vast complex of changes the world is now undergoing, not the class struggle whose spirit and method are opposed to science. If we lay hold upon the causal force exercised by this embodiment of intelligence we shall know where to turn for the means of directing further change.

When I say that scientific method and technology have been the active force in producing the revolutionary transformations society is undergoing, I do not imply no other forces have been at work to arrest, deflect and corrupt their operation. Rather this fact is positively implied. At this point, indeed, is located the conflict that underlies the confusions and uncertainties of the present scene. The conflict is between institutions and habits originating in the pre-scientific and pre-technological age and the new forces generated by science and technology. The application of science, to a considerable degree, even its own growth, has been conditioned by the system to which the name of capitalism is given, a rough designation of a complex of political and legal arrangements centering about a particular mode of economic relations. Because of the conditioning of science and technology by this setting, the second and humanly most important part of Bacon's prediction has so far largely missed realization. The conquest of natural energies has not accrued to the betterment of the common human estate in anything like the degree he anticipated.

Because of conditions that were set by the legal institutions and the moral ideas existing when the scientific and industrial revolutions came into being, the chief usufruct of the latter has been appropriated by a relatively small class. Industrial entrepreneurs have reaped out of all proportion to what they sowed. By obtaining private ownership of the means of production and exchange they deflected a considerable share of the results of increased productivity to their private pockets. This appropriation was not the fruit of criminal conspiracy or of sinister intent. It was sanctioned not only by legal institutions of age-long standing but by the entire prevailing moral code. The institution of private property long antedated feudal times. It is the institution with which men have lived, with few exceptions, since the dawn of civilization. Its existence has deeply impressed itself upon mankind's moral conceptions. Moreover, the new industrial forces tended to break down many of the rigid class barriers that had been in force, and to give to millions a new outlook and inspire a new hope;—especially in this country with no feudal background and no fixed class system.

Since the legal institutions and the patterns of mind characteristic of ages of civilization still endure, there exists the conflict that brings confusion into every phase of present life. The problem of bringing into being a new social orientation and organization is, when reduced to its ultimates, the problem of using the new resources of production, made possible by the advance of physical science, for social ends, for what Bentham called the greatest good of the greatest number. Institutional relationships fixed in the pre-scientific age stand in the way of accomplishing this great transformation. Lag in mental and moral patterns provides the bulwark of the older institutions; in expressing the past they still express present beliefs, outlooks and purposes. Here is the place where the problem of liberalism centres today.

The argument drawn from past history that radical change must be effected by means of class struggle, culminating in open war, fails to discriminate between the two forces, one active, the other resistant and deflecting, that have produced the social scene in which we live. The active force is, as I have said, scientific method and technological application. The opposite force is that of older institutions and the habits that have grown up around them. Instead of discrimination between forces and distribution of their consequences, we find the two things lumped together. The compound is labeled the capitalistic or the bourgeois class, and to this class as a class is imputed all the important features of present industrialized society—much as the defenders of the régime of economic liberty exercised for private property are accustomed to attribute every improvement made in the last century and a half to the same capitalistic régime. Thus in orthodox communist literature, from the *Communist Manifesto* of 1848 to the present day, we are told that the bourgeoisie, the name for a distinctive class, has done this and that. It has, so it is said, given a cosmopolitan character to production and consumption; has destroyed the national basis of industry; has agglomerated population in urban centres; has transferred power from the country to the city, in the process of creating colossal productive force, its chief achievement. In addition, it has created crises of ever renewed intensity; has created imperialism of a new type in frantic effort to control raw materials and markets. Finally, it has created a new class, the proletariat, and has created it as a class having a common interest opposed to that of the bourgeoisie, and is giving an irresistible stimulus to its organization, first as a class and then as a political power. According to the economic version of the Hegelian dialectic, the bourgeois class is thus creating its own complete and polar opposite, and this in time will end the old power and rule. The class struggle of veiled civil war will finally burst into open revolution and the result will be either the common ruin of the contending parties or a revolutionary reconstitution of society at large through a transfer of power from one class to another.

The position thus sketched unites vast sweep with great simplicity. I am concerned with it here only as far as it emphasizes the idea of a struggle between classes, culminating in open and violent warfare as being the method for production of radical social change. For, be it noted, the issue is not whether some amount of violence will accompany the effectuation of radical change of institutions. The question is whether force of intelligence is to be the method upon which we consistently rely and to whose promotion we devote our energies. Insistence that the use of violent force is *inevitable* limits the use of available intelligence, for wherever the inevitable reigns intelligence cannot be used. Commitment to inevitability is always the fruit of dogma; intelligence does not pretend to *know* save as a result of experimentation, the opposite of preconceived dogma. Moreover, acceptance in advance of the inevitability of violence tends to produce the use of violence in cases where peaceful methods might otherwise avail. The curious fact is that while it is generally admitted that this and that particular social problem, say of the family, or railroads or banking, must be solved, if at all, by the method of intelligence, yet there is supposed to be some one all-inclusive social problem which can be solved only by the use of violence. This fact would be inexplicable were it not a conclusion from dogma as its premise.

It is frequently asserted that the method of experimental intelligence can be applied to physical facts because physical nature does not present conflicts of class interests, while it is inapplicable to society because the latter is so deeply marked by incompatible interests. It is then assumed that the "experimentalist" is one who has chosen to ignore the uncomfortable fact of conflicting interests. Of course, there *are* conflicting interests; otherwise there would be no social problems. The problem under discussion is precisely *how* conflicting claims are to be settled in the interest of the widest possible contribution to the interests of all—or at least of the great majority. The method of democracy—inasfar as it is that of organized intelligence—is to bring these conflicts out into the open where their special claims can be seen and appraised, where they can be discussed and judged in the light of more inclusive interests than are represented by either of them separately. There is, for example, a clash of interests between munition manufacturers and most of the rest of the population. The more the respective claims of the two are publicly and scientifically weighed, the more likely it is that the public interest will be disclosed and be made effective. There is an undoubted objective clash of interests between finance-capitalism that controls the means of production and whose profit is served by maintaining relative scarcity, and idle workers and hungry consumers. But what generates violent strife is failure to bring the conflict into the light of intelligence where the conflicting interests can be adjudicated in behalf of the interest of the great majority. Those most committed to the dogma of inevitable force recognize the need for intelligently discovering and expressing the dominant social interest up to a certain point and then draw back. The "experimentalist" is one who would see to it that the method depended upon by all in some degree in every democratic community be followed through to completion. . . .

It is true that in this country, because of the interpretations made by courts of a written constitution, our political institutions are unusually inflexible. It is also true, as well as even more important (because it is a factor in causing this rigidity) that our institutions, democratic in form, tend to favor in substance a privileged plutocracy. Nevertheless, it is sheer defeatism to assume in advance of actual trial that democratic political institutions are incapable either of further development or of constructive social application. . . .

. . . It requires an unusually credulous faith in the Hegelian dialectic of opposites to think that all of a sudden the use of force by a class will be transmuted into a democratic classless society. Force breeds counterforce; the Newtonian law of action and reaction still holds in physics, and violence is physical. To profess democracy as an ultimate ideal and the suppression of democracy as a means to the ideal may be possible in a country that has never known even rudimentary democracy, but when professed in a country that has anything of a genuine democratic spirit in its traditions, it signifies desire for possession and retention of power by a class, whether that class be called Fascist or Proletarian. In the light of what happens in non-democratic countries, it is pertinent to ask whether the rule of a class signifies the dictatorship of the majority, or dictatorship over the chosen class by a minority party; whether dissenters are allowed even within the class the party claims to represent; and whether the development of literature and the other arts proceeds according to a formula prescribed by a party in conformity with a doctrinaire dogma of history and of infallible leadership, or whether artists are free from regimentation? Until these questions are satisfactorily answered, it is permissible to look with considerable suspicion upon those who assert that suppression of democracy is the road to the adequate establishment of genuine democracy. The one exception—and that apparent rather than real—to dependence upon organized intelligence as the method for directing social change is found when society through an authorized majority has entered upon the path of social experimentation leading to great social change, and a minority refuses by force to permit the method of intelligent action to go into effect. Then force may be intelligently employed to subdue and disarm the recalcitrant minority.

There may be some who think I am unduly dignifying a position held by a comparatively small group by taking their arguments as seriously as I have done. But their position serves to bring into strong relief the alternatives before us. It makes clear the meaning of renascent liberalism. The alternatives are continuation of drift with attendant improvisations to meet special emergencies; dependence upon violence; dependence upon socially organized intelligence. The first two alternatives, however, are not mutually exclusive, for if things are allowed to drift the result may be some sort of social change effected by the use of force, whether so planned or not. Upon the whole, the recent policy of liberalism has been to further "social legislation"; that is, measures which add performance of social services to the older functions of government. The value of this addition is not to be despised. It marks a decided move away from *laissez faire* liberalism, and has considerable importance in educating the public mind to a realization of the possibilities of organized social control. It has helped to develop some of the techniques that in any case will be needed in a socialized economy. But the cause of liberalism will be lost for a considerable period if it is not prepared to go further and socialize the forces of production, now at hand, so that the liberty of individuals will be supported by the very structure of economic organization.

The ultimate place of economic organization in human life is to assure the secure basis for an ordered expression of individual capacity and for the satisfaction of the needs of man in non-economic directions. The effort of mankind in connection with material production belongs, as I said earlier, among interests and activities that are, relatively speaking, routine in character, "routine" being defined as that which, without absorbing attention and energy, provides a constant basis for liberation of the values of intellectual, esthetic and companionship life. Every significant religious and moral teacher and prophet has asserted that the material is instrumental to the good life. Nominally at least, this idea is accepted by every civilized community. The transfer of the burden of material production from human muscles and brain to steam, electricity and chemical processes now makes possible the effective actualization of this ideal. Needs, wants and desires are always the moving force in generating creative action. When these wants are compelled by force of conditions to be directed for the most part, among the mass of mankind, into obtaining the means of subsistence, what should be a means becomes perforce an end in itself. Up to the present the new mechanical forces of production, which are the means of emancipation from this state of affairs, have been employed to intensify and exaggerate the reversal of the true relation between means and ends. Humanly speaking, I do not see how it would have been possible to avoid an epoch having this character. But its perpetuation is the cause of the continually growing social chaos and strife. Its termination cannot be effected by preaching to individuals that they should place spiritual ends above material means. It can be brought about by organized social reconstruction that puts the results of the mechanism of abundance at the free disposal of individuals. The actual corrosive "materialism" of our times does not proceed from science. It springs from the notion, sedulously cultivated by the class in power, that the creative capacities of individuals can be evoked and developed only in a struggle for material possessions and material gain. We either should surrender our professed belief in the supremacy of ideal and spiritual values and accommodate our beliefs to the predominant material orientation, or we should through organized endeavor institute the socialized economy of material security and plenty that will release human energy for pursuit of higher values.

Since liberation of the capacities of individuals for free, self-initiated expression is an essential part of the creed of liberalism, liberalism that is sincere must will the means that condition the achieving of its ends. Regimentation of material and mechanical forces is the only way by which the mass of individuals can be released from regimentation and consequent suppression of their cultural possibilities. The eclipse of liberalism is due to the fact that it has not faced the alternatives and adopted the means upon which realization of its professed aims depends. Liberalism can be true to its ideals only as it takes the course that leads to their attainment. The notion that organized social control of economic forces lies outside the historic path of liberalism shows that liberalism is still impeded by remnants of its earlier *laissez faire* phase, with its opposition of society and the individual. The thing which now dampens liberal ardor and paralyzes its efforts is the conception that liberty and development of individuality as ends exclude the use of organized social effort as means. Earlier liberalism regarded the separate and competing economic action of individuals as the means to social well-being as the end. We must reverse the perspective and see that socialized economy is the means of free individual development as the end.

That liberals are divided in outlook and endeavor while reactionaries are held together by community of interests and the ties of custom is well-nigh a commonplace. Organization of standpoint and belief among liberals can be achieved only in and by unity of endeavor. Organized unity of action attended by consensus of beliefs will come about in the degree in which social control of economic forces is made the goal of liberal action. The greatest educational power, the greatest force in shaping the dispositions and attitudes of individuals, is the social medium in which they live. The medium that now lies closest to us is that of unified action for the inclusive end of a socialized economy. . . .

. . . Democracy has been a fighting faith. When its ideals are reenforced by those of scientific method and experimental intelligence, it cannot be that it is incapable of evoking discipline, ardor and organization. To narrow the issue for the future to a struggle between Fascism and Communism is to invite a catastrophe that may carry civilization down in the struggle. Vital and courageous democratic liberalism is the one force that can surely avoid such a disastrous narrowing of the issue. I for one do not believe that Americans living in the tradition of Jefferson and Lincoln will weaken and give up without a whole-hearted effort to make democracy a living reality. This, I repeat, involves organization.

The question cannot be answered by argument. Experimental method means experiment, and the question can be answered only by trying, by organized effort. The reasons for making the trial are not abstract or recondite. They are found in the confusion, uncertainty and conflict that mark the modern world. The reasons for thinking that the effort if made will be successful are also not abstract and remote. They lie in what the method of experimental and cooperative intelligence has already accomplished in subduing to potential human use the energies of physical nature. In material production, the method of intelligence is now the established rule; to abandon it would be to revert to savagery. The task is to go on, and not backward, until the method of intelligence and experimental control is the rule in social relations and social direction. Either we take this road or we admit that the problem of social organization in behalf of human liberty and the flowering of human capacities is insoluble.

It would be fantastic folly to ignore or to belittle the obstacles that stand in the way. But what has taken place, also against great odds, in the scientific and industrial revolutions, is an accomplished fact; the way is marked out. It may be that the way will remain untrodden. If so, the future holds the menace of confusion moving into chaos, a chaos that will be externally masked for a time by an organization of force, coercive and violent, in which the liberties of men will all but disappear. Even so, the cause of the liberty of the human spirit, the cause of opportunity of human beings for full development of their powers, the cause for which liberalism enduringly stands, is too precious and too ingrained in the human constitution to be forever obscured. Intelligence after millions of years of errancy has found itself as a method, and it will not be lost forever in the blackness of night. The business of liberalism is to bend every energy and exhibit every courage so that these precious goods may not even be temporarily lost but be intensified and expanded here and now.

The Pathos of Liberalism

Reinhold Niebuhr

No one in America has a more generally conceded right to speak in the name of liberalism than John Dewey. He has been for many years not only the leading philosophical exponent of liberal doctrine but the fountain and source of liberal pedagogical theory and method. He has furthermore been active in a score of political and social movements in which he has proved not only his interest in the practical application of his theories but also a courageous willingness to extend both his theory and his practice beyond the limits set by traditional liberalism.

A new book by Professor Dewey[1] therefore offers excellent opportunity to assess the resources of liberalism in the present social scene, particularly since the book is a theoretic elaboration of his advanced position. The great contribution of historic liberalism, declares Professor Dewey, was its emphasis upon liberty and intelligence. Its great need today is to serve the cause of liberty by helping to create a social structure in which the ideal will become a reality for the many and not the few; and to make "freed intelligence" socially effective. All that is good in a modern advanced liberalism is revealed in the development of the first point and all that is dubious betrays itself in the second.

"Liberalism," declares Professor Dewey, "must now become radical, meaning by 'radical' perception of thoroughgoing changes in the set-up of institutions and corresponding activity to bring the changes to pass." This social radicalism is gradualistic in method but not reformist: "The process of producing changes will in any case be a gradual one. But 'reforms,' which deal now with this abuse and now with that without having a social goal based upon an inclusive plan, differ entirely from effort at reforming, in its literal sense, the institutional scheme of things." The motive of advanced or radical liberalism in seeking this thoroughgoing reorganization of the social order is to secure the value of liberty, to which liberalism is committed, in economic and not merely in legal terms: "The majority who call themselves liberals today are committed to the principle that organized society must use its powers to establish conditions under which the mass of individuals can possess actual as

[First published in *The Nation*, Vol. 141, No. 3662 (11 September 1935).]
1. *Liberalism and Social Action.* By John Dewey. G. P. Putnam's Sons. $1.50.

distinct from merely legal liberty. . . . They believe that the conception of the state which limits the activities of the latter to keeping order between individuals and to securing redress for one person when another infringes the liberty existing law has given him is in effect simply a justification of the brutalities and inequities of the existing system."

The ultimate end toward which Professor Dewey's liberalism strives is socialistic: "The only form of enduring social organization that is now possible is one in which the new forces of productivity are cooperatively controlled and used in the interest of the effective liberty and the cultural development of the individuals that constitute society." This end "can now be achieved only by a reversal of the means to which early liberalism was committed." Professor Dewey's devotion to liberty has, in short, nothing in common with that of Herbert Hoover, who has given such a perfect statement of the plutocratic corruption of the creed of liberalism. Nor has it much in common with the piecemeal reformism of the more timid liberals. His statement of faith is typical of a large body of intellectual liberalism, which resists the dishonest appropriation and corruption of the liberal creed by the plutocratic oligarchs of our society and which sees the problem of social change in larger terms that those of mere reformism.

So far, so good. It is in his discussion of the function of intelligence in the process of social change that the limitations of Professor Dewey's liberalism appear. No one would quarrel with him in his insistence on the necessity of avoiding drift into chaos and the corresponding necessity of an intelligent direction of social change. Nor is he wrong when he protests against the dogmatism of certain types of radicalism. Nevertheless, every argument used in developing his theme of the function of "freed intelligence" in social change betrays a constitutional weakness in the liberal approach to politics. It does not recognize the relation of social and economic interest to the play of intelligence upon social problems. It does not perceive the perennial and inevitable character of the subordination of reason to interest in the social struggle. Its ideal of a "freed intelligence" expects a degree of rational freedom from the particular interests and perspectives of those who think about social problems which is incompatible with the very constitution of human nature.

This weakness reveals itself at every turn. The possibilities of intelligence in social action are supposedly proved by the achievements of science in the development of a technical civilization: "What are the modern forces of production save those of scientific technology? And what is scientific technology save a large-scale demonstration of organized intelligence in action?" This is supposed to refute the Marxian

thesis of the revolutionary dynamic created by the incompatibility between new forces of production and the legal property system. Why, then,
did not this "organized intelligence" which created a technical civilization create also an economic and political system which would make such
a civilization sufferable? The answer is given in the theory of a cultural
lag. "The release of productivity is the product of cooperatively organized intelligence," and the "institutional framework is precisely that
which is not yet subjected to any considerable degree to the impact of
inventive and instructive intelligence." An example of this cultural lag is
the notion that social insecurity is an incentive to diligence. "Early liberalism emphasized the importance of insecurity as a fundamentally necessary economic motive." But the "conditions of insecurity now no longer
spring from nature," and therefore "insecurity is *not now* the motive to
work and sacrifice but to despair." But the habits of mind and action of
the earlier period still persist and operate to retard social change in the
interest of greater security. This theory actually assumes that there was a
time in which social insecurity was a generator of diligence, and does not
recognize that the earlier liberalism, in spite of its greater honesty, was
just as much as capitalistic liberalism a tool of class interest. The idea
that social insecurity is a necessary incentive to diligence was not true
when it was first propounded and is not held now merely because old
patterns of thought persist.

The same inability to recognize the perennial enslavement of even
"freed intelligence" to partial and particular interests is revealed in Professor Dewey's discussion of violence and social change. With every
responsible analyst of the modern social crisis, Professor Dewey would
like to resolve our social difficulties without violence. There can be no
quarrel with him over his thesis of the perils of violence not only to the
proletarian proponents of a new social order but to civilization itself. But
the discussion of the possibility of avoiding violence lacks realism because Professor Dewey again sees violence only as a consequence of a
social ignorance which a more perfect intelligence will be able to eliminate. Unlike many liberals he sees the coercive and even violent character of present society: "It is not pleasant to face the extent to which, as a
matter of fact, coercive and violent force are relied upon in the present
social system as a means of social control." The assumption "that the
method of intelligence already rules and that those who urge the use of
violence are introducing a new element into the social picture may not be
hypocritical but it is unintelligently unaware of what is actually involved
in intelligence as an alternative method of social action." In other words,
the real question is how the holders of privilege and power are to be

dissuaded from violence as a means of preventing necessary social change. This must be done by destroying the "ingrained habit of regarding intelligence as an individual possession and its exercise as an individual right"—"Liberalism must assume the responsibility for making it clear that intelligence is a social asset and is clothed with a function as public as is its origin." A liberalism which defends liberty as a public necessity rather than a private right will supposedly sooth the savage breast of an imperiled and frantic oligarchy, while the older and more individualistic liberalism merely succeeded in maintaining liberty "as long as it did not menace the status quo." One might as well expect to beguile the gentlemen of the Liberty League to modify their touching devotion to the Constitution by proving to them logically, rationally, and intellectually that the flexibility of the Constitution is a necessary prerequisite of orderly social change.

To say all this is not to assume that violence and civil war are absolutely inevitable in basic social change. But their avoidance depends upon quite different considerations from those advanced by Professor Dewey; upon the possibility, for instance, of securing some modicum of political cooperation between the industrial workers, the farmers, and the lower middle classes. If that cannot be achieved, and if the lower middle classes must inevitably become the allies of an imperiled plutocracy, violence will scarcely be avoided, no matter how much intellectuals may bewail the tragic and tortuous character of the processes of history.

It must be said in conclusion that Professor Dewey expressly denies that liberalism ignores the fact that conflicting interests in society prevent the method of experimental intelligence from being as effective in social problems as in the physical sciences. "The method of democracy is to bring these conflicting interests out into the open, where their special claims can be seen and appraised and where they can be discussed and judged in the light of more inclusive interests." Now it is a fact that many conflicts of interest are thus arbitrated, at least when the contrast between them is not too sharp and when the contending parties do not absorb the total community and therefore destroy the last remnant of impartiality and neutrality in the community with reference to a particular dispute. It is when that happens that we have a revolutionary situation.

In envisaging the possibilities of a rational arbitration of conflicting interests Professor Dewey hopes for a day in which party disputes will give way to an impartial and scientific inquiry into the cause and effect of social realities and the means and ends of social policies. "The idea that the conflict of parties will, by means of public discussion, bring out necessary public truths" has nothing "in common with the procedure of organized cooperative inquiry, which has won the triumphs of science in the field of physical nature." We are back, in other words, where we began, on the thesis that nothing but a cultural lag prevents men from viewing the social policies in which they are involved with the same degree of objectivity they use in delving into the mysteries of biochemistry or astronomy. Whatever the possibilities and necessities of social intelligence in social action, that thesis is a hopeless one. In so far as a "renascent liberalism" rests upon it, it will confuse the political problem. Its stubbornness in maintaining the thesis imparts an aspect of pathos to even so courageous and honest a liberalism as that of Professor Dewey.

Liberty and Social Control

Today there is no word more bandied about than liberty. Every effort at planned control of economic forces is resisted and attacked, by a certain group, in the name of liberty. The slightest observation shows that this group is made up of those who are interested, from causes that are evident, in the preservation of the economic status quo; that is to say, in the maintenance of the customary privileges and legal rights they already possess. When we look at history in the large we find that the demand for liberty and efforts to achieve it have come from those who wanted to *alter* the institutional set-up. This striking contrast is a stimulus to thoughtful inquiry. What does liberty mean anyway? Why should the cause of liberty have been identified in the past with efforts at change of laws and institutions while at the present time a certain group is using all its vast resources to convince the public that change of economic institutions is an attack upon liberty?

Well, in the first place, liberty is not just an idea, an abstract principle. It is power, effective power to do specific things. There is no such thing as liberty in general; liberty, so to speak, at large. If one wants to know what the condition of liberty is at a given time, one has to examine what persons *can* do and what they *cannot* do. The moment one examines the question from the standpoint of effective action, it becomes evident that the demand for liberty is a demand for power, either for possession of powers of action not already possessed or for retention and expansion of powers already possessed. The present ado in behalf of liberty by the managers and beneficiaries of the existing economic system is immediately explicable if one views it as a demand for preservation of the powers they already possess. Since it is the existing system that gives them these powers, liberty is thus inevitably identified with the perpetuation of that system. Translate the present hullaballoo about liberty into struggle to retain powers already possessed, and it has a meaning.

In the second place, the possession of effective power is always a matter of the *distribution* of power that exists at the time. A physical analogy may make clear what I mean. Water runs down hill and electric currents flow because of *difference in potentials*. If the ground is level, water is stagnant. If on the level ocean, there are dashing waves, it is because there is another power operating, that of the winds, occasioned

[First published in *Social Frontier* 2 (November 1935); reprinted in *The Later Works*, Vol. 11.]

ultimately by a difference in the distribution of temperature at different points. There is no such thing physically as manifestation of energy or effective power by one thing except in relation to the energy manifested by other things. There is no such thing as the liberty or effective power of an individual, group, or class, except in relation to the liberties, the effective powers, of *other* individuals, groups, and classes.

Demand for retention of powers already possessed on the part of a particular group means, therefore, that other individuals and groups shall continue to possess only the capacities in and for activity which *they* already possess. Demand for increased power at one point means demands for change in the distribution of powers, that is, for less power somewhere else. You cannot discuss or measure the liberty of one individual or group of individuals without thereby raising the question of the effect upon the liberty of others, any more than you can measure the energy of a head water at the head without measuring the difference of levels.

In the third place, this relativity of liberty to the existing distribution of powers of action, while meaning that there is no such thing as absolute liberty, also necessarily means that wherever there is liberty at one place there is restraint at some other place. *The system of liberties that exists at any time is always the system of restraints or controls that exists at that time.* No one can *do* anything except in relation to what others can do and cannot do.

These three points are general. But they cannot be dismissed as mere abstractions. For when they are applied either in idea or in action they mean that liberty is always a *social* question, not an individual one. For the liberties that any individual actually has depends upon the distribution of powers or liberties that exists, and this distribution is identical with actual social arrangements, legal and political—and, at the present time, economic, in a peculiarly important way.

Return now to the fact that historically the great movements for human liberation have always been movements to change institutions and not to preserve them intact. It follows from what has been said that there have been movements to bring about a changed distribution of power to do—and power to think and to express thought is a power to do—such that there would be a more balanced, a more equal, even, and equitable system of human liberties.

The present movement for social control of industry, money and credit, is simply a part of this endless human struggle. The present attempt to define liberty in terms of the existing distribution of liberty is an attempt to maintain the existing system of control of power, of social restraints and regimentations. I cannot go here into the nature and consequences of this system. If one is satisfied with it, let him support the conception of liberty put forth by, say, the Liberty League which represents the present economic system. But let him not be fooled into thinking that the issue is liberty versus restraint and regimentation. For the issue is simply that of one system of control of the social forces upon which the distribution of liberties depends, versus some other system of social control which would bring about another distribution of liberties. And let those who are struggling to replace the present economic system by a cooperative one also remember that in struggling for a new system of social restraints and controls they are also struggling for a more equal and equitable balance of powers that will enhance and multiply the effective liberties of the mass of individuals. Let them not be jockeyed into the position of supporting social control at the expense of liberty, when what they want is another method of social control than the one that now exists, one that will increase significant human liberties.

It is nonsense to suppose that we do not have social control *now*. The trouble is that it is exercised by the few who have economic power, at the expense of the liberties of the many and at the cost of increasing disorder, culminating in that chaos of war which the representatives of liberty for the possessive class identify with true discipline.

The Need for a New Party

THE PRESENT CRISIS

There is a deep-seated reason why the common man is convinced that neither the Democratic nor the Republican party represents him or his interests. The Republican party has played the role of Providence. It has told the people that its leaders in alliance with big business are the guardians of that general prosperity which is attained under the direction of organized capital. It has declared that when big capitalists were made prosperous, a general state of welfare would seep down and be enjoyed by the masses. It was not for the masses to do anything; they had only to wait, hold out their hands and receive what the gods above would give them. The masses did not exactly believe this gospel, but they saw nothing that they could do—and so they waited. The conviction that prosperity begins above and then descends has been the underlying doctrine of every Republican policy since the War. It is typified in every utterance and every act of that representative of the Messiahship of big business—Secretary Mellon.

President Hoover is a willing and to all appearances a sincere believer in the gospel. There were those who thought the "engineering mind" would effect some healthful regeneration. They forgot that the engineer at present looks two ways. On the one hand, he looks to the efficient use of materials and processes: he is the servant of technological progress. But on the other hand, he is the servant of capital employed for private profit. He is used to thinking in the same terms and speaking the same language as his masters. And when his engineering ability has been employed, not in actual engineering enterprises, but in some eminently profitable undertaking, he is completely identified with the gospel current among men of large business and wealth, who have to rationalize their behavior by making themselves believe that it is in the interest of general welfare. However, this gospel begins to be questioned when the income of the majority of the people falls below a decent subsistence level, as it has during the present depression. Providence can maintain itself securely only when it provides. A self-professed Providence which not only does not provide, but shakes the very structure of economic society and endangers the elementary securities of life, is a self-confessed fraud.

[First published in four parts in *New Republic* 66 (18 March, 25 March, 1 April, 8 April 1931); reprinted in *The Later Works*, Vol. 6.]

Unfortunately for the permanent prospects of the Democratic party, its leaders prematurely accepted the gospel truth of the doctrine that prosperity descends from above. For the Democrats during the process of assuring the people that they would be just as "safe" as the Republicans, and in assuring big business—and asking for campaign contributions on that basis—that they would be as good and obedient boys as the Republican leaders, not only habituated themselves to the Republican mode of thought, but committed themselves to the policy of alliance with big business. Many independents who voted for Smith in the last presidential campaign did so under mental protest. They disliked the leadership of Raskob and the campaign of "hush-hush" on the economic issues which he fostered. Their fears of what would happen under this overt committal, which was the culmination of the covert committals practised for some time, were borne out by the feeble action of the Democratic party in the new tariff legislation, and in the subservience of the leaders to the demands of finance in connection with drought relief and unemployment. The generally acknowledged absence of genuine leadership in the Democratic party is a necessary by-product. No carbon copy of an original can pretend to leadership or force.

There is no hope that either of the old main parties is going to change. The reason lies even deeper than the self-interest which binds leaders and office holders so closely to "business" that they can be freed only by acts of treachery. Their mental habits are formed in the pattern of this alliance. Conservatism tends to come with age, and the two parties are old. It comes the more surely and exercises its reactionary effect the more disastrously when professed leaders have based the very structure of their beliefs on the doctrine of popular salvation by means of dependence on property interests. Whatever may be the convictions of individuals within the parties, the parties themselves are property-minded. In the clash between property interests and human interests, all their habits of thought and action fatally impel them to side with the former. They make concessions, but do not change the direction of their belief or behavior. . . .

When the country was enjoying what was called prosperity, the doctrine that big industrialists are the true guardians of the welfare of society in general had a temporary appeal. It is hard to imagine any doctrine more inept than this is now, when such "leadership" has brought the country to the present impasse, marked by widespread human woe. The wise and powerful leaders are still disputing among themselves how the present crisis came about; they assign this and that cause. They have no idea how long it will last or how we shall get out of it. They are gambling with chance; they put their faith in the blind goddess of luck. They could not, most of them, even guess right on their own specialty, the stock market. Their pretension to social leadership has been exploded. The bursting of the loaded shell has left loss and ruin behind it.

American memory is notoriously short; we go from incident to episode in the briefest moment. But it is possible to recall the time when we were told that delay in passing the tariff bill was the major obstruction to the revival of business and prosperity; the day when the organs of big industry were holding up recalcitrant Senators as the only significant obstacle. Well, the tariff bill was passed, raising our tariff walls still higher. The Democratic party, having decided that the way to win power was to wear the Republican uniform, made no effective opposition; it was, on the whole, an accomplice to the passage of the bill, passive and even active. The result was just what impartial economists predicted. It was a challenge to the world to engage in economic war. The response was prompt. Imports were curtailed and production at home was lessened because the access to the market was hindered. Exports fell off. The consumer paid a higher price for what he was still able to buy, but the manufacturing interest lost rather than gained, because the margin supplied by export trade was cut down.

The tariff situation is significant far beyond itself. It exemplifies the bankruptcy of archaic political ideas and policies. It demonstrates the bankruptcy of industry as now conducted in conserving even its own economic interests. There were indeed some industrialists, drawn chiefly from the new, expanding lines of manufacture, who had no sympathy with making tariff walls higher and more obstructive. But they made no active and aggressive campaign in opposition; they were afraid to do so, because the whole economic system was so interwoven with the political policy of favoring production at the expense of consumption. They disliked particular instances of the policy, but they endured them rather than do anything which might alter the system itself.

There can be little doubt, I think, that the new tariff was unpopular with people in general. But they were unable to make an effective protest; they were too bewildered to attempt to protest. They had no organ of opposition, because both old parties were tied to the system of fostering the immediate short-time interests of production without reference to its effect on the consumer and the standard of living. It has seemed over and over again as if the limit had been reached in the way of high tariffs; there are many who predict that the last tariff is the expiring move of the ultra-protectionists. But I should hesitate to join these prophets. For the tariff policy is not an isolated thing. It has been the mistake of those in favor of lower tariffs to treat the matter as if it were isolated and could be treated by itself. A general reversal of the trend of political life can alone emancipate the tariff from the clutches of parties which are themselves in the hands of the dominant economic interests. . . .

WHO MIGHT MAKE A NEW PARTY?

Discontent with the two old parties does not of itself compel the formation of a new one. The realization that both are alike because both are servants of big business is a step toward the creation of a new alignment of political forces. However, it is a step which does not necessarily lead to organized action. For, one might ask, why cannot and should not a new alignment grow out of or within one of the old parties? This question is asked by those who are thoroughly dissatisfied with the old parties as they stand; who want to see radical changes in their conduct; who believe, to state it briefly, in new purposes, new policies and new methods in politics.

The question deserves an answer. On the one hand, it implies the possibility and the desirability of boring from within by methods which will eventually produce a complete face-about and reorganization. And on the other hand, it implies the organization of independent progressive voters so that they will hold the balance of power and be able to throw their weight in every election on the side of candidates who stand for progressive measures. One or the other of these tactics is usually urged by persons having a practical experience with politics, a practical experience which the present writer lacks. Moreover, they consider any other strategy utopian and doomed to failure.

Let us take, for example, a Democrat in one of the Northeastern states, in New York or Massachusetts. He will point to the progressive leaders in his party and to the great measure of popular response they evoke. Why not, he will ask, utilize the liberal leaders and elements in the Democratic party as the basis for new methods and goals? Though he will admit that the present difference between express policies of the two parties is slight, he will go on to point out that, historically and temperamentally, the Democratic party is the party of the common people, of the industrial laborers and the relatively poor, and that its tradition commits it to opposition to the privileged, and to support of the masses, in distinction from the "aristocratic affiliations" of the Republican party. On the other hand, if we take a Republican from the Middle West, we will get an opposite reaction. He will point to the insurgency within the Republican party of the West; to the fact that historically the Republican party originated in support of liberty. If brief, he will invoke Lincoln, as the Eastern Democrat invokes the Jeffersonian tradition. Furthermore, he will point out that the Democratic party in the East is the party of Tammany Hall and of corrupt city machines; that the Southern wing is the very stronghold of conservatism, and that its historical conservatism is reinforced at present by an industrial development. And anyway, he will conclude, the Northern and Southern wings of the Democratic party have nothing in common save the desire for party victory. But to all these accusations the Eastern progressive Democrat will reply: And what is there in common between the Eastern reactionary and the Western insurgent wing of the Republican party, and which wing dictates national policies and candidates?

To my mind, the two sets of statements are facts which completely neutralize each other. Taken in conjunction they give the answer to the question: Why not bore from within and reform one of the old parties? I speak as one who as far back as 1912 hoped for a resurrection of the Republican party, as one who has at times in national elections hoped for a revival within the Democratic party. But at last I am disillusioned; I am humiliated at the recollection of the length of time it has taken me to pass to something like political maturity. For, I submit, it is an infantile cherishing of illusions, a withdrawal from the realities of economic and political facts, to pin one's hopes and put one's trust on the possibilities of organic change in either of the old major parties. . . .

Then there are the Socialist and Communist parties. Why should not political discontent and unrest express itself through them? Not much need be said about joining the Communists. As a party, they are directly governed from Moscow, and foreign control is simply out of the question for any party in the United States that means to be a going concern. And, aside from the fact that the Communist party does not speak the American idiom or think in terms relevant to the American situation, it is identified with a fanatical and doctrinaire inflexibility.

The Socialist party, on the other hand, has lost much of its alien atmosphere—once mainly German as the Communist is Russian. It has freed itself to a large extent from doctrinaire dogmas, though internal division within the party on this score has still to be taken into account. Let me anticipate my later discussion by saying that I think a new party will have to adopt many measures which are now labeled socialistic—measures which are discounted and condemned because of that tag. But while support for such measures in the concrete, when they are adapted to actual situations, will win support from American people, I cannot imagine the American people supporting them on the ground of Socialism, or any other sweeping ism, laid down in advance. The greatest handicap from which special measures favored by the Socialists suffer is that they are advanced by the Socialist party as Socialism. . . .

. . . The first appeal of a new party must be to what is called the middle class: to professional people, including, of course, teachers, the average retail merchant, the fairly well-to-do householder, the struggling white-collar worker, including his feminine counterpart, and the farmer—

even the farmer who has not as yet reached the ragged edge of despair. In spite of the disparaging tone in which "bourgeois" is spoken, this is a bourgeois country; and an American appeal couched in the language which the American people understand must start from this fact. Equality of opportunity is still an American ideal. The middle class is now concerned as to whether it will be able to maintain this ideal for itself, and it believes in a realization of the ideal for those less fortunately situated. A new political movement should aim to protect and render secure the standard of living enjoyed by the middle class and to extend the advantages of this standard, in both its cultural and economic aspects, to those who do not enjoy it. This should be attended with whatever leveling down of the idle, luxurious and predatory group such a goal necessitates. . . .

POLICIES FOR A NEW PARTY

In order to be workable, the policies of a new political movement must be elastic and must have unified appeal. Recovery of the agencies of the government by the national community for the service of the nation meets both conditions. It is neither rigid and doctrinaire nor so vague that it cannot be translated into definite legislative measures. It is not committed to any dogma about ultimate ideals, not to any preordained theoretical scheme as to the way in which desirable social changes must be brought about. Negatively, there is a foe that can be located and identified. The usurpation of functions of government by an economic group in its own interests gives the opportunity for aggressive attack; and a sense of conflict and battle is a necessary part of any movement which enlists the imagination and the emotions. Much of the confusion and fatigue of tired liberals has been due to the fact that they felt the situation to be so complicated that they could not focus their attack. The present depression has made clear the incapacity of captains of industry and finance to lead the social host into anything but chaos, suffering and insecurity.

Mere attack without a constructive counterpart is always futile in the long run. The recovery of the agencies of legislation, administrative and judicial decision to serve social ends, which the Preamble to the Constitution declares to be the object of government, translates itself almost automatically into terms of a flexible political program. No commitment to dogma or fixed doctrine is necessary. The program can be defined in terms of direct social needs and can develop as these change. While opportunistic in application, it will be definite and concentrated in purpose. It will not get lost in a dispersed inventory of scattered items of reform so long as it sticks to the unifying principle of the use of government to effect the subordination of economic forces to the maintenance of human justice and happiness. The unregulated play of these forces has brought us to our present condition. Even if the leaders of finance and industry were so frightened by the work they have accomplished as to make an effort at coordination and stabilization, governmental action must come into play. President Hoover's constant appeal to self-reliance, enterprise, private initiative, is simply puerile; it is a voice from the grave in which human hopes and happiness are buried. Not that these words do not represent excellent qualities, but that their exercise *under existing conditions* is just what has brought society to its present catastrophe. Governmental action is necessary to change these conditions and give them a new direction; only then can the honored qualities have a chance for expression. . . .

Since private control of natural resources, of the land with its mines, mineral deposits, water power, oil, natural gas, is the stronghold of monopolistic privilege, it must be attacked in its fortress. Society always controls the agency of taxation; taxation of land values, which are due to the requirements of society, is the only adequate method. Since industry under present conditions is dependent upon transportation and communication, since the consumer as well is at the mercy of the same agencies, and since these agencies tend automatically to become monopolistic, they must, by municipal, state and federal action, pass into the hands of the public.

Control of opinion is the greatest weapon of anti-social forces. We are ruled by headlines, publicity agents and "counsellors of public relations." Propaganda can be attacked and its force weakened only by one agency— informed publicity. The steady encroachment by organized capital upon guaranteed civil liberties can be met only by organized vigilance in behalf of free speech, free press and peaceable assembly. The forces which are undermining these instrumentalities, upon which all other forms of freedom depend, are so subtle and efficient that there is no hope of recovering these fundamental rights, unless they are made an open issue. A free circulation of the pure air of intelligence is a prerequisite in any attempt to cleanse society of its corruptions and enable it to lift its load of oppression. . . .

When economic power is social and political power on a large scale and yet is irresponsible, a change from chaos and anarchy to order is inevitable. Civilizations have gone down because of eruptions from without or exhaustion from within. But a society possessed of science and technological equipment will not commit voluntary suicide. The alternative is planned economy. At present there are no signs that "business adrift" has the will or the intelligence to coordinate itself in the social interest. Politics on the other hand cannot do everything. Even if the Russian experiment succeeds in accomplishing economic planning by political means, Russia is Russia, and the United States is the United States. Starting from scratch, industrially speaking, with a people which lacks the individualistic tradition psychologically as well as economically and politically is a very different thing from reorganizing advanced industrialism saturated with traditions of liberty and self-help.

But a planned economy cannot come into existence without political action. George Soule has recently indicated in these columns some definite ways in which the government can intervene through boards of control. Industry self-regulating in behalf of social interest is a remote ideal. Even if the more intelligent among industrial captains were desirous of effecting a movement in this direction, they cannot accomplish much unless organized society lays down general conditions and provides a mechanism. The people's recovery of the control of government from the usurpation by interests which, as I have said, reign but do not govern, is not an end in itself; it is a precondition for the adoption of measures and policies which will make economic power responsible. . . .

The Economic Basis
of the New Society

What gain has been made in the matter of establishing conditions that give the mass of workers not only what is called "security" but also constructive interest in the work they do? What gain has been made in giving individuals, the great mass of individuals, an opportunity to find themselves and then to educate themselves for what they can best do in work which is socially useful and such as to give free play in development of themselves? The managers of industries here and there have learned that it pays to have conditions such that those who are employed know enough about what they are doing so as to take an interest in it. Educators here and there are awake to the need of discovering vocational and occupational abilities and to the need of readjusting the school system to build upon what is discovered. But the basic trouble is not the scantiness of efforts in these directions, serious as is their paucity. It is again that the whole existing industrial system tends to nullify in large measure the effects of these efforts even when they are made. The problem of the adjustment of individual capacities and their development to actual occupations is not a one-sided or unilateral one. It is bilateral and reciprocal. It is a matter of the state of existing occupations, of the whole set-up of productive work;—of the structure of the individual system. Even if there were a much more widespread and searching concern with the capacities of individuals and much more preparation of them along the lines of their inherent fitness and needs than now exists, what assurance is there in the existing system that there will be opportunity to use their gifts and the education they have obtained? As far as the mass is concerned, we are now putting the social cart before the social horse.

If we take the question of production, what do we find? I pass by the basic fact that real production is completed only through distribution and consumption, so that mere improvement in the mechanical means of mass production may—and does—intensify the problem instead of solving it. I pass it over here because recurring crisis and depressions, with the paradox of want amid plenty, has forced the fact upon the attention of every thoughtful person. The outcome is sufficient proof that the problem of production cannot be solved in isolation from distribution and

[First published in *Intelligence in the Modern World,* ed. Joseph Ratner (New York: Modern Library, 1939); reprinted in *The Later Works,* Vol. 13.]

consumption. I want here to call attention rather to the fact that the present method of dealing with the problem is *restriction* of productive capacity. For scarcity of materials and surplus of those who want to work in the ideal situation for profit on the part of those situated to take advantage of it. *Restriction of production* at the very time when *expansion* of production is most needed has long been the rule of *industrialists.* Now the Government is adopting the same policy for agriculturalists. Those who practice restriction of production in their own businesses cry out loudly when the Government, following their example, intervenes to kill pigs, plow under cotton, and reduce the crop of cereals, and does it moreover when there is the most urgent need for food. Here again, as in the case of public relief, critics prefer to complain about symptoms rather than to face the cause:—The inherent exigencies of the existing social-economic system. Anyone can wax eloquent about the high social function of those who farm, mine and quarry, providing the raw materials not only of food, clothing and shelter but also of all later forms of production of both capital and consumer goods. Anyone can wax pathetic over the plight of agriculture. But under present conditions, the former course is to put the burden of carrying society upon the class now least competent to bear it and the latter course is to engage in idle sentiment.

The ultimate problem of production is the production of human beings. To this end, the production of goods is intermediate and auxiliary. It is by this standard that the present system stands condemned. "Security" is a means, and although an indispensable social means it is not the end. Machinery and technological improvements are means, but again are not the end. Discovery of individual needs and capacities is a means to the end, but only a means. The means have to be implemented by a social-economic system that establishes and uses the means for the production of free human beings associating with one another on terms of equality. Then and then only will these means be an integral part of the end, not frustrated and self-defeating, bringing new evils and generating new problems.

The problem today remains one of using available intelligence; of employing the immense resources science has put at our disposal. A pooled and coordinated social intelligence, not the mere scattered individualized intelligences of persons here and there, however, high their I.Qs. may be. Mere individual intellectual capacities are as ineffective as are mere personal good intentions. The existence of social objective intelligence brings us back to the point where we started. Social control effected through organized application of social intelligence is the sole form of social control that can and will get rid of existing evils without landing us finally in some form of coercive control from above and outside.

A great tragedy of the present situation may turn out to be that those most conscious of present evils and of the need of thoroughgoing change in the social-economic system will trust to some short-cut way out, like the method of civil war and violence. Instead of relying upon the constant application of all socially available resources of knowledge and continuous inquiry they may rely upon the frozen intelligence of some past thinker, sect and party cult: frozen because arrested into a dogma.

That "intelligence," when frozen in dogmatic social philosophies, themselves the fruit of arrested philosophies of history, generates a vicious circle of blind oscillation is tragically exemplified in the present state of the world. What *claims* to be social planning is now found in Communist and Fascist countries. The *social* consequence is complete suppression of freedom of inquiry, communication and voluntary association, by means of a combination of personal violence, culminating in extirpation, and systematic partisan propaganda. The results are such that in the minds of many persons the very idea of social planning and of violation of the integrity of the individual are becoming intimately bound together. But an immense difference divides the plann*ed* society from a *continuously* plann*ing* society. The former requires fixed blue-prints imposed from above and therefore involving reliance upon physical and psychological force to secure conformity to them. The latter means the release of intelligence through the widest form of cooperative give-and-take. The attempt to *plan* social organization and association without the freest possible play of intelligence contradicts the very idea in *social* plann*ing.* For the latter is an operative method of activity, not a predetermined set of final "truths."

When social "planning" is predicated on a set of *"final"* truths, the social end is fixed once for all, and the "end" is then used to justify whatever means are deemed necessary to attain it. "Planning" then takes place only with respect to means of the latter sort, not with respect to ends, so that planning with respect to even means is constrained and coercive. The social result is that the means used have quite other consequences than the end originally set up in idea and afterwards progressively reduced to mere words. As the events of the past twenty years have shown, the seizure of political power by force signifies the continued maintenance of power by force with its continued suppression of the most precious freedoms of the individual spirit. Maintenance of power in order to use force becomes the actual end. Means used determine the end actually reached. The end justifies the means only when the means used are such as actually bring about the desired and desirable end.

Only when reflection upon means and choice of ends are free can there be actual social planning. Every arrest of intelligence (and every form of social dogma is an arrest) obstructs and finally suppresses free consideration and choice of means. The method of social intelligence is primarily concerned with free determination of means to be employed. Until that method of social action is adopted we shall remain in a period of drift and unrest whose final outcome is likely to be force and counter force, with temporary victory to the side possessed of the most machine guns.

"FROM ABSOLUTISM
TO EXPERIMENTALISM":
THE DEMOCRATIC
PUBLIC AND THE
WAR QUESTION

The
Democratic
State

Democracy is a word of many meanings. Some of them are of such a broad social and moral import as to be irrelevant to our immediate theme. But one of the meanings is distinctly political, for it denotes a mode of government, a specified practice in selecting officials and regulating their conduct as officials. This is not the most inspiring of the different meanings of democracy; it is comparatively special in character. But it contains about all that is relevant to *political* democracy. Now the theories and practices regarding the selection and behavior of public officials which constitute political democracy have been worked out against the historical background just alluded to. They represent an effort in the first place to counteract the forces that have so largely determined the possession of rule by accidental and irrelevant factors, and in the second place an effort to counteract the tendency to employ political power to serve private instead of public ends. To discuss democratic government at large apart from its historic background is to miss its point and to throw away all means for an intelligent criticism of it. In taking the distinctively historical point of view we do not derogate from the important and even superior claims of democracy as an ethical and social ideal. We limit the topic for discussion in such a way as to avoid "the great bad," the mixing of things which need to be kept distinct.

Viewed as a historical tendency exhibited in a chain of movements which have affected the forms of government over almost the entire globe during the last century and a half, democracy is a complex affair. There is a current legend to the effect that the movement originated in a single clear-cut idea, and has proceeded by a single unbroken impetus to unfold itself to a predestined end, whether triumphantly glorious or fatally catastrophic. The myth is perhaps rarely held in so simple and

[From *The Public and Its Problems* (New York: Henry Holt and Co., 1927); reprinted in *The Later Works*, Vol. 2.]

unmixed a form. But something approaching it is found whenever men either praise or damn democratic government absolutely, that is, without comparing it with alternative polities. Even the least accidental, the most deliberately planned, political forms do not embody some absolute and unquestioned good. They represent a choice, amid a complex of contending forces, of that particular possibility which appears to promise the most good with the least attendant evil.

Such a statement, moreover, immensely oversimplifies. Political forms do not originate in a once for all way. The greatest change, once it is accomplished, is simply the outcome of a vast series of adaptations and responsive accommodations, each to its own particular situation. Looking back, it is possible to make out a trend of more or less steady change in a single direction. But it is, we repeat, mere mythology to attribute such unity of result as exists (which is always easy to exaggerate) to single force or principle. Political democracy has emerged as a kind of net consequence of a vast multitude of responsive adjustments to a vast number of situations, no two of which were alike, but which tended to converge to a common outcome. The democratic convergence, moreover, was not the result of distinctively political forces and agencies. Much less is democracy the product *of* democracy, of some inherent nisus, or immanent idea. The temperate generalization to the effect that the unity of the democratic movement is found in effort to remedy evils experienced in consequence of prior political institutions realizes that it proceeded step by step, and that each step was taken without foreknowledge of any ultimate result, and, for the most part, under the immediate influence of a number of differing impulses and slogans. . . .

. . . In any case, the complexity of the historic events which have operated is such as to preclude any thought of rehearsing them in these pages, even if I had a knowledge and competency which are lacking. Two general and obvious considerations need, however, to be mentioned. Born in revolt against established forms of government and the state, the events which finally culminated in democratic political forms were deeply tinged by fear of government, and were actuated by a desire to reduce it to a minimum so as to limit the evil it could do.

Since established political forms were tied up with other institutions, especially ecclesiastical, and with a solid body of tradition and inherited belief, the revolt also extended to the latter. Thus it happened that the intellectual terms in which the movement expressed itself had a negative import even when they seemed to be positive. Freedom presented itself as an end in itself, though it signified in fact liberation from oppression and tradition. Since it was necessary, upon the intellectual side, to find justification for the movements of revolt, and since established authority was upon the side of institutional life, the natural recourse was appeal to some inalienable sacred authority resident in the protesting individuals. Thus "individualism" was born, a theory which endowed singular persons in isolation from any associations, except those which they deliberately formed for their own ends, with native or natural rights. The revolt against old and limiting associations was converted, intellectually, into the doctrine of independence of any and all associations.

Thus the practical movement for the limitation of the powers of government became associated, as in the influential philosophy of John Locke, with the doctrine that the ground and justification of the restriction was prior non-political rights inherent in the very structure of the individual. From these tenets, it was a short step to the conclusion that the sole end of government was the protection of individuals in the rights which were theirs by nature. The American revolution was a rebellion against an established government, and it naturally borrowed and expanded these ideas as the ideological interpretation of the effort to obtain independence of the colonies. It is now easy for the imagination to conceive circumstances under which revolts against prior governmental forms would have found its theoretical formulation in an assertion of the rights of groups, of other associations than those of a political nature. There was no logic which rendered necessary the appeal to the individual as an independent and isolated being. In abstract logic, it would have sufficed to assert that some primary groupings had claims which the state could not legitimately encroach upon. In that case, the celebrated modern antithesis of the Individual and Social, and the problem of their reconciliation, would not have arisen. The problem would have taken the form of defining the relationship which non-political groups bear to political union. But, as we have already remarked, the obnoxious state was closely bound up in fact and in tradition with other associations, ecclesiastic (and through its influence with the family), and economic, such as gilds and corporations, and, by means of the church-state, even with unions for scientific inquiry and with educational institutions. The easiest way out was to go back to the naked individual, to sweep away all associations as foreign to his nature and rights save as they proceeded from his own voluntary choice, and guaranteed his own private ends.

Nothing better exhibits the scope of the movement than the fact that philosophic theories of knowledge made the same appeal to the self, or ego, in the form of personal consciousness identified with mind itself, that political theory made to the natural individual, as the court of ultimate resort. The schools of Locke and Descartes, however much they were opposed in other respects, agreed in this, differing only as to whether the sentient or rational nature of the individual was the fundamental thing. From philosophy the idea crept into psychology, which became an introspective and introverted account of isolated and ultimate private consciousness. Henceforth moral and political individualism could appeal to "scientific" warrant for its tenets and employ a vocabulary made current by psychology:—although in fact the psychology appealed to as its scientific foundation was its own offspring.

The "individualistic" movement finds a classic expression in the great documents of the French Revolution, which at one stroke did away with all forms of association, leaving, in theory, the bare individual face to face with the state. It would hardly have reached this point, however, if it had not been for a second factor, which must be noted. A new scientific movement had been made possible by the invention and use of new mechanical appliances—the lens is typical—which focused attention upon tools like the lever and pendulum, which, although they had long been in use, had not formed points of departure for scientific theory. This new development in inquiry brought, as Bacon foretold, great economic changes in its wake. It more than paid its debt to tools by leading to the invention of machines. The use of machinery in production and commerce was followed by the creation of new powerful social conditions, personal opportunities and wants. Their adequate manifestation was limited by established political and legal practices. The legal regulations so affected every phase of life which was interested in taking advantage of the new economic agencies as to hamper and oppress the free play of manufacture and exchange. The established custom of states, expressed intellectually in the theory of mercantilism against which Adam Smith wrote his account of *The* (True) *Wealth of Nations,* prevented the expansion of trade between nations, a restriction which reacted to limit domestic industry. Internally, there was a network of restrictions inherited from feudalism. The prices of labor and staples were not framed in the market by higgling but were set by justices of the peace. The development of industry was hampered by laws regulating choice of a calling, apprenticeship, migration of workers from place to place,—and so on.

Thus fear of government and desire to limit its operations, because they were hostile to the development of the new agencies of production and distribution of services and commodities, received powerful reenforcement. The economic movement was perhaps the more influential because it operated, not in the name of the individual and his inherent rights, but in the name of Nature. Economic "laws," that of labor springing from natural wants and leading to the creation of wealth, of present abstinence in behalf of future enjoyment leading to creation of capital effective in piling up still more wealth, the free play of competitive exchange, designated the law of supply and demand, were "natural" laws.

They were set in opposition to political laws as artificial, man-made affairs. The inherited tradition which remained least questioned was a conception of Nature which made Nature something to conjure with. The older metaphysical conception of Natural Law was, however, changed into an economic conception; laws of nature, implanted in human nature, regulated the production and exchange of goods and services, and in such a way that when they were kept free from artificial, that is political, meddling, they resulted in the maximum possible social prosperity and progress. Popular opinion is little troubled by questions of logical consistency. The economic theory of *laissez-faire,* based upon belief in beneficent natural laws which brought about harmony of personal profit and social benefit, was readily fused with the doctrine of natural rights. They both had the same practical import, and what is logic between friends? Thus the protest of the utilitarian school, which sponsored the economic theory of natural law in economics, against natural right theories had no effect in preventing the popular amalgam of the two sides. . . .

. . . The essential problem of government thus reduces itself to this: What arrangements will prevent rulers from advancing their own interests at the expense of the ruled? Or, in positive terms, by what political means shall the interests of the governors be identified with those of the governed?

The answer was given, notably by James Mill, in a classic formulation of the nature of political democracy. Its significant features were popular election of officials, short terms of office and frequent elections. If public officials were dependent upon citizens for official position and its rewards, their personal interests would coincide with those of people at large—at least of industrious and property-owning persons. Officials chosen by popular vote would find their election to office dependent upon presenting evidence of their zeal and skill in protecting the interests of the populace. Short terms and frequent elections would ensure their being held to regular account; the polling-booth would constitute their day of judgment. The fear of it would operate as a constant check.

Of course in this account I have oversimplified what was already an oversimplification. The dissertation of James Mill was written before the passage of the Reform Bill of 1832. Taken pragmatically, it was an argument for the extension of the suffrage, then largely in the hands of hereditary landowners, to manufacturers and merchants. James Mill had nothing but dread of pure democracies. He opposed the extension of the franchise to women.[1] He was interested in the new "middle-class" form-

---

1. This last position promptly called forth a protest from the head of the utilitarian school, Jeremy Bentham.

ing under the influence of the application of steam to manufacture and trade. His attitude is well expressed in his conviction that even if the suffrage were extended downwards, the middle-class "which gives to science, art and legislation itself its most distinguished ornaments, and which is the chief source of all that is refined and exalted in human nature, is that portion of the community of which the influence would ultimately decide." In spite, however, of oversimplification, and of its special historic motivation, the doctrine claimed to rest upon universal psychological truth; it affords a fair picture of the principles which were supposed to justify the movement toward democratic government. It is unnecessary to indulge in extensive criticism. The differences between the conditions postulated by the theory and those which have actually obtained with the development of democratic governments speak for themselves. The discrepancy is a sufficient criticism. This disparity itself shows, however, that what has happened sprang from no theory but was inherent in what was going on not only without respect to theories but without regard to politics: because, generally speaking, of the use of steam applied to mechanical inventions.

It would be a great mistake, however, to regard the idea of the isolated individual possessed of inherent rights "by nature" apart from association, and the idea of economic laws as natural, in comparison with which political laws being artificial are injurious (save when carefully subordinated), as idle and impotent. The ideas were something more than flies on the turning wheels. They did not originate the movement toward popular government, but they did profoundly influence the forms which it assumed. Or perhaps it would be truer to say that persistent older conditions, to which the theories were more faithful than to the state of affairs they professed to report, were so reenforced by the professed philosophy of the democratic state, as to exercise a great influence. The result was a skew, a deflection and distortion, in democratic forms. Putting the "individualistic" matter in a gross statement, which has to be corrected by later qualifications, we may say that "the individual," about which the new philosophy centered itself, was in process of complete submergence in fact at the very time in which he was being elevated on high in theory. As to the alleged subordination of political affairs to natural forces and laws, we may say that actual economic conditions were thoroughly artificial, in the sense in which the theory condemned the artificial. They supplied the man-made instrumentalities by which the new governmental agencies were grasped and used to suit the desires of the new class of business men.

Both of these statements are formal as well as sweeping. To acquire intelligible meaning they must be developed in some detail. Graham

Wallas prefixed to the first chapter of his book entitled *The Great Society* the following words of Woodrow Wilson, taken from *The New Freedom:* "Yesterday and ever since history began, men were related to one another as individuals. . . . To-day, the every-day relationships of men are largely with great impersonal concerns, with organisations, not with other individuals. Now this is nothing short of a new social age, a new age of human relationships, a new stage-setting for the drama of life." If we accept these words as containing even a moderate degree of truth, they indicate the enormous ineptitude of the individualistic philosophy to meet the needs and direct the factors of the new age. They suggest what is meant by saying the theory of an individual possessed of desires and claims and endued with foresight and prudence and love of bettering himself was framed at just the time when the individual was counting for less in the direction of social affairs, at a time when mechanical forces and vast impersonal organizations were determining the frame of things.

The statement that "yesterday and ever since history began, men were related to one another as individuals" is not true. Men have always been associated together in living, and association in conjoint behavior has affected their relations to one another as individuals. It is enough to recall how largely human relations have been permeated by patterns derived directly and indirectly from the family; even the state was a dynastic affair. But none the less the contrast which Mr. Wilson had in mind is a fact. The earlier associations were mostly of the type well termed by Cooley[2] "face-to-face." Those which were important, which really counted in forming emotional and intellectual dispositions, were local and contiguous and consequently visible. Human beings, if they shared in them at all, shared directly and in a way of which they were aware in both their affections and their beliefs. The state, even when it despotically interfered, was remote, an agency alien to daily life. Otherwise it entered men's lives through custom and common law. No matter how widespread their operation might be, it was not their breadth and inclusiveness which counted but their immediate local presence. The church was indeed both a universal and an intimate affair. But it entered into the life of most human beings not through its universality, as far as their thoughts and habits were concerned, but through an immediate ministration of rites and sacraments. The new technology applied in production and commerce resulted in a social revolution. The local communities without intent or forecast found their affairs conditioned by remote and invisible organizations. The scope of the latter's activities was so vast and their impact upon face-to-face associations so pervasive and

---

2. C. H. Cooley, *Social Organization*, Ch. 3, on "Primary Groups."

unremitting that it is no exaggeration to speak of "a new age of human relations." The Great Society created by steam and electricity may be a society, but it is no community. The invasion of the community by the new and relatively impersonal and mechanical modes of combined human behavior is the outstanding fact of modern life. In these ways of aggregate activity the community, in its strict sense, is not a conscious partner, and over them it has no direct control. They were, however, the chief factors in bringing into being national and territorial states. The need of some control over them was the chief agency in making the government of these states democratic or popular in the current sense of these words.

Why, then, was a movement, which involved so much submerging of personal action in the overflowing consequences of remote and inaccessible collective actions, reflected in a philosophy of individualism? A complete answer is out of the question. Two considerations are, however, obvious and significant. The new conditions involved a release of human potentialities previously dormant. While their impact was unsettling to the community, it was liberating with respect to single persons, while its oppressive phase was hidden in the impenetrable mists of the future. Speaking with greater correctness, the oppressive phase affected primarily the elements of the community which were also depressed in the older and semi-feudal conditions. Since they did not count for much anyway, being traditionally the drawers of water and hewers of wood, having emerged only in a legal sense from serfdom, the effect of new economic conditions upon the laboring masses went largely unnoted. Day laborers were still in effect, as openly in the classic philosophy, underlying conditions of community life rather than members of it. Only gradually did the effect upon them become apparent; by that time they had attained enough power—were sufficiently important factors in the new economic régime—to obtain political emancipation, and thus figure in the forms of the democratic state. Meanwhile the liberating effect was markedly conspicuous with respect to the members of the "middle-class," the manufacturing and mercantile class. It would be short-sighted to limit the release of powers to opportunities to procure wealth and enjoy its fruits, although the creation of material wants and ability to satisfy them are not to be lightly passed over. Initiative, inventiveness, foresight and planning were also stimulated and confirmed. This manifestation of new powers was on a sufficiently large scale to strike and absorb attention. The result was formulated as the discovery of the individual. The customary is taken for granted; it operates subconsciously. Breach of wont and use is focal; it forms "consciousness." The necessary and persistent modes of association went unnoticed. The new ones, which were voluntarily undertaken, occupied thought exclusively. They monopolized the observed horizon. "Individualism" was a doctrine which stated what was focal in thought and purpose.

The other consideration is akin. In the release of new powers singular persons were emancipated from a mass of old habits, regulations and institutions. We have already noted how the methods of production and exchange made possible by the new technology were hampered by the rules and customs of the prior régime. The latter were then felt to be intolerably restrictive and oppressive. Since they hampered the free play of initiative and commercial activity, they were artificial and enslaving. The struggle for emancipation from their influence was identified with the liberty of the individual as such; in the intensity of the struggle, associations and institutions were condemned wholesale as foes of freedom save as they were products of personal agreement and voluntary choice. That many forms of association remained practically untouched was easily overlooked, just because they were matters of course. Indeed, any attempt to touch them, notably the established form of family association and the legal institution of property, were looked upon as subversive, as license, not liberty, in the sanctified phrase. The identification of democratic forms of government with this individualism was easy. The right of suffrage represented for the mass a release of hitherto dormant capacity and also, in appearance at least, a power to shape social relations on the basis of individual volition. . . .

The opponents of popular government were no more prescient than its supporters, although they showed more logical sense in following the assumed individualistic premise to its conclusion: the disintegration of society. Carlyle's savage attacks upon the notion of a society held together only by a "cash-nexus" are well known. Its inevitable terminus to him was "anarchy plus a constable." He did not see that the new industrial régime was forging social bonds as rigid as those which were disappearing and much more extensive—whether desirable ties or not is another matter. . . .

Associated behavior directed toward objects which fulfill wants not only produces those objects, but brings customs and institutions into being. The indirect and unthought-of consequences are usually more important than the direct. The fallacy of supposing that the new industrial régime would produce just and for the most part only the consequences consciously forecast and aimed at was the counterpart of the fallacy that the wants and efforts characteristic of it were functions of "natural" human beings. They arose out of institutionalized action and they resulted in institutionalized action. The disparity between the results of the industrial revolution and the conscious intentions of those engaged in it is a remarkable case of the extent to which indirect consequences of conjoint activity outweigh, beyond the possibility of reckoning, the results directly contemplated. Its outcome was the development of those extensive and invisible bonds, those "great impersonal concerns, organizations," which now pervasively affect the thinking, willing and doing of everybody, and which have ushered in the "new era of human relationships."

Equally undreamed of was the effect of the massive organizations and complicated interactions upon the state. Instead of the independent, self-moved individuals contemplated by the theory, we have standardized interchangeable units. Persons are joined together, not because they have voluntarily chosen to be united in these forms, but because vast currents are running which bring men together. Green and red lines, marking out political boundaries, are on the maps and affect legislation and jurisdiction of courts, but railways, mails and telegraph-wires disregard them. The consequences of the latter influence more profoundly those living within the legal local units than do boundary lines. The forms of associated action characteristic of the present economic order are so massive and extensive that they determine the most significant constituents of the public and the residence of power. Inevitably they reach out to grasp the agencies of government; they are controlling factors in legislation and administration. Not chiefly because of deliberate and planned self-interest, large as may be its role, but because they are the most potent and best organized of social forces. In a word, the new forms of combined action due to the modern economic régime control present politics, much as dynastic interests controlled those of two centuries ago. They affect thinking and desire more than did the interests which formerly moved the state.

We have spoken as if the displacement of old legal and political institutions was all but complete. That is a gross exaggeration. Some of the most fundamental of traditions and habits have hardly been affected at all. It is enough to mention the institution of property. The naïveté with which the philosophy of "natural" economics ignored the effect upon industry and commerce of the legal status of property, the way in which it identified wealth and property in the legal form in which the latter had existed, is almost incredible to-day. But the simple fact is that technological industry has not operated with any great degree of freedom. It has been confined and deflected at every point; it has never taken its own course. The engineer has worked in subordination to the business manager whose primary concern is not with wealth but with the interests of property as worked out in the feudal and semi-feudal period. Thus the one point in which the philosophers of "Individualism" predicted truly was that in which they did not predict at all, but in which they merely clarified and simplified established wont and use: when, that is, they asserted that the main business of government is to make property interests secure.

A large part of the indictments which are now drawn against technological industry are chargeable to the unchanged persistence of a legal institution inherited from the pre-industrial age. It is confusing, however, to identify in a wholesale way this issue with the question of private property. It is conceivable that private property may function socially. It does so even now to a considerable degree. Otherwise it could not be supported for a day. The extent of its social utility is what blinds us to the numerous and great social disutilities that attend its present working, or at least reconcile us to its continuation. The real issue or at least the issue to be first settled concerns the conditions under which the institution of private property legally and politically functions.

We thus reach our conclusion. The same forces which have brought about the forms of democratic government, general suffrage, executives and legislators chosen by majority vote, have also brought about conditions which halt the social and humane ideals that demand the utilization of government as the genuine instrumentality of an inclusive and fraternally associated public. "The new age of human relationships" has no political agencies worthy of it. The democratic public is still largely inchoate and unorganized.

The Problem of Method

One reason for the comparative sterility of discussion of social matters is because so much intellectual energy has gone into the supposititious problem of the relations of individualism and collectivism at large, wholesale, and because the image of the antithesis infects so many specific questions. Thereby thought is diverted from the only fruitful questions, those of investigation into factual subject-matter, and becomes a discussion of concepts. The "problem" of the relation of the concept of authority to that of freedom, of personal rights to social obligations, with only a subsumptive illustrative reference to empirical facts, has been substituted for inquiry into the *consequences* of some particular distribution, under given conditions, of specific freedoms and authorities, and for inquiry into what altered distribution would yield more desirable consequences. . . .

. . . That social "evolution" has been either from collectivism to individualism or the reverse is sheer superstition. It has consisted in a continuous re-distribution of social integrations on the one hand and of capacities and energies of individuals on the other. Individuals find themselves cramped and depressed by absorption of their potentialities in some mode of association which has been institutionalized and become dominant. They may think they are clamoring for a purely personal liberty, but what they are doing is to bring into being a greater liberty to share in other associations, so that more of their individual potentialities will be released and their personal experience enriched. Life has been impoverished, not by a predominance of "society" in general over individuality, but by a domination of one form of association, the family, clan, church, economic institutions, over other actual and possible forms. On the other hand, the problem of exercising "social control" over individuals is in its reality that of regulating the doings and results of some individuals in order that a larger number of individuals may have a fuller and deeper experience. Since both ends can be intelligently attained only by knowledge of actual conditions in their modes of operation and their consequences, it may be confidently asserted that the chief enemy of a social thinking which would count in public affairs is the sterile and impotent, because totally irrelevant, channels in which so much intellectual energy has been expended.

[From *The Public and Its Problems* (New York: Henry Holt and Co., 1927); reprinted in *The Later Works*, Vol. 2.]

The second point with respect to method is closely related. Political theories have shared in the absolutistic character of philosophy generally. By this is meant something much more than philosophies of the Absolute. Even professedly empirical philosophies have assumed a certain finality and foreverness in their theories which may be expressed by saying that they have been non-historical in character. They have isolated their subject-matter from its connections, and any isolated subject-matter becomes unqualified in the degree of its disconnection. In social theory dealing with human nature, a certain fixed and standardized "individual" has been postulated, from whose assumed traits social phenomena could be deduced. . . . While it is evidently important to take this into account, it is also evident that none of the *distinctive* features of *human* association can be deduced from it. Thus, in spite of Mill's horror of the metaphysical absolute, his leading social conceptions were, logically, absolutistic. Certain social laws, normative and regulative, at all periods and under all circumstances of proper social life were assumed to exist.

The doctrine of evolution modified this idea of method only superficially. For "evolution" was itself often understood non-historically. That is, it was assumed that there is a predestined course of fixed stages through which social development must proceed. Under the influence of concepts borrowed from the physical science of the time, it was taken for granted that the very possibility of a social science stood or fell with the determination of fixed uniformities. Now every such logic is fatal to free experimental social inquiry. Investigation into empirical facts was undertaken, of course, but its results had to fit into certain ready-made and second-hand rubrics. . . .

What we have termed the absolutistic logic ends, as far as method in social matters is concerned, in a substitution of discussion of concepts and their logical relations to one another for inquiry. Whatever form it assumes, it results in strengthening the reign of dogma. Their contents may vary, but dogma persists. At the outset we noted in discussion of the state the influence of methods which look for causal forces. Long ago, physical science abandoned this method and took up that of detection of correlation of events. Our language and our thinking is still saturated with the idea of laws which phenomena "obey." But in his actual procedures, the scientific inquirer into physical events treats a law simply as a stable correlation of changes in what happens, a statement of the way in which one phenomenon, or some aspect or phase of it, varies when some other specified phenomenon varies. "Causation" is an affair of historical sequence, of the order in which a series of changes takes place. To know cause and effect is to know, in the abstract, the formula of correlation in change, and, in the concrete, a certain historical career of sequential events. The appeal to causal forces at large not only misleads inquiry into social facts, but it affects equally seriously the formation of purposes and policies. The person who holds the doctrine of "individualism" or "collectivism" has his program determined for him in advance. It is not with him a matter of finding out the particular thing which needs to be done and the best way, under the circumstances, of doing it. It is an affair of applying a hard and fast doctrine which follows logically from his preconception of the nature of ultimate causes. He is exempt from the responsibility of discovering the concrete correlation of changes, from the need of tracing particular sequences or histories of events through their complicated careers. He knows in advance the sort of thing which must be done, just as in ancient physical philosophy the thinker knew in advance what must happen, so that all he had to do was to supply a logical framework of definitions and classifications.

When we say that thinking and beliefs should be experimental, not absolutistic, we have then in mind a certain logic of method, not, primarily, the carrying on of experimentation like that of laboratories. Such a logic involves the following factors: First, that those concepts, general principles, theories and dialectical developments which are indispensable to any systematic knowledge be shaped and tested as tools of inquiry. Secondly, that policies and proposals for social action be treated as working hypotheses, not as programs to be rigidly adhered to and executed. They will be experimental in the sense that they will be entertained subject to constant and well-equipped observation of the consequences they entail when acted upon, and subject to ready and flexible revision in the light of observed consequences. The social sciences, if these two stipulations are fulfilled, will then be an apparatus for conducting investigation, and for recording and interpreting (organizing) its results. The apparatus will no longer be taken to be itself knowledge, but will be seen to be intellectual means of making discoveries of phenomena having social import and understanding their meaning. Differences of opinion in the sense of differences of judgment as to the course which it is best to follow, the policy which it is best to try out, will still exist. But opinion in the sense of beliefs formed and held in the absence of evidence will be reduced in quantity and importance. No longer will views generated in view of special situations be frozen into absolute standards and masquerade as eternal truths.

This phase of the discussion may be concluded by consideration of the relation of experts to a democratic public. . . .

The strongest point to be made in behalf of even such rudimentary political forms as democracy has already attained, popular voting, majority rule and so on, is that to some extent they involve a consultation and discussion which uncover social needs and troubles. This fact is the great asset on the side of the political ledger. De Tocqueville wrote it down almost a century ago in his survey of the prospects of democracy in the United States. Accusing a democracy of a tendency to prefer mediocrity in its elected rulers, and admitting its exposure to gusts of passion and its openness to folly, he pointed out in effect that popular government is educative as other modes of political regulation are not. It forces a recognition that there are common interests, even though the recognition of *what* they are is confused; and the need it enforces of discussion and publicity brings about some clarification of what they are. The man who wears the shoe knows best that it pinches and where it pinches, even if the expert shoemaker is the best judge of how the trouble is to be remedied. Popular government has at least created public spirit even if its success in informing that spirit has not been great.

A class of experts is inevitably so removed from common interests as to become a class with private interests and private knowledge, which in social matters is not knowledge at all. The ballot is, as often said, a substitute for bullets. But what is more significant is that counting of heads compels prior recourse to methods of discussion, consultation and persuasion, while the essence of appeal to force is to cut short resort to such methods. Majority rule, just as majority rule, is as foolish as its critics charge it with being. But it never is *merely* majority rule. As a practical politician, Samuel J. Tilden, said a long time ago: "The means by which a majority comes to be a majority is the more important thing": antecedent debates, modification of views to meet the opinions of minorities, the relative satisfaction given the latter by the fact that it has had a chance and that next time it may be successful in becoming a majority. Think of the meaning of the "problem of minorities" in certain European states, and compare it with the status of minorities in countries having popular government. It is true that all valuable as well as new ideas begin with minorities, perhaps a minority of one. The important consideration is that opportunity be given that idea to spread and to become the possession of the multitude. No government by experts in which the masses do not have the chance to inform the experts as to their needs can be anything but an oligarchy managed in the interests of the few. And the enlightenment must proceed in ways which force the administrative specialists to take account of the needs. The world has suffered more from leaders and authorities than from the masses.

The essential need, in other words, is the improvement of the methods and conditions of debate, discussion and persuasion. That is *the* problem of the public. We have asserted that this improvement depends essentially upon freeing and perfecting the processes of inquiry and of dissemination of their conclusions. Inquiry, indeed, is a work which devolves upon experts. But their expertness is not shown in framing and executing policies, but in discovering and making known the facts upon which the former depend. They are technical experts in the sense that scientific investigators and artists manifest *expertise.* It is not necessary that the many should have the knowledge and skill to carry on the needed investigations; what is required is that they have the ability to judge of the bearing of the knowledge supplied by others upon common concerns.

It is easy to exaggerate the amount of intelligence and ability demanded to render such judgments fitted for their purpose. In the first place, we are likely to form our estimate on the basis of present conditions. But indubitably one great trouble at present is that the data for good judgment are lacking; and no innate faculty of mind can make up for the absence of facts. Until secrecy, prejudice, bias, misrepresentation, and propaganda as well as sheer ignorance are replaced by inquiry and publicity, we have no way of telling how apt for judgment of social policies the existing intelligence of the masses may be. It would certainly go much further than at present. In the second place, *effective* intelligence is not an original, innate endowment. No matter what are the differences in native intelligence (allowing for the moment that intelligence can be native), the actuality of mind is dependent upon the education which social conditions effect. Just as the specialized mind and knowledge of the past is embodied in implements, utensils, devices and technologies which those of a grade of intelligence which could not produce them can now intelligently use, so it will be when currents of public knowledge blow through social affairs.

The level of action fixed by *embodied* intelligence is always the important thing. In savage culture a superior man will be superior to his fellows, but his knowledge and judgment will lag in many matters far behind that of an inferiorly endowed person in an advanced civilization. Capacities are limited by the objects and tools at hand. They are still more dependent upon the prevailing habits of attention and interest which are set by tradition and institutional customs. Meanings run in the channels formed by instrumentalities of which, in the end, language, the vehicle of thought as well as of communication, is the most important. A mechanic can discourse of ohms and amperes as Sir Isaac Newton could not in his day. Many a man who has tinkered with radios can judge of things which Faraday did not dream of. It is aside from the point to say that if Newton and Faraday were now here, the amateur and mechanic would be infants beside them. The retort only brings out the point: the difference made by different objects to think of and by different meanings in circulation. A more intelligent state of social affairs, one more

informed with knowledge, more directed by intelligence, would not improve original endowments one whit, but it would raise the level upon
which the intelligence of all operates. The height of this level is much
more important for judgment of public concerns than are differences in
intelligence quotients. As Santayana has said: "Could a better system
prevail in our lives a better order would establish itself in our thinking. It
has not been for want of keen senses, or personal genius, or a constant
order in the outer world, that mankind has fallen back repeatedly into
barbarism and superstition. It has been for want of good character, good
example, and good government." The notion that intelligence is a personal endowment or personal attainment is the great conceit of the
intellectual class, as that of the commercial class is that wealth is something which they personally have wrought and possess.

A point which concerns us in conclusion passes beyond the field of
intellectual method, and trenches upon the question of practical reformation of social conditions. In its deepest and richest sense a community must always remain a matter of face-to-face intercourse. This is
why the family and neighborhood, with all their deficiencies, have always
been the chief agencies of nurture, the means by which dispositions are
stably formed and ideas acquired which laid hold on the roots of character. The Great Community, in the sense of free and full intercommunication, is conceivable. But it can never possess all the qualities
which mark a local community. It will do its final work in ordering the
relations and enriching the experience of local associations. The invasion
and partial destruction of the life of the latter by outside uncontrolled
agencies is the immediate source of the instability, disintegration and
restlessness which characterize the present epoch. Evils which are un-
critically and indiscriminately laid at the door of industrialism and democracy might, with greater intelligence, be referred to the dislocation
and unsettlement of local communities. Vital and thorough attachments
are bred only in the intimacy of an intercourse which is of necessity
restricted in range. . . .

It is outside the scope of our discussion to look into the prospects of
the reconstruction of face-to-face communities. But there is something
deep within human nature itself which pulls toward settled relationships.
Inertia and the tendency toward stability belong to emotions and desires
as well as to masses and molecules. That happiness which is full of
content and peace is found only in enduring ties with others, which reach
to such depths that they go below the surface of conscious experience to
form its undisturbed foundation. No one knows how much of the frothy
excitement of life, of mania for motion, of fretful discontent, of need for
artificial stimulation, is the expression of frantic search for something to

fill the void caused by the loosening of the bonds which holds persons together in immediate community of experience. If there is anything in human psychology to be counted upon, it may be urged that when man is satiated with restless seeking for the remote which yields no enduring satisfaction, the human spirit will return to seek calm and order within itself. This, we repeat, can be found only in the vital, steady, and deep relationships which are present only in an immediate community.

The psychological tendency can, however, manifest itself only when it is in harmonious conjunction with the objective course of events. Analysis finds itself in troubled waters if it attempts to discover whether the tide of events is turning away from dispersion of energies and acceleration of motion. Physically and externally, conditions have made, of course, for concentration; the development of urban, at the expense of rural, populations; the corporate organization of aggregated wealth, the growth of all sorts of organizations, are evidence enough. But enormous organization is compatible with demolition of the ties that form local communities and with substitution of impersonal bonds for personal unions, with a flux which is hostile to stability. The character of our cities, of organized business and the nature of the comprehensive associations in which individuality is lost, testify also to this fact. Yet there are contrary signs. "Community" and community activities are becoming words to conjure with. The local is the ultimate universal, and as near an absolute as exists. It is easy to point to many signs which indicate that unconscious agencies as well as deliberate planning are making for such an enrichment of the experience of local communities as will conduce to render them genuine centres of the attention, interest and devotion for their constituent members.

The unanswered question is how far these tendencies will reestablish the void left by the disintegration of the family, church and neighborhood. We cannot predict the outcome. But we can assert with confidence that there is nothing intrinsic in the forces which have effected uniform standardization, mobility and remote invisible relationships that is fatally obstructive to the return movement of their consequences into the local homes of mankind. Uniformity and standardization may provide an underlying basis for differentiation and liberation of individual potentialities. They may sink to the plane of unconscious habituations, taken for granted in the mechanical phases of life, and deposit a soil from which personal susceptibilities and endowments may richly and stably flower. Mobility may in the end supply the means by which the spoils of remote and indirect interaction and interdependence flow back into local life, keeping it flexible, preventing the stagnancy which has attended stability in the past, and furnishing it with the elements of a variegated and many-hued experience. Organization may cease to be taken as an end in itself. Then it will no longer be mechanical and external, hampering the free play of artistic gifts, fettering men and women with chains of conformity, conducing to abdication of all which does not fit into the automatic movement of organization as a self-sufficing thing. Organization as a means to an end would reenforce individuality and enable it to be securely itself by enduing it with resources beyond its unaided reach.

Whatever the future may have in store, one thing is certain. Unless local communal life can be restored, the public cannot adequately resolve its most urgent problem: to find and identify itself. But if it be reestablished, it will manifest a fullness, variety and freedom of possession and enjoyment of meanings and goods unknown in the contiguous associations of the past. For it will be alive and flexible as well as stable, responsive to the complex and world-wide scene in which it is enmeshed. While local, it will not be isolated. Its larger relationships will provide an inexhaustible and flowing fund of meanings upon which to draw, with assurance that its drafts will be honored. Territorial states and political boundaries will persist; but they will not be barriers which impoverish experience by cutting man off from his fellows; they will not be hard and fast divisions whereby external separation is converted into inner jealousy, fear, suspicion and hostility. . . .

Conscience and Compulsion

Those in contact with youth know that a considerable number have undergone a serious moral strain in the weeks since war was declared by the United States. Much larger numbers have had to make a moral adjustment which if not involving a tragedy of the inner life has been effected only with some awkward trampling of what has been cherished as the finer flowers of the soul. And how could it have been otherwise? I doubt if any propaganda has ever been carried on with greater persistence or with greater success—so far as affecting feelings was concerned—than that for peace during the decade prior to 1914. The times were so ripe that the movement hardly had to be pushed. Our remoteness from the immediate scene of international hatreds, the bad aftertaste from the Spanish-American War, the contentment generated by successful industrialism, the general humanitarianism of which political progressivism was as much a symptom as social settlements, the gradual substitution of calculating rationalism for the older romantic patriotism—all of these things and many more fell in with that general spirit of goodwill which is essential America, to create a sense of war as the supreme stupidity. War came. But there persisted the feeling that it was "over there" and that we at peace were the preservers of sanity in a world gone mad. Some of the phrases used in this sense by President Wilson gave great offense to our present allies, but they were the phrases which best expressed the average American feeling.

At last we were in it ourselves. And is it strange that thousands of young people who had taken the peace movement with moral seriousness found themselves upset? Already an attempt is making to befog the past. It is intimated that our ante-bellum pacifism was a compound of sentimentality, cowardice and a degenerate materialism bred of excessive comfort. Nothing could be further from the truth. Current pacifism was identified with good business, philanthropy, morality and religion. Combine Mr. Carnegie and Mr. Bryan and you have as near the typical American as you are likely to find. Especially is it true that the churches took up the cause of peace as a great moral issue. Clergymen obliged to shun political issues because they were so closely linked with struggle for economic power gladly added peace to divorce and temperance as sub-

[First published in *New Republic* 11 (1917). Republished in *Characters and Events*, ed. Joseph Ratner (New York: Henry Holt and Co., 1929); reprinted in *The Middle Works*, Vol. 10.]

jects which were safe and also "live." The American habit of discussing political questions in a moral vocabulary found full scope with peace and war. In our colleges the Y.M.C.A.'s were even more ardent promoters of peace sentiments than were intercollegiate socialist clubs.

We are not an over-agile people morally. No one has yet depicted the immense moral wrench involved in our passage from friendly neutrality to participation in war. I hardly believe the turnover could have been accomplished under a leadership less skilful than that of President Wilson, so far as he succeeded in creating the belief that just because the pacific moral impulse retained all its validity Germany must be defeated in order that it find full fruition. That was a bridge on which many a conscience crossed with no greater dexterity in balancing than conscience frequently finds necessary. But there were many who still had doubts, qualms, clouds of bewilderment. How could wrong so suddenly become right? Among the questioners were many whom we are wont to term idealistic, men and women who have the most difficulty in identifying the conventional and the popular with the right and good. And it is among these that there was enacted a genuine tragedy when the impulse to loyalty, to service, to unity came into conflict with their moral abhorrence of war, which they had learned to look upon as murder, and murder of a peculiarly stupid sort. Conscription did not originate the crisis in moral experience, but it brought it acutely to a focus.

I can but think that such young people deserve something better than accusations, varying from pro-Germanism and the crime of Socialism to traitorous disloyalty, which the newspapers so readily "hurl" at them—to borrow their own language. Nor does it quite cover the ground to urge that genuinely conscientious objectors be given that work, when they are drafted, which will put the least heavy load possible upon their consciences. The country ought to be great enough in spirit as it is great enough in men and in the variety of tasks to be performed to make this a matter of course. But it is to be feared that if local tribunals take their cue from current newspaper objurgations they will regard it as their duty to punish the objectors as dangerous malefactors instead of asking to what tasks they may most usefully be assigned. It is not, however, the problem of practical administration that I raise, but the nature of the moral education which has been revealed in our American aversion to war and in the ways in which persons perplexed by the coercions of wartime have met their dilemmas. For at the very worst most of these young people appear to me victims of a moral innocency and an inexpertness which have been engendered by the moral training which they have undergone.

It is perhaps a penalty which we have paid for our unusual development of good nature and goodwill that our moral training emphasizes the emotions rather than intelligence, ideals rather than specific purposes, the nurture of personal motives rather than the creation of social agencies and environments. The tendency to dispose of war by bringing it under the commandment against murder, the belief that by *not* doing something, by keeping out of a declaration of war, our responsibilities could be met, a somewhat mushy belief in the existence of disembodied moral forces which require only an atmosphere of feelings to operate so as to bring about what is right, the denial of the efficacy of force, no matter how controlled, to modify disposition; in short, the inveterate habit of separating ends from means and then identifying morals with ends thus emasculated, such things as these are the source of much of the perplexity of conscience from which idealistic youth has suffered. The evangelical Protestant tradition has fostered the tendency to locate morals in personal feelings instead of in the control of social situations, and our legal tradition has bred the habit of attaching feelings to fixed rules and injunctions instead of to social conditions and consequences of action as these are revealed to the scrutiny of intelligence. . . .

The Future of Pacifism

There is no paradox in the fact that the American people is profoundly pacifist and yet highly impatient of the present activities of many professed or professional pacifists. The disposition to call the latter pro-German and to move for their suppression is an easy way of expressing a sense of the untimely character of their moves at the present juncture. But the war will pass, and the future of the profound American desire for peace, for amity, for unhampered and prosperous intercourse, is a topic which is intimately connected with the war itself. For upon its constant consideration depends whether the impulse to a better ordered world which reconciled America to war shall find satisfaction or meet frustration. And I know no better way to introduce the subject than a consideration of the failure of the pacifist propaganda to determine finally the course of a nation which was converted to pacifism in advance.

The explanation, I take it, is that it takes two to make peace as well as to make war; or, as the present situation abundantly testifies, a much larger number than two. He was a poor judge of politics who did not know from the very day of the *Lusitania* message—or at all events from that of the *Sussex* message—that the entrance of the United States into the war depended upon the action of Germany. Any other notion was totally inconsistent with any belief in President Wilson's sincerity; it imputed to him an almost inconceivable levity in a time when seriousness was the chief need. Those who voted for him for President on the ground that he "kept us out of war" and who felt aggrieved when we got into war have only themselves to blame. He had unmistakably plotted a line which led inevitably to conflict with Germany in case the latter should take the course which she finally adopted.

This indictment of professional pacifism for futile gesturing may seem to rest upon acceptance of the belief in the political omnipotence of the executive; it may seem to imply the belief that his original step committed the nation irretrievably. Such an inference, however, is merely formal. It overlooks the material fact that President Wilson's action had the sanction of the country. I will not enter into the question of legal neutrality, but morally neutral the country never was, and probably the only stupid thing President Wilson did was to suppose, in his early proclamation, that it could be. And this brings us back to the basic fact

[First published in *New Republic* 11 (1917). Republished in *Characters and Events*, ed. Joseph Ratner (New York: Henry Holt and Co., 1929); reprinted in *The Middle Works*, Vol. 10.]

that in a world organized for war there are as yet no political mechanisms which enable a nation with warm sympathies to make them effective, save through military participation. It is, again, an instinctive perception of this fact which encourages the idea that pacifists who do not support the war must be pro-German at heart.

The best statement which I have seen made of the pacifist position since we entered the war is that of Miss Addams. She earnestly protests against the idea that the pacifist position was negative or laissez-faire. She holds that the popular impression that pacifism meant abstinence and just keeping out of trouble is wrong; that it stood for a positive international polity in which this country should be the leader of the nations of the world "into a wider life of coördinated activity"; she insists that the growth of nations under modern conditions involves of necessity international complications which admit "of adequate treatment only through an international agency not yet created." In short, the pacifists "urge upon the United States not indifference to moral issues and to the fate of liberty and democracy, but a strenuous endeavor to lead all nations of the earth into an organized international life."

That intelligent pacifism stands for this end, and that the more intelligent among the pacifists, like Miss Addams, saw the situation in this fashion need not be doubted. But as Miss Addams recognized in the same address there are many types of pacifists. I question whether any one who followed the pacifist literature which appeared in the year or two before we got into the war derived from it the conception that the dominant ideal was that ascribed to pacifism by Miss Addams, namely, that the United States should play a "vitally energetic rôle" in a political reorganization of the world. But even if this had been the universal idea of what was theoretically desirable, the force of circumstances forbade pacifists who drew back at war as a means of bringing about this role from pressing it.

The pacifist literature of the months preceding our entrance into war was opportunistic—breathlessly, frantically so. It did not deal in the higher strategy of international politics, but in immediate day-by-day tactics for staving off the war. Because the professional pacifists were committed to the idea that anything was better than our getting into the war, their interest in general international reorganization had no chance for expression. They were in the dilemma of trying to accomplish what only definite political agencies could effect, while admitting these agencies had not been created. Thus they were pushed out of the generic position of work for the development of such agencies into the very elementary attitude that if no nation ever allowed itself to be drawn into war, no matter how great the provocation, wars would cease to be. Hence the continuous recourse to concessions and schemes, devised *ad hoc* over night, to meet each changing aspect of the diplomatic situation so as to ward off war. The logic seems sound. But the method is one of treating symptoms and ignoring the disease. At the best, such a method is likely to remain some distance behind newly appearing symptoms, and in a critical disease the time is bound to come (as events demonstrated in our case) when the disease gets so identified with the symptoms that nothing can be done. All this seems to concern the past of pacifism rather than its future. But it indicates, by elimination, what that future must be if it is to be a prosperous one. It lies in furthering whatever will bring into existence those new agencies of international control whose absence has made the efforts of pacifists idle gestures in the air. Its more immediate future lies in seeing to it that the war itself is turned to account as a means for bringing these agencies into being. To go on protesting against war in general and this war in particular, to direct effort to stopping the war in particular, to direct effort to stopping the war rather than to determining the terms upon which it shall be stopped, is to repeat the earlier tactics after their ineffectualness has been revealed. Failure to recognize the immense impetus to reorganization afforded by this war; failure to recognize the closeness and extent of true international combinations which it necessitates, is a stupidity equaled only by the militarist's conception of war as a noble blessing in disguise.

I have little patience with those who are so anxious to save their influence for some important crisis that they never risk its use in any present emergency. But I can but feel that the pacifists wasted rather than invested their potentialities when they turned so vigorously to opposing entrance into a war which was already all but universal, instead of using their energies to form, at a plastic juncture, the conditions and objects of our entrance. How far this wasted power is recoverable it is hard to say. Certainly an added responsibility is put upon those who still think of themselves as fundamentally pacifists in spite of the fact that they believed our entrance into the war a needed thing. For the only way in which they can justify their position is by using their force to help make the war, so far as this country can influence its final outcome, a factor in realizing the ideals which President Wilson expressed for the American people before and just upon entering the war. All such pacifists—and they comprise in my opinion the great mass of the American people— must see to it that these ideals are forced upon our allies, however unwilling they may be, rather than covered up by the débris of war. If the genuine pacifism of our country, a pacifism interested in permanent results rather than in momentary methods, had had leadership, it is not likely that we should have entered without obtaining in advance some stipulations. As it is, we (so far, at least, as any one knows) romantically abstained from any bargaining and thereby made our future task more difficult. . . .

Conscience and
Intelligence in War

Randolph Bourne

The merely "conscientious objector" has absorbed too much attention from those who are concerned about understanding the non-popularity of our participation in the war. Not all the pacifist feeling has had an evangelical color. There is an element of anti-war sentiment which has tried to be realistic, and does not hope to defeat war merely by not doing something. Though events have been manipulated against it, this element neither welcomes martyrdom nor hopes to be saved for its amiable sentiments. And it is just this attitude, far more significantly "American" than "conscientious objection," that John Dewey has ignored in his recent article on "Conscience and Compulsion." The result has been to apply his pragmatic philosophy in its least convincing form.

His criticism is of the merely good and merely conscientious souls whose moral training has emphasized sentiments rather than specific purposes, and who are always found helpless before the coercion of events. His argument follows the well-known lines of his instrumental use of the intelligence for the realization of conscious social purpose. The conscience, he implies, is balked by an unpleasant situation, is futile unless it attaches itself to forces moving in another, and more desirable, direction. Dissatisfied with the given means or end, one chooses another alternative, either a new end to which the means may be shaped, or a new means to effect the desired end. But in applying this theory to the war situation, does not the philosopher ignore the fact that it is exactly in war that alternatives are rigorously limited? Is not war perhaps the one social absolute, the one situation where the choice of ends ceases to function? Obviously in a world of choice one may hope intelligently to select and manipulate some social mechanism by which a desired social arrangement may be brought about. But war always comes to seem just that urgent, inevitable crisis of the nation's life where everything must be yielded to one purpose. For a few months, the public may retain the illusion of freedom, of mastery over social forces. But as war continues, there comes the deep popular recognition that there is now but one end—victory; and but one means—the organization of all the resources of the nation into a conventional war technique. "Peace without victory"

[First published in *The Dial* (13 September 1917).]

becomes a logical and biological contradiction. Belligerent peoples will have long ago realized that war is its own end, and that, to paraphrase a popular ditty, they fight because they fight because they fight. This was the real basis of the opposition to the President's gesture for peace—the realization that though America might still be living in a pragmatic world, war had made Europe a realm of the absolute. And in our own country, war had not been with us for ten weeks before "peace without victory" changed officially into "conquer or submit!"

In wartime, there is literally no other end but war, and the objector, therefore, lives no longer with a choice of alternatives. The pacifist conscience attaches itself to no end because no end exists which connects with its desires. Plans and programmes may exist which have not to do with war, but they exist only in the realm of fantasy, not in the realm of practical politics. Peace comes through victory or exhaustion, and not through creative intelligence. The appeal to force removes everything automatically to a non-intelligent sphere of thinking and acting. Mr. Dewey is depressed at the number of conscientious young men who exchanged their "Thou shalt not kill" into an "Obey the law," though they saw the situation exactly as before. But his depression is due only to that inexorability which every pragmatist must resent. It is not just to be depressed at their poverty of imagination. For he is dealing with precisely the one situation in which his philosophy will no longer work. He implies that there was some way by which conscience could operate very differently from that whose main concern is to "remain itself unspotted from within." Well, in what way? Where does one find "forces moving in another direction"? One may find forces moving against the war, resisting the organization for war, agitating for a speedy peace. But such forces are not merely alternative social policies. They are not morally equivalent to the policy of war. They have the unique quality of disloyalty. They challenge the entire force of the nation. As soon as they threaten to become at all effective, they are automatically crushed out, under even the most democratic of governments. Never has a government in wartime been known to refuse the use of relentless coercion against "forces moving in another direction." The attaching of one's conscience to any such forces is infallibly taken to be the allying of oneself with the disloyal, and the inadvertent aiding of the nation's enemies. There is, of course, the alternative of revolution, which would have much the same effect as disloyalty. Does Mr. Dewey mean to urge the "conscientious objector" to take to disloyalty or revolution in his efforts to attach his conscience to intelligent alternatives? And if not, will he tell us what social mechanism he knows of that is considered relevant or even permissible in wartime that does not contribute to the war technique? One resists or one obeys. If one resists, one is martyred or coerced. If one obeys, the effect is just as if one accepted the war.

In wartime, then, one's pragmatic conscience moves in a vacuum. There is no leverage to clutch. To a philosopher of the creative intelligence, the fact that war blots out the choice of ends and even of means should be the final argument against its use as a technique for any purpose whatever. War once entered upon, neither means nor ends can really be revised or altered. The acceptance of the war by Mr. Dewey can only be explained by the prevailing sentiment that this was a war in which we had to be. I have heard him say that it was far better to enter the war intelligently than blindly or hysterically. This is not quite the same as saying that deliberate murder is more creatively intelligent than murder committed in the heat of sudden passion. For what Mr. Dewey meant was probably that if we entered the war intelligently we would choose the ends which the war technique might serve. But is it not a little curious to find the men who thought the war inevitable—"what could we do?"—and who could neither prevent it nor devise an alternative, still confident that they can control its terrible force for beneficent purposes? Having accepted the inevitable of war, one can more easily accept other inevitables.

At the back of Mr. Dewey's mind was perhaps the hope that the pacifist conscience, though hating war and everything connected with it, might aid this war because of the radical social reforms it was sure to bring. But the same people who thought of this as an end for which the pacifist should be willing to accept the instrument, are now complaining that labor, though it consecrated itself to the nation's service, is not now receiving the nation's gratitude; that the war-swollen fortune is sliding free of paying for the war; that education is being impoverished, and national demoralization rather than integration taking place. These ironic frustrations of the social purpose were foreseen by the realistic pacifists. They were the best of reasons for finding an alternative to war. They were the best of motives for not attaching one's conscience to forces that involved a technique which infallibly trailed along these social evils. Once you accept war, there is no choice but to be shoved along the line of inevitables with which war is organically bound up.

In wartime, therefore, the "forces moving in another direction," to which Mr. Dewey invites the objecting conscience to attach itself, are illusory. War is just that absolute situation which is its own end and its own means, and which speedily outstrips the power of intelligent and creative control. As long as you are out of war, events remain to some degree malleable. This was the argument for "armed neutrality." But clamp down the psychic pattern of war on the nation, and you have precipitated an absolute where mastery becomes a mockery. Mere conscientious objection in wartime is not so uncreative or unintelligent as Mr. Dewey represents it. No social machinery exists to make dissent effective. Alternative ends are illusory. You can only accept, or rebel, or remain apathetic. This is not true of other social situations. It is true of war. If you are skeptical of the technique of war, or of the professed aims, a negative attitude is the only possible one. It may not be noble to cencentrate on your own integrity, but it is perhaps better than to be a hypocrite or a martyr. And if pragmatists like Mr. Dewey are going to accept "inevitables," you at least have an equal right to choose what shall seem inevitable to you.

To many pragmatists the impotence of the pacifists in the period preceding the war has been a sore point. They are scolded for their lack of organization and their mere obstructiveness. Actually, they were fertile in constructive suggestions. But no social machinery existed for harnessing their conscience to action. The referendum would have been a slight democratic clutch. It was hooted out of court. Armed neutrality was foozled. The forces that were irresistibly for war had control of the war-making machinery. The pacifists sounded ridiculous and unreasonable, because the drive was the other way. The war suction had begun. Choices were already abolished, and the most realistic and constructive pacifism in the world would have been helpless.

In all this chain of events, those minds were able to retain a feeling of alternative forces and of free choice which were in sympathy with the announced purpose of the war and not temporarily hostile to its technique. The philosophy of creative intelligence still seemed to be working because there was no need to test its applicability. The dissenter, however, felt cruelly the coercive forces. Suppose I really believe that world peace will more likely come exactly "by not doing something," by a collusive neglect of imperialistic policy on the new Russian model. Suppose I believe that a federalism of sovereign nations will only mean more competitive wars. What forces are there then to which I can assimilate this war of ours, and so make my intelligence and conscience count for what little they may? Is not Mr. Dewey's case against the merely passive built on an assumption that if one chose freely one would choose the present inevitable forces? But the mind that is skeptical of these present forces,—is it not thrown back to a choice of resistance or apathy? Can one do more than wait and hope for wisdom when the world becomes pragmatic and flexible again?

Morals and the
Conduct of States

The plea that nations *ought* to regulate themselves by the moral code which obtains among individuals is likely to degenerate into a sentimentalism which projects action on the base of wishes instead of facts. It escapes this sentimentalism only as it is a symptom of a discontent with the present social order which will momentarily express itself in a demand for a new social organization. To indulge in vituperations at the wickedness of war and in asseverations of the obligations of states to act upon the basis of the most enlightened code is merely to permit one's self a Pharisaic luxury—unless one is willing to fight for the establishment of a social organization which will make moral responsibilities and regulations a fact.

We are still incredibly subjectivistic in our moral ideas. The common assumption of the Protestant world is that men are gifted as individuals with conscience and that this conscience brings into existence acts and social relations which may approximate its high dictates. So far as anything objective, anything external to the individual is recognized, it is usually something supernatural, God or some of those mitigated substitutes for theological supernaturalism which modern thought calls transcendental absolutes and values. A pacifist clergyman in California recently proclaimed his supreme right to follow not only for himself but for propaganda among others the dictates of his own conscience even when they brought him into conflict with the law of the land: his right to do it not only in the sense of willingness to stand the penalties which would follow, but in the sense that the state had no right to inflict any penalties if he chose to obey what his conscience told him was the law of God. He doubtless offended the loyalty of thousands of his fellow citizens. It may be doubted how many of them recognized that he was asserting the essence of moral anarchy, by which I mean a course which would not only lead to practical anarchy but to a destruction of all moral distinctions whatever. For "conscience," that is the aggregate of the moral

[First published in *New Republic* 14 (1918). Republished in *Characters and Events* (New York: Henry Holt and Co., 1929), and in *Intelligence in the Modern World* (New York: Modern Library, 1939), with the title "Preconditions of the Security of Nations," both edited by Joseph Ratner. Reprinted in *The Middle Works*, Vol. 11.]

sentiments and ideas of man, is not the author and judge of social institutions, but the product and reflex of the latter. They are functions of social organization. They reflect criticism of the existing social order as well as approval of it. But in this capacity they are heralds of a changed social order. They are significant only as they become the pivots about which turn active efforts for the reconstruction of the social order. The notion that it is possible to get bodies of men to act in accord with finer moral sentiments while the general scheme of social organization remains the same is not only futile, it is a mark of the subtlest form of conceit, moral egotism.

If only there were a general recognition of the dependence of moral control upon social order, all of the sentiment and well-wishing opinion that is now dissipated would be centred. It would aim at the establishment of a definitely organized federation of nations not merely in order that certain moral obligations might be effectively enforced but in order that a variety of obligations might come into existence. The weakness on the ethical side of previous discussions of international courts and leagues has been that these have so largely assumed that moral considerations are already adequately cared for, and that it remains only to give them, through proper agencies, legal effect. The result was that moral enthusiasm was no sooner aroused than it was chilled by finding only legal technicalities with which to occupy itself, more international laws, treaties, courts, diplomats and lawyers. It wanted machinery to propel a great new idea and it found itself confronting additions to make the old machinery work better, to keep going the old idea of ultimate national sovereignty and irresponsibility. It found itself confronted with negative provisions for making war more difficult to enter upon, but which refrained from dealing in any positively organized way with those defects in social organization from which wars proceed. All proposals short of a league of nations whose object is not the negative one of preventing war but the positive one of looking after economic and social needs which are now at the mercy of chance and the voracity of isolated states, assume that war is the effect of bellicosity—which is exactly on the intellectual level of the famous idea that it is the dormitive power of opium which puts men to sleep.

Warlikeness is not of itself the cause of war; a clash of interests due to absence of organization is its cause. A supernational organization which oversees, obviates and adjusts these clashes, an organization which, as Mr. Levinson points out, is possible only with coincident outlawing of war itself, will focus moral energies now scattered and make operative moral ideas now futile. It will align the moral code of state behavior with the best which obtains as to personal conduct. But it will do more than that. It will give personal conscience a new stay and outlook. It will permit the social principle which is the heart of all morals to find full instead of hampered expression; it will enable it to be courageous because consistent. It will generalize that secularization or humanization of morals which is now so halting and vagrant that it leads many persons to escape supernaturalism only to land in a half-suppressed scepticism as to the possibility of any intelligent and objective morals, anything beyond social convention on one hand and personal taste on the other.

When I said that it is mere sentimentalism to deplore the deviation of the moral standard of states from that of persons unless one is willing to fight for a social organization which will permit moral relations and regulations to exist, I meant fight in every sense of the word. War to put a stop to war is no new thing. History shows a multitude of wars which have been professedly waged in order that a future war should not arrive. History also shows that as a pacifist, Mars has not been a success. But a war waged to establish an international order and by that means to outlaw war is something hitherto unknown. In just the degree in which the American conception of the war gains force, and *this* war becomes a war for a new type of social organization, it will be a war of compelling moral import.

Democratic Ends Need Democratic Methods for Their Realization

Unforeseen commitments out of town have prevented me from attending the meeting at Town Hall to which I have looked forward with such great interest. I am proud of the work of the Committee for Cultural Freedom, and its efforts to defend and advance the integrity of cultural and intellectual life.

As we listen to accounts of the repression of cultural freedom in countries which have been swept by totalitarian terror, let us bear in mind that our chief problems are those within our own culture. In the modern world, every country under some circumstances becomes fertile soil for seeds out of which grow fanatical conflict, intolerance, racial oppression.

The attitude which prevails in some parts of the country towards Negroes, Catholics and Jews is spiritually akin to the excesses that have made a shambles of democracy in other countries of the world.

The conflict between the methods of freedom and those of totalitarianism, insofar as we accept the democratic ideals to which our history commits us, is within our own institutions and attitudes. It can be won only by extending the application of democratic methods, methods of consultation, persuasion, negotiation, cooperative intelligence in the task of making our own politics, industry, education—our culture generally— a servant and an evolving manifestation of democratic ideas.

Resort to military force is a first sure sign that we are giving up the struggle for the democratic way of life, and that the Old World has conquered morally as well as geographically.

If there is one conclusion to which human experience unmistakably points, it is that democratic ends demand democratic methods for their realization. Authoritarian methods now offer themselves to us in new guises. They come to us claiming to serve the ultimate ends of freedom by immediate, and allegedly temporal, techniques of suppression.

[First published in *New Leader* 22 (21 October 1939); from a message read at the first public meeting of the Committee for Cultural Freedom on 13 October 1939 at Town Hall in New York City. Reprinted in *The Later Works*, Vol. 14.]

Or they recommend adoption of a totalitarian regime in order to fight totalitarianism. In whatever form they offer themselves, they owe their seductive power to their claim to serve ideal ends.

Our first defense is to realize that democracy can be served only by the slow day by day adoption and contagious diffusion in every phase of our common life of methods that are identical with the ends to be reached.

There is no substitute for intelligence and integrity in cultural life. Anything else is a betrayal of human freedom no matter in what guise it presents itself.

An American democracy can serve the world only as it demonstrates in the conduct of its own life the efficacy of plural, partial, and experimental methods in securing and maintaining an ever-increasing release of the powers of human nature, in service of a freedom which is cooperative and a cooperation which is voluntary.

We cannot sit back in complacent optimism. History will not do our work for us. Neither is there any call for panic or pessimism.

We, members and friends of the Committee for Cultural Freedom, must dedicate ourselves to the task of securing and widening cultural freedom with eyes open and minds alert to every danger which threatens it. We must always remember that the dependence of ends upon means is such that the only ultimate result is the result that is attained today, tomorrow, the next day, and day after day, in the succession of years and generations.

Only thus can we be on guard against those who paint a rosy future which has no date in order to cover up their theft of our existing liberties. Only thus can we be sure that we face our problems in details one by one as they arise, and with all the resources provided by collective intelligence operating in cooperative action.

The Basic Values and
Loyalties of Democracy

Values and loyalties go together, for if you want to know what a man's values are do not ask him. One is rarely aware, with any high degree of perception, what are the values that govern one's conduct. Observe a person's conduct over a period long enough to note the direction in which his activities tend and you will be able to tell where his loyalties lie, and knowing them, you will know the ends which stir and guide his actions: that is to say, the things that are values in actuality, not just in name. And if I begin with emphasizing the importance of observing the direction taken by behavior over a period of time rather than judging by words, it is because at no time in history have words meant as little as they do today.

One of the worst corruptions that totalitarianism has engendered is its complete violation of integrity of language. There is some truth in the saying, "at the border line, it is not easy to tell where education stops and propaganda begins." But the propaganda of the Soviet Union, Italy, Germany and Japan is easily identified by the fact that in every important matter the words used have to be read in reverse. They are selected and weighed with no reference to anything but their effect upon others. Criteria for judging slight deviations from fact are in the possession of every reasonably mature person, for his experience enables him to judge of probabilities. But complete inversions of truth are astonishingly confusing. They produce a state of daze that endures long enough to enable its creators to accomplish their will while darkness still prevails.

In short, a primary, perhaps *the* primary, loyalty of democracy at the present time is to communication. It cannot be denied that our American democracy has often made more in words of the liberties of free speech, free publication and free assembly than in action. But that the spirit of democracy is, nevertheless, alive and active is proved by the fact that publicity is a well established habit. It gives the opportunity for many silly and many false things to be uttered. But experience has confirmed the faith that silly things are of so many different kinds that they cancel each

[First published in *American Teacher* 25 (May 1941); reprinted in *The Later Works*, Vol. 14.]

other over a period of time, and that falsities come out in the wash of experience as dirt comes out in soap and water.

The freedom which is the essence of democracy is above all the freedom to develop intelligence; intelligence consisting of judgment as to what facts are relevant to action and how they are relevant to things to be done, and a corresponding alertness in the quest for such facts. To what extent we are actually democratic will in the end be decided by the degree to which the existing totalitarian menace awakens us to deeper loyalty to intelligence, pure and undefiled, and to the intrinsic connection between it and free communication: the method of conference, consultation, discussion, in which there takes place purification and pooling of the net results of the experiences of multitudes of people. It is said that "talk" is cheap. But the hundreds and hundreds of thousands of persons who have been tortured, who have died, who are rotting in concentration camps, prove that talk may also be tragically costly, and that democracy to endure must hold it immensely precious.

It has been discouraging to American democrats to see how shallow has been loyalty to this value in those fellow Americans who, while professing democracy, have still defended suppression of liberty of speech, press and creed in the Soviet Union. One would have supposed that any American would by this time have enough of the democratic spirit in his very blood so that he would need nothing more than suppression to enable him to judge the policy of a country, no matter what one supposes it can say for itself on other matters. We are warned that we must feed and nourish this particular loyalty with much more energy and deliberate persistence than we have done in the past—beginning in the family and the school.

Since I cannot discuss all the loyalties that define the values of the democratic way of life, I confine myself to those which are emphasized by contrast with contemporary totalitarianism. In theory, democracy has always professed belief in the potentialities of every human being, and all the need for providing conditions that will enable these potentialities to come to realization. We shall miss the second most important lesson the present state of the world has to teach us if we fail to see and to feel intensely that this belief must now be greatly extended and deepened. It is a faith which becomes sentimental when it is not put systematically into practice every day in all the relationships of living. There are phrases, sanctioned by religion, regarding the sacredness of personality. But glib reciting of the verbal creed is no protection against snobbishness, intolerance and taking advantage of others when opportunity offers. Our anti-democratic heritage of Negro slavery has left us with habits of intolerance toward the colored race—habits which belie profession of democratic loyalty. The very tenets of religion have been employed to foster anti-semitism. There are still many, too many, persons who feel free to cultivate and express racial prejudices as if they were within their personal rights, not recognizing how the attitude of intolerance infects, perhaps fatally as the example of Germany so surely proves, the basic humanities without which democracy is but a name.

For it is humanity and the human spirit that are at stake, and not just what is sometimes called the "individual," since the latter is a value in potential humanity and not as something separate and atomic. The attempt to identify democracy with economic individualism as the essence of free action has done harm to the reality of democracy and is capable of doing even greater injury than it has already done.

So I close by saying that the third loyalty which measures democracy is the will to transform passive toleration into active cooperation. The "fraternity" which was the third member of the democratic trinity of the France of the Revolution has never been practiced on a wide scale. Nationalism, expressed in our country in such phrases as "America First," is one of the strongest factors in producing existing totalitarianism, just as a promise of doing away with it has caused some misguided persons to be sympathetic with Naziism. Fraternity is the will to work together; it is the essence of cooperation. As I have said, it has never been widely practiced, and this failure is a large factor in producing the present state of the world. We may hope that it, not the equality produced by totalitarian suppression, will constitute the "wave of the future."

REAFFIRMING DEMOCRATIC INDIVIDUALISM: THE REJECTION OF COMMUNISM

Culture and Human Nature

In the American as in the English liberal tradition, the idea of freedom has been connected with the idea of individuality, of *the* individual. The connection has been so close and so often reiterated that it has come to seem inherent. Many persons will be surprised if they hear that freedom has ever been supposed to have another source and foundation than the very nature of individuality. Yet in the continental European tradition the affiliation of the idea of freedom is with the idea of rationality. Those are free who govern themselves by the dictates of reason; those who follow the promptings of appetite and sense are so ruled by them as to be unfree. Thus it was that Hegel at the very time he was glorifying the State wrote a philosophy of history according to which the movement of historical events was from the despotic state of the Oriental World in which only one was free to the era dawning in Germany in the Western World in which *all* are free. The same difference in contexts that give freedom its meaning is found when representatives of totalitarian Germany at the present time claim their regime is giving the subjects of their state a "higher" freedom than can be found in democratic states, individuals in the latter being unfree because their lives are chaotic and undisciplined. The aroma of the continental tradition hangs about the sayings of those who settle so many social problems to their own satisfaction by invoking a distinction between liberty and license, identifying the former with "liberty under law"—for in the classic tradition law and reason are related as child and parent. So far as the saying assigns to law an origin and authority having nothing to do with freedom, so far, that is, as it affirms the impossibility of free conditions determin-

[From *Freedom and Culture* (New York: G. P. Putnam's Sons, 1939); reprinted in *The Later Works*, Vol. 13.]

ing their own law, it points directly, even if unintentionally, to the totalitarian state.

We do not, however, have to go as far abroad as the European continent to note that freedom has had its practical significance fixed in different ways in different cultural contexts. For in the early nineteenth century there was a great practical difference between the English and the American theories, although both associated freedom with qualities that cause human beings to be *individuals* in the distinctive sense of that word. The contrast is so flat that it would be amusing if it were not so instructive. Jefferson, who was the original and systematic promulgator of the doctrine of free, self-governing institutions, found that the properties of individuals with which these institutions were most closely associated were traits found in the farming class. In his more pessimistic moments he even went so far as to anticipate that the development of manufacturing and commerce would produce a state of affairs in which persons in this country "would eat one another" as they did in Europe. In England, on the other hand, landed proprietors were the great enemy of the new freedom, which was connected in its social and political manifestations with the activities and aims of the manufacturing class.

It is not, of course, the bare fact of contrast which is instructive but the causes for its existence. They are not far to seek. Landed proprietors formed the aristocracy in Great Britain. The hold landed interests had over law-making bodies due to feudalism was hostile to the development of manufacturing and commerce. In the United States traces of feudalism were so faint that laws against primogeniture were about all that was needed to erase them. It was easy in this country to idealize the farmers as the sturdy yeomanry who embodied all the virtues associated with the original Anglo-Saxon love of liberty, the Magna Charta, and the struggle against the despotism of the Stuarts. Farmers were the independent self-supporting class that had no favors to ask from anybody, since they were not dependent for their livelihood nor their ideas upon others, owning and managing their own farms. It is a history that again would be amusing, were it not instructive, to find that as this country changed from an agrarian one to an urban industrial one, the qualities of initiative, invention, vigor and intrinsic contribution to progress which British *laissez-faire* liberalism had associated with manufacturing pursuits were transferred by American Courts and by the political representatives of business and finance from Jeffersonian individuals and given to the entrepreneurs who were individuals in the British sense.

In such considerations as these—which would be reinforced by an extensive survey of the history of the meaning given to freedom under different conditions—we have one instance and an important one of the relation of culture to the whole problem of freedom. The facts fall directly in line with the conclusion of the previous chapter:—a conclusion summed up in saying that the idea of Culture, which has become a central idea of anthropology, has such a wide sociological application that it puts a new face upon the old, old problem of the relation of the individual and the social. The idea of culture even outlaws the very terms in which the problem has been conceived, independently of its effect upon solutions proposed. For most statements of the problem have been posed as if there were some inherent difference amounting to opposition between what is called the individual and the social. As a consequence there was a tendency for those who were interested in theory to line up in two parties, which at the poles were so far apart that one denied whatever the other asserted. One party held that social conventions, traditions, institutions, rules are maintained only by some form of coercion, overt or covert, which encroaches upon the natural freedom of individuals; while the other school held that individuals are such by nature that the one standing social problem is the agencies by which recalcitrant individuals are brought under social control or "socialized." The term of honor of one school has been that of reproach of the other. The two extremes serve to define the terms in which the problem was put. Most persons occupy an intermediate and compromise position, one whose classic expression is that the basic problem of law and politics is to find the line which separates legitimate liberty from the proper exercise of law and political authority, so that each can maintain its own province under its own jurisdiction; law operating only when liberty oversteps its proper bounds, an operation supposed, during the heights of *laissez-faire* liberalism, to be legitimate only when police action was required to keep the peace. . . .

It is extremely difficult at a distance to judge just what are the appeals made to better elements in human nature by, say, such policies as form the Nazi faith. We may believe that aside from appeal to fear; from desire to escape responsibilities imposed by free citizenship; from impulses to submission strengthened by habits of obedience bred in the past; from desire for compensation for past humiliations, and from the action of nationalistic sentiments growing in intensity for over a century (and not in Germany alone), there is also love for novelty which in this particular case has taken the form of idealistic faith, among the youth in particular, of being engaged in creating a pattern for new institutions which the whole world will in time adopt. For one of the elements of human nature that is often discounted in both idea and practice is the satisfaction derived from a sense of sharing in creative activities; the satisfaction increasing in direct ratio to the scope of the constructive work engaged in.

Other causes may be mentioned, though with the admission that it is quite possible in good faith to doubt or deny their operation. There is the satisfaction that comes from a sense of union with others, a feeling capable of being intensified till it becomes a mystical sense of fusion with others and being mistaken for love on a high level of manifestation. The satisfaction obtained by the sentiment of communion with others, of the breaking down of barriers, will be intense in the degree in which it has previously been denied opportunity to manifest itself. The comparative ease with which provincial loyalties, which in Germany had been at least as intense and as influential as state-rights sentiments ever were in this country, were broken down; the similar ease, though less in degree, with which habitual religious beliefs and practices were subordinated to a feeling of racial and social union, would seem to testify that underneath there was yearning for emotional fusion. Something of this kind showed itself in most countries when they were engaged in the World War. For the time being it seemed as if barriers that separated individuals from one another had been swept away. Submission to abolition of political parties and to abolition of labor unions which had had great power, would hardly have come about so readily had there not been some kind of a void which the new regime promised to fill. Just how far the fact of uniformity is accompanied by a sense of equality in a nation where class distinctions had been rigid, one can only guess at. But there is considerable ground for believing that it has been a strong factor in reconciling "humbler" folk to enforced deprivation of material benefits, so that, at least for a time, a sense of honorable equality more than compensates for less to eat, harder and longer hours of work—since it is psychologically true that man does not live by bread alone.

It might seem as if belief in operation of "idealistic" factors was contradicted by the cruel persecutions that have taken place, things indicative of a reign of sadism rather than of desire for union with others irrespective of birth and locale. But history shows that more than once social unity has been promoted by the presence, real or alleged, of some hostile group. It has long been a part of the technique of politicians who wish to maintain themselves in power to foster the idea that the alternative is the danger of being conquered by an enemy. Nor does what has been suggested slur over in any way the effect of powerful and unremitting propaganda. For the intention has been to indicate some of the conditions whose interaction produces the social spectacle. Other powerful factors in the interaction are those technologies produced by modern science which have multiplied the means of modifying the dispositions of the mass of the population; and which, in conjunction with economic centralization, have enabled mass opinion to become like physical goods a matter of mass production. Here also is both a warning and a suggestion to those concerned with cultural conditions which will maintain democratic freedom. The warning is obvious as to the role of propaganda, which now operates with us in channels less direct and less official. The suggestion is that the printing press and radio have made the problem of the intelligent and honest use of means of communication in behalf of openly declared public ends a matter of fundamental concern.

What has been said is stated by way of illustration, and it may, if any one desires, be treated as hypothetical. For even so, the suggestions serve to enforce the point that a social regime can come into enduring existence only as it satisfies some elements of human nature not previously afforded expression. On the other hand getting relief from saturation of elements that have become stale makes almost anything welcome if only it is different. The general principle holds even if the elements that are provided a new outlet are the baser things in human nature: fear, suspicion, jealousy, inferiority complexes; factors that were excited by earlier conditions but that are now given channels of fuller expression. Common observation, especially of the young, shows that nothing is more exasperating and more resented than stirring up certain impulses and tendencies and then checking their manifestation. We should also note that a period of uncertainty and insecurity, accompanied as it is by more or less unsettlement and disturbance, creates a feeling that anything would be better than what exists, together with desire for order and stability upon almost any terms—the latter being a reason why revolutions are so regularly followed by reaction, and explain the fact that Lenin expressed by saying revolutions are authoritative, though not for the reason he gave.

Just which of these factors are involved in our own maintenance of democratic conditions or whether any of them are so involved is, at this juncture, not so pertinent as is the principle they illustrate. Negatively speaking, we have to get away from the influence of belief in bald single forces, whether they are thought of as intrinsically psychological or sociological. This includes getting away from mere hatred of abominable things, and it also means refusing to fall back on such a generalized statement as that Fascist institutions are expressions of the sort of thing to be expected in a stage of contracting capitalism, since they are a kind of final spasm of protest against approaching dissolution. We cannot reject out of hand any cause assigned; it may have some truth. But the primary need is to escape from wholesale reasons, as totalitarian as are the states ruled by dictators. We have to analyze conditions by observations, which are as discriminating as they are extensive, until we discover specific interactions that are taking place, and learn to think in terms of interactions instead of force. We are led to search even for the conditions which have given the interacting factors the power they possess.

The lesson is far from being entirely new. The founders of American political democracy were not so naively devoted to pure theory that they were unaware of the necessity of cultural conditions for the successful working of democratic forms. I could easily fill pages from Thomas Jefferson in which he insists upon the necessity of a free press, general schooling and local neighborhood groups carrying on, through intimate meetings and discussions, the management of their own affairs, if political democracy was to be made secure. These sayings could be backed up by almost equally numerous expressions of his fears for the success of republican institutions in South American countries that had thrown off the Spanish yoke.

He expressly set forth his fear that their traditions were such that domestic military despotisms would be substituted for foreign subjugations. A background of "ignorance, bigotry and superstition" was not a good omen. On one occasion he even went so far as to suggest that the best thing that could happen would be for the South American states to remain under the nominal supremacy of Spain, under the collective guarantee of France, Russia, Holland and the United States, until experience in self-government prepared them for complete independence.

The real source of the weakness that has developed later in the position of our democratic progenitors is not that they isolated the problem of freedom from the positive conditions that would nourish it, but that they did not—and in their time could not—carry their analysis far enough. The outstanding examples of this inability are their faith in the public press and in schooling. They certainly were not wrong in emphasizing the need of a free press and of common public schools to provide conditions favorable to democracy. But to them the enemy of freedom of the press was official governmental censorship and control; they did not foresee the non-political causes that might restrict its freedom, nor the economic factors that would put a heavy premium on centralization. And they failed to see how education in literacy could become a weapon in the hands of an oppressive government, nor that the chief cause for promotion of elementary education in Europe would be increase of military power. . . .

After many centuries of struggle and following of false gods, the natural sciences now possess methods by which particular facts and general ideas are brought into effective cooperation with one another. But with respect to means for understanding social events, we are still living in the pre-scientific epoch, although the events to be understood are the consequences of application of scientific knowledge to a degree unprecedented in history. With respect to information and understanding of social events, our state is that on one side of an immense number of undigested and unrelated facts, reported in isolation (and hence easily colored by some twist of interest) and large untested generalizations on the other side.

The generalizations are so general in the sense of remoteness from the events to which they are supposed to apply that they are matters of opinion, and frequently the rallying cries and slogans of factions and classes. They are often expressions of partisan desire clothed in the language of intellect. As matters of opinion, they are batted hither and yon in controversy and are subject to changes of popular fashion. They differ at practically every point from scientific generalizations, since the latter express the relations of facts to one another and, as they are employed to bring together more facts, are tested by the material to which they are applied.

If a glance at an editorial page of a newspaper shows what is meant by untested opinions put forth in the garb of the general principles of sound judgment, the items of the news columns illustrate what is meant by a multitude of diverse unrelated facts. The popular idea of "sensational," as it is derived from the daily press, is more instructive as to meaning of *sensations* than is the treatment accorded that subject in books on psychology. Events are sensational in the degree in which they make a strong impact in isolation from the relations to other events that give them their significance. They appeal to those who like things raw. Ordinary reports of murders, love nests, etc., are of this sort, with an artificial intensity supplied by unusual size or color of type. To say that a response is intellectual, not sensational, in the degree in which its significance is supplied by relations to other things is to state a truism. They are two sets of words used to describe the same thing.

One effect of literacy under existing conditions has been to create in a large number of persons an appetite for the momentary "thrills" caused by impacts that stimulate nerve endings but whose connections with cerebral functions are broken. Then stimulation and excitation are not so ordered that intelligence is produced. At the same time the habit of using judgment is weakened by the habit of depending on external stimuli. Upon the whole it is probably a tribute to the powers of endurance of human nature that the consequences are not more serious than they are.

The new mechanisms resulting from application of scientific discoveries have, of course, immensely extended the range and variety of particular events, or "news items" which are brought to bear upon the senses and the emotions connected with them. The telegraph, telephone, and radio report events going on over the whole face of the globe. They are for the most part events about which the individuals who are told of them can do nothing, except to react with a passing emotional excitation. For, because of lack of relation and organization in reference to one another, no imaginative reproduction of the situation is possible, such as might make up for the absence of personal response. Before we engage in too much pity for the inhabitants of our rural regions before the days of invention of modern devices for circulation of information, we should recall that they knew more about the things that affected their own lives than the city dweller of today is likely to know about the causes of his affairs. They did not possess nearly as many separate items of information, but they were compelled to know, in the sense of *understanding,* the conditions that bore upon the conduct of their own affairs. Today the influences that affect the actions performed by individuals are so remote as to be unknown. We are at the mercy of events acting upon us in unexpected, abrupt, and violent ways.

The bearing of these considerations upon the cultural conditions involved in maintenance of freedom is not far to seek. It is very directly connected with what now seems to us the over-simplification of the democratic idea indulged in by the authors of our republican government. They had in mind persons whose daily occupations stimulated initiative and vigor, and who possessed information which even if narrow in scope, bore pretty directly upon what they had to do, while its sources were pretty much within their control. Their judgment was exercised upon things within the range of their activities and their contacts. The press, the telegraph, the telephone and radio have broadened indefinitely the range of information at the disposal of the average person. It would be foolish to deny that a certain quickening of sluggish minds has resulted. But quite aside from having opened avenues through which organized propaganda may operate continuously to stir emotion and to leave behind a deposit of opinion, there is much information about which judgment is not called upon to respond, and where even if it wanted to, it cannot act effectively so dispersive is the material about which it is called upon to exert itself. The average person is surrounded today by readymade intellectual goods as he is by readymade foods, articles, and all kinds of gadgets. He has not the personal share in making either intellectual or material goods that his pioneer ancestors had. Consequently they knew better what they themselves were about, though they knew infinitely less concerning what the world at large was doing.

Self-government of the town-meeting type is adequate for management of local affairs, such as school buildings, district revenues, local roads and local taxation. Participation in these forms of self-government was a good preparation for self-government on a larger scale. But such matters as roads and schools under existing conditions have more than local import even in country districts; and while participation in town meetings is good as far as it arouses public spirit, it cannot provide the information that enables a citizen to be an intelligent judge of national affairs—now also affected by world conditions. Schooling in literacy is no substitute for the dispositions which were formerly provided by direct experiences of an educative quality. The void created by lack of relevant personal experiences combines with the confusion produced by impact of multitudes of unrelated incidents to create attitudes which are responsive to organized propaganda, hammering in day after day the same few and relatively simple beliefs asseverated to be "truths" essential to national welfare. In short, we have to take into account the attitudes of human nature that have been created by the immense development in mechanical instrumentalities if we are to understand the present power of organized propaganda. . . .

Democracy and Human Nature

The subject matter which follows is that of a drama in three acts, of which the last is the unfinished one now being enacted in which we, now living, are the participants. The first act, as far as it is possible to tell its condensed story, is that of a one-sided simplification of human nature which was used to promote and justify the new political movement. The second act is that of the reaction against the theory and the practices connected with it, on the ground that it was the forerunner of moral and social anarchy, the cause of dissolution of the ties of cohesion that bind human beings together in organic union. The third act, now playing, is that of recovery of the moral significance of the connection of human nature and democracy, now stated in concrete terms of existing conditions and freed from the one-sided exaggerations of the earlier statement. I give this summary first because in what follows I have been compelled to go in some detail into matters that if pursued further are technically theoretical.

I begin by saying that the type of theory which isolated the "external" factor of interactions that produce social phenomena is paralleled by one which isolated the "internal" or human factor. Indeed, if I had followed the historic order the latter type of theory would have been discussed first. And this type of theory is still more widely and influentially held than we might suppose. For its vogue is not now adequately represented by those professional psychologists and sociologists who claim that all social phenomena are to be understood in terms of the mental operations of individuals, since society consists in the last analysis only of individual persons. The practically effective statement of the point of view is found in economic theory, where it furnished the backbone of laissez-faire economics; and in the British political liberalism which developed in combination with this economic doctrine. A particular view of human motives in relation to social events, as explanations of them and as the basis of all sound social policy, has not come to us labeled psychology. But as a theory about human nature it is essentially psychological. We still find a view put forth as to an intrinsic and necessary connection between democracy and capitalism which has a psychological foundation and temper. For it is only because of belief in a certain theory of human

[From *Freedom and Culture* (New York: G. P. Putnam's Sons, 1939); reprinted in *The Later Works*, Vol. 13.]

nature that the two are said to be Siamese twins, so that attack upon one is a threat directed at the life of the other.

The classic expression of the point of view which would explain social phenomena by means of psychological phenomena is that of John Stuart Mill in his *Logic*—a statement that probably appeared almost axiomatic when it was put forth. "All phenomena of society are phenomena of human nature . . . and if therefore the phenomena of human thought, feeling and action are subject to fixed laws, the phenomena of society cannot but conform to law." And again, "The laws of the phenomena of society are and can be nothing but the laws of the actions and passions of human beings united in the social state." And then, as if to state conclusively that being "united in the social state" makes no difference as to the laws of individuals and hence none in those of society, he adds, "Human beings in society have no properties but those which are derived from and may be resolved into the laws of the nature of individual man."

This reference to "individual man" discloses the nature of the particular simplification which controlled the views and the policies of this particular school. The men who expressed and entertained the type of philosophy whose method was summed up by Mill were in their time revolutionaries. They wished to liberate a certain group of individuals, those concerned in new forms of industry, commerce and finance, from shackles inherited from feudalism which were endeared by custom and interest to a powerful landed aristocracy. If they do not appear now to be revolutionary (operating to bring about social change by change in men's opinions not by force), it is because their views are now the philosophy of conservatives in every highly industrialized country.

They essayed an intellectual formulation of principles which would justify the success of the tendencies which present day revolutionaries call the bourgeois capitalism they are trying to overthrow. The psychology in question is not that of present textbooks. But it expressed the individualistic ideas that animated the economic and political theories of the radicals of the time. Its "individualism" supplied the background of a great deal of even the technical psychology of the present day—pretty much all of it, save that which has started on a new tack because of biological and anthropological considerations. At the time of its origin, it was not a bookish doctrine even when written down in books. The books were elaborations of ideas that were propounded in electoral campaigns and offered as laws to be adopted by parliament.

Before engaging in any detailed statements, I want to recall a statement made earlier; namely, that the popular view of the constitution of human nature at any given time is a reflex of social movements which have either become institutionalized or else are showing themselves against opposing social odds and hence need intellectual and moral formulation to increase their power. I may seem to be going far afield if I refer to Plato's statement of the way by which to determine the constituents of human nature. The proper method, he said, was to look at the version of human nature written in large and legible letters in the organization of classes in society, before trying to make it out in the dim petty edition found in individuals. And so on the basis of the social organization with which he was acquainted he found that since in society there was a laboring class toiling to find the means of satisfying the appetites, a citizen soldiery class loyal even to death to the laws of the state, and a legislative class, so the human soul must be composed of appetite at the base—in both significations of "base"—of generous spirited impulses which looked beyond personal enjoyment, while appetite was engaged only in taking in and absorbing for its own satisfaction, and finally reason, the legislative power.

Having found these three things in the composition of human nature, he had no difficulty in going back to social organization and proving that there was one class which had to be kept in order by rules and laws imposed from above, since otherwise its action was without limits, and would in the name of liberty destroy harmony and order; another class, whose inclinations were all towards obedience and loyalty to law, towards right beliefs, although itself incapable of discovering the ends from which laws are derived; and at the apex, in any well-ordered organization, the rule of those whose predominant natural qualities were reason, after that faculty had been suitably formed by education.

It would be hard to find a better illustration of the fact that any movement purporting to discover the psychological causes and sources of social phenomena is in fact a reverse movement, in which current social tendencies are read back into the structure of human nature; and are then used to explain the very things from which they are deduced. It was then "natural" for the men who reflected the new movement of industry and commerce to erect the appetites, treated by Plato as a kind of necessary evil, into the cornerstone of social well-being and progress. Something of the same kind exists at present when love of power is put forward to play the role taken a century ago by self-interest as the dominant "motive"—and if I put the word motive in quotation marks, it is for the reason just given. What are called motives turn out upon critical examination to be complex attitudes patterned under cultural conditions, rather than simple elements in human nature.

Even when we refer to tendencies and impulses that actually are genuine elements in human nature we find, unless we swallow whole some current opinion, that of themselves they explain nothing about social phenomena. For they produce consequences only as they are shaped into acquired dispositions by interaction with environing cultural conditions. Hobbes, who was the first of the moderns to identify the "state of nature" and its laws—the classic background of all political theories—with the raw uneducated state of human nature, may be called as witness. According to Hobbes, "In the nature of man we find three principal causes of quarrel. First competition, secondly diffidence, thirdly glory. The first maketh men invade for gain; the second for safety; and the third for reputation. The first use violence to make themselves the masters of other persons; the second to defend them; the third for trifles as a word, a smile, a different opinion or any other sign of undervalue, either direct in their persons or by reflection in their kindred, their friends, their nation."

That the qualities mentioned by Hobbes actually exist in human nature and that they may generate "quarrel," that is, conflict and war between states and civil war within a nation—the chronic state of affairs when Hobbes lived—is not denied. Insofar, Hobbes' account of the natural psychology which prevents the state of security which is a pre-requisite for civilized communities shows more insight than many attempts made today to list the traits of raw human nature that are supposed to cause social phenomena. Hobbes thought that the entire natural state of men in their relations to one another was a war of all against all, man being naturally to man "as a wolf." The intent of Hobbes was thus a glorification of deliberately instituted relations, authoritative laws and regulations which should rule not just overt actions, but the impulses and ideas which cause men to hold up certain things as ends or goods. Hobbes himself thought of this authority as a political sovereign. But it would be in the spirit of his treatment to regard it as glorification of culture over against raw human nature, and more than one writer has pointed out the likeness between his Leviathan and the Nazi totalitarian state.

There are more than one instructive parallelisms that may be drawn between the period in which Hobbes lived and the present time, especially as to insecurity and conflict between nations and classes. The point here pertinent, however, is that the qualities Hobbes selected as the causes of disorders making the life of mankind "brutish and nasty," are the very "motives" that have been selected by others as the cause of *beneficent* social effects; namely, harmony, prosperity, and indefinite progress. The position taken by Hobbes about competition as love of gain was completely reversed in the British social philosophy of the nineteenth century. Instead of being a source of war, it was taken to be the means by which individuals found the occupation for which they were best fitted;

by which needed goods reached the consumer at least cost, and by which a state of ultimate harmonious interdependence would be produced—provided only competition were allowed to operate without "artificial" restriction. Even today one reads articles and hears speeches in which the cause of our present economic troubles is laid to political interference with the beneficent workings of private competitive effort for gain.

The object of alluding to these two very different conceptions of this component in human nature is not to decide or discuss which is right. The point is that both are guilty of the same fallacy. In itself, the impulse (or whatever name be given it) is neither socially maleficent nor beneficent. Its significance depends upon consequences actually produced; and these depend upon the conditions under which it operates and with which it interacts. The conditions are set by tradition, by custom, by law, by the kind of public approvals and disapprovals; by all conditions constituting the environment. These conditions are so pluralized even in one and the same country at the same period that love of gain (regarded as a trait of human nature) may be both socially useful and socially harmful. And, in spite of the tendency to set up cooperative impulses as thoroughly beneficial, the same thing is true of them—regarded simply as components of human nature. Neither competition nor cooperation can be judged as traits of human nature. They are names for certain relations among the actions of individuals as the relations actually obtain in a community.

This would be true even if there were tendencies in human nature so definitely marked off from one another as to merit the names given them and even if human nature were as fixed as it is sometimes said to be. For even in that case, human nature operates in a multitude of different environing conditions, and it is interaction with the latter that determines the consequences and the social significance and value, positive or negative, of the tendencies. The alleged fixity of the structure of human nature does not explain in the least the differences that mark off one tribe, family, people, from another—which is to say that in and of itself it explains no state of society whatever. It issues no advice as to what policies it is advantageous to follow. It does not even justify conservatism as against radicalism.

But the alleged unchangeableness of human nature cannot be admitted. For while certain needs in human nature are constant, the consequences they produce (because of the existing state of culture—of science, morals, religion, art, industry, legal rules) react back into the original components of human nature to shape them into new forms. The total pattern is thereby modified. The futility of exclusive appeal to psychological factors both to explain what takes place and to form policies as to what *should* take place, would be evident to everybody—had it not proved to be a convenient device for "rationalizing" policies that are urged on other grounds by some group or faction. While the case of "competition" urging men both to war and to beneficent social progress is most obviously instructive in this respect, examination of the other elements of Hobbes supports the same conclusion.

There have been communities, for example, in which regard for the honor of one's self, one's family, one's class, has been the chief conservator of all worth while social values. It has always been the chief virtue of an aristocratic class, civil or military. While its value has often been exaggerated, it is folly to deny that in interaction with certain cultural conditions, it has had valuable consequences. "Diffidence" or fear as a motive is an even more ambiguous and meaningless term as far as its consequences are concerned. It takes any form, from craven cowardice to prudence, caution, and the circumspection without which no intelligent foresight is possible. It may become reverence—which has been exaggerated in the abstract at times but which may be attached to the kind of objects which render it supremely desirable. "Love of power," to which it is now fashionable to appeal, has a meaning only when it applies to everything in general and hence explains nothing in particular.

Discussion up to this point has been intended to elicit two principles. One of them is that the views about human nature that are popular at a given time are usually derived from contemporary social currents; currents so conspicuous as to stand out or else less marked and less effective social movements which a special group believes *should* become dominant:—as for example, in the case of the legislative reason with Plato, and of competitive love of gain with classical economists. The other principle is that reference to components of original human nature, even if they actually exist, explains no social occurrence whatever and gives no advice or direction as to what policies it is better to adopt. This does not mean that reference to them must necessarily be of a "rationalizing" concealed apologetic type. It means that whenever it occurs with practical significance it has *moral* not psychological import. For, whether brought forward from the side of conserving what already exists or from that of producing change, it is an expression of valuation, and of purpose determined by estimate of values. When a trait of human nature is put forward on this basis, it is in its proper context and is subject to intelligent examination.

The prevailing habit, however, is to assume that a social issue does not concern values to be preferred and striven for, but rather something predetermined by the constitution of human nature. This assumption is the source of serious social ills. Intellectually it is a reversion to the type of explanation that governed physical science until say, the seventeenth century: a method now seen to have been the chief source of the long-continued retardation of natural science. For this type of theory consists of appeal to general forces to "explain" what happens.

Natural science began to progress steadily only when general forces were banished and inquiry was directed instead of ascertaining correlations that exist between observed changes. Popular appeal to, say, electricity, light or heat, etc., as a force to account for some particular event still exists, as to electricity to explain storms attended by thunder and lightning. Scientific men themselves often talk in similar words. But such general terms are in their case shorthand expressions. They stand for uniform relations between events that are observed to occur; they do not mark appeal to something behind what happens and which is supposed to produce it. If we take the case of the lightning flash and electricity, Franklin's identification of the former as of the electrical kind brought it into connection with things from which it had been formerly isolated, and knowledge about them was available in dealing with it. But instead of electricity being an explanatory force, knowledge that lightning is an electrical phenomenon opened a number of special problems, some of which are still unsolved. . . .

The present predicament may be stated as follows: Democracy does involve a belief that political institutions and law be such as to take fundamental account of human nature. They must give it freer play than any non-democratic institutions. At the same time, the theory, legalistic and moralistic, about human nature that has been used to expound and justify this reliance upon human nature has proved inadequate. Upon the legal and political side, during the nineteenth century it was progressively overloaded with ideas and practices which have more to do with business carried on for profit than with democracy. On the moralistic side, it has tended to substitute emotional exhortation to act in accord with the Golden Rule for the discipline and the control afforded by incorporation of democratic ideals into *all* the relations of life. Because of lack of an adequate theory of human nature in its relations to democracy, attachment to democratic ends and methods has tended to become a matter of tradition and habit—an excellent thing as far as it goes, but when it becomes routine is easily undermined when change of conditions changes other habits.

Were I to say that democracy needs a new psychology of human nature, one adequate to the heavy demands put upon it by foreign and domestic conditions, I might be taken to utter an academic irrelevancy. But if the remark is understood to mean that democracy has always been allied with humanism, with faith in the potentialities of human nature, and that the present need is vigorous reassertion of this faith, developed in relevant ideas and manifested in practical attitudes, it but continues the American tradition. For belief in the "common man" has no significance save as an expression of belief in the intimate and vital connection of democracy and human nature.

We cannot continue the idea that human nature when left to itself, when freed from external arbitrary restrictions, will tend to the production of democratic institutions that work successfully. We have now to state the issue from the other side. We have to see that democracy means the belief that humanistic culture *should* prevail; we should be frank and open in our recognition that the proposition is a moral one—like any idea that concerns what *should* be.

Strange as it seems to us, democracy is challenged by totalitarian states of the Fascist variety on moral grounds just as it is challenged by totalitarianisms of the left on economic grounds. We may be able to defend democracy on the latter score, as far as comparative conditions are involved, since up to the present at least the Union of Soviet Socialist Republics has not "caught up" with us, much less "surpassed" us, in material affairs. But defense against the other type of totalitarianism (and perhaps in the end against also the Marxist type) requires a positive and courageous constructive awakening to the significance of faith in human nature for development of every phase of our culture:—science, art, education, morals and religion, as well as politics and economics. No matter how uniform and constant human nature is in the abstract, the conditions within which and upon which it operates have changed so greatly since political democracy was established among us, that democracy cannot now depend upon or be expressed in political institutions alone. We cannot even be certain that they and their legal accompaniments are actually democratic at the present time—for democracy is expressed in the attitudes of human beings and is measured by consequences produced in their lives.

The impact of the humanist view of democracy upon all forms of culture, upon education, science and art, morals and religion, as well as upon industry and politics, saves it from the criticism passed upon moralistic exhortation. For it tells us that we need to examine every one of the phases of human activity to ascertain what effects it has in release, maturing and fruition of the potentialities of human nature. It does not tell us to "re-arm morally" and all social problems will be solved. It says, Find out how all the constituents of our existing culture are operating and then see to it that whenever and wherever needed they be modified in order that their workings may release and fulfill the possibilities of human nature.

It used to be said (and the statement has not gone completely out of fashion) that democracy is a by-product of Christianity, since the latter teaches the infinite worth of the individual human soul. We are now told by some persons that since belief in the soul has been discredited by science, the moral basis for democracy supposed to exist must go into the discard. We are told that if there are reasons for preferring it to other arrangements of the relations of human beings to one another, they must be found in specialized external advantages which outweigh the advantages of other social forms. From a very different quarter, we are told that weakening of the older theological doctrine of the soul is one of the reasons for the eclipse of faith in democracy. These two views at opposite poles give depth and urgency to the question whether there are adequate grounds for faith in the potentialities of human nature and whether they can be accompanied by the intensity and ardor once awakened by religious ideas upon a theological basis. Is human nature intrinsically such a poor thing that the idea is *absurd?* I do not attempt to give any answer, but the word *faith* is intentionally used. For in the long run democracy will stand or fall with the possibility of maintaining the faith and justifying it by works.

Take, for example, the question of intolerance. Systematic hatred and suspicion of any human group, "racial," sectarian, political, denotes deep-seated scepticism about the qualities of human nature. From the standpoint of a faith in the possibilities of human nature possessing religious quality it is blasphemous. It may start by being directed at a particular group, and be supported in name by assigning special reasons why that group is not worthy of confidence, respect, and decent human treatment. But the underlying attitude is one of fundamental distrust of human nature. Hence it spreads from distrust and hatred of a particular group until it may undermine the conviction that any group of persons has any intrinsic right for esteem or recognition—which, then, if it be given, is for some special and external grounds, such as usefulness to our particular interests and ambitions. There is no physical acid which has the corrosive power possessed by intolerance directed against persons because they belong to a group that bears a certain name. Its corrosive potency gains with what it feeds on. An anti-humanist attitude is the essence of every form of intolerance. Movements that begin by stirring up hostility against a group of people end by denying to them all human qualities.

The case of intolerance is used as an illustration of the intrinsic connection between the prospects of democracy and belief in the potentialities of human nature—not for its own sake, important as it is on its own account. How much of our past tolerance was positive and how much of it a toleration equivalent to "standing" something we do not like, "putting up" with something because it involves too much trouble to try to change it? For a good deal of the present reaction against democracy is probably simply the disclosure of a weakness that was there before; one that was covered up or did not appear in its true light. Certainly racial prejudice against Negroes, Catholics, and Jews is no new thing in our life. Its presence among us is an intrinsic weakness and a handle for the accusation that we do not act differently from Nazi Germany.

The greatest practical inconsistency that would be revealed by searching our own habitual attitudes is probably one between the democratic method of forming opinions in political matters and the methods in common use in forming beliefs in other subjects. In theory, the democratic method is persuasion through public discussion carried on not only in legislative halls but in the press, private conversations and public assemblies. The substitution of ballots for bullets, of the right to vote for the lash, is an expression of the will to substitute the method of discussion for the method of coercion. With all its defects and partialities in determination of political decisions, it has worked to keep factional disputes within bounds, to an extent that was incredible a century or more ago. While Carlyle could bring his gift of satire into play in ridiculing the notion that men by talking to and at each other in an assembly hall can settle what is true in social affairs any more than they can settle what is true in the multiplication table, he failed to see that if men had been using clubs to maim and kill one another to decide the product of 7 times 7, there would have been sound reasons for appealing to discussion and persuasion even in the latter case. The fundamental reply is that social "truths" are so unlike mathematical truths that unanimity of uniform belief is possible in respect to the former only when a dictator has the power to tell others what they must believe—or profess they believe. The adjustment of interests demands that diverse interests have a chance to articulate themselves.

The real trouble is that there is an intrinsic split in our habitual attitudes when we profess to depend upon discussion and persuasion in politics and then systematically depend upon other methods in reaching conclusions in matters of morals and religion, or in anything where we depend upon a person or group possessed of "authority." We do not have to go to theological matters to find examples. In homes and in schools, the places where the essentials of character are supposed to be formed, the usual procedure is settlement of issues, intellectual and moral, by appeal to the "authority" of parent, teacher, or textbook. Dispositions formed under such conditions are so inconsistent with the democratic method that in a crisis they may be aroused to act in positively anti-democratic ways for anti-democratic ends; just as resort to coercive force and suppression of civil liberties are readily palliated in nominally democratic communities when the cry is raised that "law and order" are threatened.

It is no easy matter to find adequate authority for action in the demand, characteristic of democracy, that conditions be such as will enable the potentialities of human nature to reach fruition. Because it is not easy the democratic road is the hard one to take. It is the road which places the greatest burden of responsibility upon the greatest number of human beings. Backsets and deviations occur and will continue to occur. But that which is its weakness at particular times is its strength in the long course of human history. Just because the cause of democratic freedom is the cause of the fullest possible realization of human potentialities, the latter when they are suppressed and oppressed will in time rebel and demand an opportunity for manifestation. With the founders of American democracy, the claims of democracy were inherently one with the demands of a just and equal morality. We cannot now well use their vocabulary. Changes in knowledge have outlawed the significations of the words they commonly used. But in spite of the unsuitability of much of their language for present use, what they asserted was that self-governing institutions are the means by which human nature can secure its fullest realization in the greatest number of persons. The question of what is involved in self-governing methods is now much more complex. But for this very reason, the task of those who retain belief in democracy is to revive and maintain in full vigor the original conviction of the intrinsic moral nature of democracy, now stated in ways congruous with present conditions of culture. We have advanced far enough to say that democracy is a way of life. We have yet to realize that it is a way of personal life and one which provides a moral standard for personal conduct.

Means and Ends

THEIR INTERDEPENDENCE, AND LEON TROTSKY'S ESSAY ON "THEIR MORALS AND OURS"

The relation of means and ends has long been an outstanding issue in morals. It has also been a burning issue in political theory and practise. Of late the discussion has centered about the later developments of Marxism in the U.S.S.R. The course of the Stalinists has been defended by many of his adherents in other countries on the ground that the purges and prosecutions, perhaps even with a certain amount of falsification, were necessary to maintain the alleged socialistic régime of that country. Others have used the measures of the Stalinist bureaucracy to condemn the Marxist policy on the ground that the latter leads to such excesses as have occurred in the U.S.S.R. precisely because Marxism holds that the end justifies the means. Some of these critics have held that since Trotsky is also a Marxian he is committed to the same policy and consequently if he had been in power would also have felt bound to use any means whatever that seemed necessary to achieve the end involved in dictatorship by the proletariat.

The discussion has had at least one useful theoretical result. It has brought out into the open for the first time, as far as I am aware, an explicit discussion by a consistent Marxian of the relation of means and ends in social action.[1] At the courteous invitation of one of the editors of this review, I propose to discuss this issue in the light of Mr. Trotsky's discussion of the interdependence of means and ends. Much of the earlier part of his essay does not, accordingly, enter into my discussion, though I may say that on the ground of *tu quoque* argument (suggested by the title) Trotsky has had no great difficulty in showing that some of his critics have acted in much the same way they attribute to him. Since Mr. Trotsky also indicates that the only alternative position to the idea that the end justifies the means is some form of absolutistic ethics based on the alleged deliverances of conscience, or a moral sense, or some brand of eternal truths, I wish to say that I write from a standpoint that rejects

[First published in *New International* 4 (August 1938); reprinted in *The Later Works*, Vol. 13.]
1. "Their Morals and Ours," by Leon Trotsky, the *New International*, June 1938, pp. 163–173.

all such doctrines as definitely as does Mr. Trotsky himself, and that I hold that the end in the sense of consequences provides the only basis for moral ideas and action, and therefore provides the only justification that can be found for means employed. . . .

Now what has given the maxim (and the practise it formulates) that the end justifies the means a bad name is that the end-in-view, the end professed and entertained (perhaps quite sincerely) justifies the use of certain means, and so justifies the latter that it is not necessary to examine what the actual consequences of the use of chosen means will be. An individual may hold, and quite sincerely as far as his personal opinion is concerned that certain means will "really" lead to a professed and desired end. But the real question is not one of personal belief but of the objective grounds upon which it is held: namely, the consequences that will actually be produced by them. So when Mr. Trotsky says that "dialectical materialism knows no dualism between means and end," the natural interpretation is that he will recommend the use of means that can be shown by their own nature to lead to the liberation of mankind as an objective consequence.

One would expect, then, that with the idea of the liberation of mankind as the end-in-view, there would be an examination of *all* means that are likely to attain this end without any fixed preconception as to what they *must* be, and that every suggested means would be weighed and judged on the express ground of the consequences it is likely to produce.

But this is *not* the course adopted in Mr. Trotsky's further discussion. He says: "The liberating morality of the proletariat is of a revolutionary character. . . . It *deduces* a rule of conduct from the laws of the development of society, thus primarily from the class struggle, the law of all laws." (Italics are mine.) As if to leave no doubt of his meaning he says: "The end flows from the historical movement"—that of the class struggle. The principle of interdependence of means and end has thus disappeared or at least been submerged. For the choice of means is not decided upon on the ground of an independent examination of measures and policies with respect to their actual objective consequences. On the contrary, means are "*deduced*" from an independent source, an alleged law of history which is *the* law of all laws of social development. Nor does the logic of the case change if the word "alleged" is stricken out. For even so, it follows that means to be used are not derived from consideration of the end, the liberation of mankind, but from another outside source. The professed end—the end-in-view—the liberation of mankind, is thus subordinated to the class struggle as the means by which it is to be attained. Instead of *inter*dependence of means and end, the end is dependent upon the means but the means are not derived from the end. Since the class struggle is regarded as the *only* means that will reach the end, and since the view that it is the only means is reached deductively and not by an inductive examination of the means-consequences in their interdependence, the means, the class struggle, does not need to be critically examined with respect to its actual objective consequences. It is automatically absolved from all need for critical examination. If we are not back in the position that the *end-in-view* (as distinct from objective consequences) justifies the use of any means in line with the class struggle and that it justifies the neglect of all other means, I fail to understand the logic of Mr. Trotsky's position.

The position that I have indicated as that of genuine interdependence of means and ends does not automatically rule out class struggle as one means for attaining the end. But it does rule out the deductive method of arriving at it as a means, to say nothing of its being the *only* means. The selection of class struggle as a means has to be justified, on the ground of the interdependence of means and end, by an examination of actual consequences of its use, not deductively. Historical considerations are certainly relevant to this examination. But the assumption of a *fixed law* of social development is not relevant. It is as if a biologist or a physician were to assert that a certain law of biology which he accepts is so related to the end of health that the means of arriving at health—and the only means—can be deduced from it, so that no further examination of biological phenomena is needed. The whole case is prejudged.

It is one thing to say that class struggle is a means of attaining the end of the liberation of mankind. It is a radically different thing to say that there is an absolute *law* of class struggle which determines the means to be used. For if it determines the means, it also determines the end—the actual consequences, and upon the principle of genuine interdependence of means and end it is arbitrary and subjective to say that that consequence will be the liberation of mankind. The liberation of mankind is the end to be striven for. In any legitimate sense of "moral," it is a moral end. No scientific law can determine a moral end save by deserting the principle of interdependence of means and end. A Marxian may sincerely believe that class struggle is *the* law of social development. But quite aside from the fact that the belief closes the doors to further examination of history—just as an assertion that the Newtonian laws are the final laws of physics would preclude further search for physical laws—it would not follow, even if it were *the* scientific law of history, that it is the means to the moral goal of the liberation of mankind. That it is such a means has to be shown not by "deduction" from a law but by examination of the actual relations of means and consequences; an examination in which given the liberation of mankind as end, there is free and unprejudiced search for the means by which it can be attained.

One more consideration may be added about class struggle as a means. There are presumably several, perhaps many, different ways by means of which the class struggle may be carried on. How can a choice be made among these different ways except by examining their consequences in relation to the goal of liberation of mankind? The belief that a law of history determines the particular way in which the struggle is to be carried on certainly seems to tend toward a fanatical and even mystical devotion to use of certain ways of conducting the class struggle to the exclusion of all other ways of conducting it. I have no wish to go outside the theoretical question of the interdependence of means and ends but it is conceivable that the course actually taken by the revolution in the U.S.S.R. becomes more explicable when it is noted that means were deduced from a supposed scientific law instead of being searched for and adopted on the ground of their relation to the moral end of the liberation of mankind.

The only conclusion I am able to reach is that in avoiding one kind of absolutism Mr. Trotsky has plunged into another kind of absolutism. There appears to be a curious transfer among orthodox Marxists of allegiance from the ideals of socialism and scientific *methods* of attaining them (scientific in the sense of being based on the objective relations of means and consequences) to the class struggle as the law of historical change. Deduction of ends set up, of means and attitudes, from this law as the primary thing makes all moral questions, that is, all questions of the end to be finally attained, meaningless. To be scientific about ends does not mean to read them out of laws, whether the laws are natural or social. Orthodox Marxism shares with orthodox religionism and with traditional idealism the belief that human ends are interwoven into the very texture and structure of existence—a conception inherited presumably from its Hegelian origin.

I Believe

My contribution to the first series of essays in *Living Philosophies* put forward the idea of faith in the possibilities of experience as the heart of my own philosophy. In the course of that contribution I said, "Individuals will always be the centre and the consummation of experience, but what the individual actually *is* in his life-experience depends upon the nature and movement of associated life." I have not changed my faith in experience nor my belief that individuality is its centre and consummation. But there has been a change in emphasis. I should now wish to emphasize more than I formerly did that individuals are the finally decisive factors of the nature and movement of associated life.

The cause of this shift of emphasis is the events of the intervening years. The rise of dictatorships and totalitarian states and the decline of democracy have been accompanied with loud proclamation of the idea that only the state, the political organization of society, can give security to individuals. In return for the security thus obtained, it is asserted even more loudly (and with much greater practical effect) that individuals owe everything to the state.

This fundamental challenge compels all who believe in liberty and democracy to rethink the whole question of the relation of individual choice, belief, and action to institutions, to reflect on the kind of social changes that will make individuals in actuality the centres and the possessors of worth-while experience. In rethinking this issue in the light of the rise of totalitarian states, I am led to emphasize the idea that only the voluntary initiative and voluntary cooperation of individuals can produce social institutions that will protect the liberties necessary for achieving development of genuine individuality.

This change of emphasis does not in any way minimize the belief that the ability of individuals to develop genuine individuality is intimately connected with the social conditions under which they associate with one another. But it attaches fundamental importance to the activities of individuals in determining the social conditions under which they live. It has been shown in the last few years that democratic *institutions* are no guarantee for the existence of democratic individuals. The alternative is that individuals who prize their own liberties and who prize the liberties

[First published in *I Believe: The Personal Philosophies of Certain Eminent Men and Women of Our Time*, ed. Clifton Fadiman (New York: Simon and Schuster, 1939); reprinted in *The Later Works*, Vol. 14.]

of other individuals, individuals who are democratic in thought and action, are the sole final warrant for the existence and endurance of democratic institutions.

The belief that the voluntary activities of individuals in voluntary association with one another is the only basis of democratic institutions does not mean a return to the older philosophy of individualism. That philosophy thought of the individual after the analogy of older physical science. He was taken to be a centre without a field. His relations to other individuals were as mechanical and external as those of Newtonian atoms to one another. Liberty was supposed to be automatically acquired by abolition of restraints and constraints; all the individual needed was to be let alone.

The negative and empty character of this individualism had consequences which produced a reaction toward an equally arbitrary and one-sided collectivism. This reaction is identical with the rise of the new form of political despotism. The decline of democracy and the rise of authoritarian states which claim they can do for individuals what the latter cannot by any possibility do for themselves are the two sides of one and the same indivisible picture.

Political collectivism is now marked in all highly industrialized countries, even when it does not reach the extreme of the totalitarian state. It is the social consequence of the development of private capitalistic collectivism in industry and finance. For this reason those who look backward to restoration of the latter system are doomed to fight a losing battle. For the tendency toward state socialism and state capitalism is the product of the economic collectivism of concentrated capital and labor that was produced by mass production and mass distribution. The inherent identity of the two forms of collectivism is disguised by the present angry and clamorous controversy waged between representatives of private and public collectivism, both claiming to speak, moreover, in the interest of the individual, one for his initiative, the other for his security.

The strict reciprocity that exists between the two collectivisms is also covered from view because they are promoted in the respective interests of different social groups. Roughly speaking, the "haves" stand for private collectivism and the "have nots" for state collectivism. The bitter struggle waged between them in the political arena conceals from recognition the fact that both favor some sort of collectivism and represent complementary aspects of the same total picture.

Between the struggles of the two parties, both purporting to serve the cause of ultimate individual freedom, the individual has in fact little show and little opportunity. Bewildered and temporarily lost anyway, the din of the contending parties increases his bewilderment. Everything is so big that he wants to ally himself with bigness, and he is told that he must make his choice between big industry and finance and the big national political state. For a long time, what political agencies did and did not do in legislation and in the courts favored the growth of private capitalistic collectivism. By way of equalizing conditions, I do not doubt that for some time to come political activity will move in the direction of support of underprivileged groups who have been oppressed and made insecure by the growth of concentrated industry and finance. The imminent danger, as events of recent years demonstrate, is that political activity will attempt to retrieve the balance by moving in the direction of state socialism.

Indeed, many persons will ask how it is possible for political action to restore the balance except by direct control over and even ownership of big industrial and financial enterprises. The answer in general is that political activity can, first and foremost, engage in aggressive maintenance of the civil liberties of free speech, free publication and intercommunication, and free assemblage. In the second place, the government can do much to encourage and promote in a positive way the growth of a great variety of voluntary cooperative undertakings.

This promotion involves abolition or drastic modification of a good many institutions that now have political support, since they stand in the way of effective voluntary association for social ends. There are tariffs and other monopoly-furthering devices that keep back individual initiative and voluntary cooperation. There is our system of land tenure and taxation that puts a premium on the holding of land—including all natural resources—for the sake of private profit in a way that effectively prevents individuals from access to the instruments of individual freedom. There is the political protection given to return on long-term capital investments which are not now accompanied by any productive work, and which are, therefore, a direct tax levied on the productive work of others: an almost incalculable restriction, in its total effect, upon individual freedom.

The intrinsic likeness of political and private collectivism is shown in the fact that the government has had recourse to promotion of a regime of scarcity instead of increased productivity. It is evident on its face that enforced restriction of productivity, whether enforced in the name of private profit or of public relief, can have only a disastrous effect, directly and indirectly, upon individual freedom. But given existing conditions, it is the sole alternative to governmental activity that would abolish such limitations upon voluntary action as have been mentioned, a list that would easily be made more specific and more extensive.

Moreover, the principle of confining political action to policies that provide the conditions for promoting the voluntary association of free individuals does not limit governmental action to negative measures. There are, for example, such political activities as are now represented by provision of public highways, public schools, protection from fire, etc., etc., supported by taxation. This type of activity can doubtless be extended in a way which will release individual liberties instead of restricting them. The principle laid down does not deter political activity from engaging in constructive measures. But it does lay down a criterion by which every political proposal shall be judged: Does it tend definitely in the direction of increase of voluntary, free choice and activity on the part of individuals?

The danger at present, as I have already said, is that in order to get away from the evils of private economic collectivism we shall plunge into political economic collectivism. The danger is so great that the course that has been suggested will be regarded as an unrealistic voice crying in the wilderness. It would be unrealistic to make light of the present drive in the direction of state socialism. But it is even more unrealistic to overlook the dangers involved in taking the latter course. For the events of recent years have demonstrated that state capitalism leads toward the totalitarian state whether of the Russian or the Fascist variety.

We now have demonstrations of the consequences of two social movements. Earlier events proved that private economic collectivism produced social anarchy, mitigated by the control exercised by an oligarchic group. Recent events have shown that state socialism or public collectivism leads to suppression of everything that individuality stands for. It is not too late for us in this country to learn the lessons taught by these two great historic movements. The way is open for a movement which will provide the fullest opportunity for cooperative voluntary endeavor. In this movement political activity will have a part, but a subordinate one. It will be confined to providing the conditions, both negative and positive, that favor the providing activity of individuals.

There is, however, a socialism which is not state socialism. It may be called functional socialism. Its nature may be illustrated by the movement for socialization of medicine. I think this socialization is bound to come anyway. But it may come about in two very different ways. It may come into existence as a state measure, under political control; or it may come about as the result of the efforts of the medical profession made aware of its social function and its responsibilities. I cannot develop the significance of the illustration. But as an illustration, its significance applies to all occupational groups; that is, to all groups that are engaged in any form of socially useful, productive, activity.

The technocrats of recent memory had a glimpse of the potentialities inherent in self-directed activities of autonomous groups performing necessary social functions. But they ruined their vision when they fell into the pit dug by Wells and Shaw, that of rule from above by an elite of experts—although according to technocracy engineers were to be the samurai. The N.I.R.A. had a glimpse of self-governing industrial groups. But, quite apart from its conflict with the existing legal system, the plan loaded the dice in favor of the existing system of control of industry— with a few sops thrown in to "labor." At best it could not have worked out in the direction of freely functioning occupational groups. The Marxists professed the idea, but they held it as an ultimate goal to be realized through seizure of political power by a single class, the proletariat. The withering away of the state which was supposed to take place is not in evidence. On the contrary, seizure of political power as the means to the ultimate end of free individuals organized in functional occupational groups has led to the production of one more autocratic political state.

The dialectic that was supposed to work in solving the contradiction between increase of political power and its abolition is conspicuous by its absence—and inherently so. The Fascists also proclaim the idea of a corporate state. But again there is reliance upon uncontrolled and irre- sponsible political power. Instead of a corporate society of functional groups there is complete suppression of every formal voluntary associa- tion of individuals.

Before concluding that in America adoption of the method of volun- tary effort in voluntary associations of individuals with one another is hopeless, one should observe the course of history. For if history teaches anything it is that judgments regarding the future have been predicated upon the basis of the tendencies that are most conspicuous at the time, while in fact the great social changes which have produced new social institutions have been the cumulative effect of flank movements that were not obvious at the time of their origin.

During the height of expanding competitive industrialism, for exam- ple, it was freely predicted that its effect would be a future society of free individuals and of free nations so interdependent that lasting peace would be achieved—*vide* Herbert Spencer. Now that the actual result has been the opposite, it is prophesied on the basis of the tendencies that are now most prominent that increased control of industrial activity by the state will usher in an era of abundance and security. Nevertheless those who can escape the hypnotic influence exercised by the immediate contempo- rary scene are aware that movements going on in the interstices of the existing order are those which will in fact shape the future. As a friend of mine puts it, the last thing the lord of the feudal castle would have imagined was that the future of society was with the forces that were represented by the humble trader who set up his post under the walls of his castle.

I am not optimistic enough to believe that voluntary associations of individuals, which are even now building up within the cracks of a crumbling social order, will speedily reverse the tendency toward political collectivism. But I am confident that the ultimate way out of the present social dead end lies with the movement these associations are initiating. Individuals who have not lost faith in themselves and in other individuals will increasingly ally themselves with these groups. Sooner or later they will construct the way out of present confusion and conflict. The sooner it is done the shorter will be the time of chaos and catastrophe.

Creative Democracy—
The Task Before Us

Under present circumstances I cannot hope to conceal the fact that I have managed to exist eighty years. Mention of the fact may suggest to you a more important fact—namely, that events of the utmost significance for the destiny of this country have taken place during the past four-fifths of a century, a period that covers more than half of its national life in its present form. For obvious reasons I shall not attempt a summary of even the more important of these events. I refer here to them because of their bearing upon the issue to which this country committed itself when the nation took shape—the creation of democracy, an issue which is now as urgent as it was a hundred and fifty years ago when the most experienced and wisest men of the country gathered to take stock of conditions and to create the political structure of a self-governing society.

For the net import of the changes that have taken place in these later years is that ways of life and institutions which were once the natural, almost the inevitable, product of fortunate conditions have now to be won by conscious and resolute effort. Not all the country was in a pioneer state eighty years ago. But it was still, save perhaps in a few large cities, so close to the pioneer stage of American life that the traditions of the pioneer, indeed of the frontier, were active agencies in forming the thoughts and shaping the beliefs of those who were born into its life. In imagination at least the country was still having an open frontier, one of unused and unappropriated resources. It was a country of physical opportunity and invitation. Even so, there was more than a marvelous conjunction of physical circumstances involved in bringing to birth this new nation. There was in existence a group of men who were capable of readapting older institutions and ideas to meet the situations provided by new physical conditions—a group of men extraordinarily gifted in political inventiveness.

At the present time, the frontier is moral, not physical. The period of free lands that seemed boundless in extent has vanished. Unused re-

[First published in *John Dewey and the Promise of America*, Progressive Education Booklet No. 14 (Columbus, Ohio: American Education Press, 1939), from an address read by Horace M. Kallen at the dinner in honor of Dewey in New York City on 20 October 1939; reprinted in *The Later Works*, Vol. 14.]

sources are now human rather than material. They are found in the waste of grown men and women who are without the chance to work, and in the young men and young women who find doors closed where there was once opportunity. The crisis that one hundred and fifty years ago called out social and political inventiveness is with us in a form which puts a heavier demand on human creativeness.

At all events this is what I mean when I say that we now have to re-create by deliberate and determined endeavor the kind of democracy which in its origin one hundred and fifty years ago was largely the product of a fortunate combination of men and circumstances. We have lived for a long time upon the heritage that came to us from the happy conjunction of men and events in an earlier day. The present state of the world is more than a reminder that we have now to put forth every energy of our own to prove worthy of our heritage. It is a challenge to do for the critical and complex conditions of today what the men of an earlier day did for simpler conditions.

If I emphasize that the task can be accomplished only by inventive effort and creative activity, it is in part because the depth of the present crisis is due in considerable part to the fact that for a long period we acted as if our democracy were something that perpetuated itself auto-matically; as if our ancestors had succeeded in setting up a machine that solved the problem of perpetual motion in politics. We acted as if democ-racy were something that took place mainly at Washington and Albany—or some other state capital—under the impetus of what happened when men and women went to the polls once a year or so—which is a some-what extreme way of saying that we have had the habit of thinking of democracy as a king of political mechanism that will work as long as citizens were reasonably faithful in performing political duties.

Of late years we have heard more and more frequently that this is not enough; that democracy is a way of life. This saying gets down to hard pan. But I am not sure that something of the externality of the old idea does not cling to the new and better statement. In any case we can escape from this external way of thinking only as we realize in thought and act that democracy is a *personal* way of individual life; that it signifies the possession and continual use of certain attitudes, forming personal character and determining desire and purpose in all the relations of life. Instead of thinking of our own dispositions and habits as accommodated to certain institutions we have to learn to think of the latter as expres-sions, projections and extensions of habitually dominant personal atti-tudes.

Democracy as a personal, an individual, way of life involves nothing fundamentally new. But when applied it puts a new practical meaning in old ideas. Put into effect it signifies that powerful present enemies of democracy can be successfully met only by the creation of personal attitudes in individual human beings; that we must get over our tendency to think that its defense can be found in any external means whatever, whether military or civil, if they are separated from individual attitudes so deep-seated as to constitute personal character.

Democracy is a way of life controlled by a working faith in the possibilities of human nature. Belief in the Common Man is a familiar article in the democratic creed. That belief is without basis and significance save as it means faith in the potentialities of human nature as that nature is exhibited in every human being irrespective of race, color, sex, birth and family, of material or cultural wealth. This faith may be enacted in statutes, but it is only on paper unless it is put in force in the attitudes which human beings display to one another in all the incidents and relations of daily life. To denounce Naziism for intolerance, cruelty and stimulation of hatred amounts to fostering insincerity if, in our personal relations to other persons, if, in our daily walk and conversation, we are moved by racial, color or other class prejudice; indeed, by anything save a generous belief in their possibilities as human beings, a belief which brings with it the need for providing conditions which will enable these capacities to reach fulfillment. The democratic faith in human equality is belief that every human being, independent of the quantity or range of his personal endowment, has the right to equal opportunity with every other person for development of whatever gifts he has. The democratic belief in the principle of leadership is a generous one. It is universal. It is belief in the capacity of every person to lead his own life free from coercion and imposition by others provided right conditions are supplied.

Democracy is a way of personal life controlled not merely by faith in human nature in general but by faith in the capacity of human beings for intelligent judgment and action if proper conditions are furnished. I have been accused more than once and from opposed quarters of an undue, a utopian, faith in the possibilities of intelligence and in education as a correlate of intelligence. At all events, I did not invent this faith. I acquired it from my surroundings as far as those surroundings were animated by the democratic spirit. For what is the faith of democracy in the role of consultation, of conference, of persuasion, of discussion, in formation of public opinion, which in the long run is self-corrective, except faith in the capacity of the intelligence of the common man to respond with commonsense to the free play of facts and ideas which are secured by effective guarantees of free inquiry, free assembly and free communication? I am willing to leave to upholders of totalitarian states of the right and the left the view that faith in the capacities of intelligence is utopian.

For the faith is so deeply embedded in the methods which are intrinsic to democracy that when a professed democrat denies the faith he convicts himself of treachery to his profession.

When I think of the conditions under which men and women are living in many foreign countries today, fear of espionage, with danger hanging over the meeting of friends for friendly conversation in private gatherings, I am inclined to believe that the heart and final guarantee of democracy is in free gatherings of neighbors on the street corner to discuss back and forth what is read in uncensored news of the day, and in gatherings of friends in the living rooms of houses and apartments to converse freely with one another. Intolerance, abuse, calling of names because of differences of opinion about religion or politics or business, as well as because of differences of race, color, wealth or degree of culture are treason to the democratic way of life. For everything which bars freedom and fullness of communication sets up barriers that divide human beings into sets and cliques, into antagonistic sects and factions, and thereby undermines the democratic way of life. Merely legal guarantees of the civil liberties of free belief, free expression, free assembly are of little avail if in daily life freedom of communication, the give and take of ideas, facts, experiences, is choked by mutual suspicion, by abuse, by fear and hatred. These things destroy the essential condition of the democratic way of living even more effectually than open coercion which—as the example of totalitarian states proves—is effective only when it succeeds in breeding hate, suspicion, intolerance in the minds of individual human beings.

Finally, given the two conditions just mentioned, democracy as a way of life is controlled by personal faith in personal day-by-day working together with others. Democracy is the belief that even when needs and ends or consequences are different for each individual, the habit of amicable cooperation—which may include, as in sport, rivalry and competition—is itself a priceless addition to life. To take as far as possible every conflict which arises—and they are bound to arise—out of the atmosphere and medium of force, of violence as a means of settlement into that of discussion and of intelligence is to treat those who disagree—even profoundly—with us as those from whom we may learn, and in so far, as friends. A genuinely democratic faith in peace is faith in the possibility of conducting disputes, controversies and conflicts as cooperative undertakings in which both parties learn by giving the other a chance to express itself, instead of having one party conquer by forceful suppression of the other—a suppression which is none the less one of violence when it takes place by psychological means of ridicule, abuse, intimidation, instead of by overt imprisonment or in concentration camps.

To cooperate by giving differences a chance to show themselves because of the belief that the expression of difference is not only a right of the other persons but is a means of enriching one's own life-experience, is inherent in the democratic personal way of life.

If what has been said is charged with being a set of moral commonplaces, my only reply is that that is just the point in saying them. For to get rid of the habit of thinking of democracy as something institutional and external and to acquire the habit of treating it as a way of personal life is to realize that democracy is a moral ideal and so far as it becomes a fact is a moral fact. It is to realize that democracy is a reality only as it is indeed a commonplace of living.

Since my adult years have been given to the pursuit of philosophy, I shall ask your indulgence if in concluding I state briefly the democratic faith in the formal terms of a philosophic position. So stated, democracy is belief in the ability of human experience to generate the aims and methods by which further experience will grow in ordered richness. Every other form of moral and social faith rests upon the idea that experience must be subjected at some point or other to some form of external control; to some "authority" alleged to exist outside the processes of experience. Democracy is the faith that the process of experience is more important than any special result attained, so that special results achieved are of ultimate value only as they are used to enrich and order the ongoing process. Since the process of experience is capable of being educative, faith in democracy is all one with faith in experience and education. All ends and values that are cut off from the ongoing process become arrests, fixations. They strive to fixate what has been gained instead of using it to open the road and point the way to new and better experiences.

If one asks what is meant by experience in this connection my reply is that it is that free interaction of individual human beings with surrounding conditions, especially the human surroundings, which develops and satisfies need and desire by increasing knowledge of things as they are. Knowledge of conditions as they are is the only solid ground for communication and sharing; all other communication means the subjection of some persons to the personal opinion of other persons. Need and desire—out of which grow purpose and direction of energy—go beyond what exists, and hence beyond knowledge, beyond science. They continually open the way into the unexplored and unattained future.

Democracy as compared with other ways of life is the sole way of living which believes wholeheartedly in the process of experience as end and as means; as that which is capable of generating the science which is the sole dependable authority for the direction of further experience and which releases emotions, needs and desires so as to call into being the things that have not existed in the past. For every way of life that fails in its democracy limits the contacts, the exchanges, the communications, the interactions by which experience is steadied while it is also enlarged and enriched. The task of this release and enrichment is one that has to be carried on day by day. Since it is one that can have no end till experience itself comes to an end, the task of democracy is forever that of creation of a freer and more humane experience in which all share and to which all contribute.

John Dewey Responds

I need hardly say that I am overwhelmed by what has been said and read on this occasion. I cannot express adequately my thanks to the Committee and to all who have come here this evening.

I am fortunate in one thing. It is not just that I have lived to complete fourscore and ten but that I have reached that age in 1949 instead of 1969 or what would have been even worse, 1979 or '89. Even now one can hardly pick up a periodical without finding an article on the social and psychological problems which are due to the increase in the span of life. If the span goes on increasing at its present rate, I can imagine that twenty or thirty years from this evening there will be no disposition to celebrate one's arriving at the age of ninety. The meeting would be more likely to be called to discuss what has become the serious social issue of longevity.

In any case, it is supposed to be the habit—if not the privilege—of old age to indulge in reminiscence. I have been reminded sufficiently of my years of late so that I have been almost forced to go back over my past and to consider how the years have been spent.

After due reflection, I have come to the conclusion that, for good or for evil, I have been first, last, and all the time, engaged in the vocation of philosophy; and that it is in the capacity of a philosopher that I am a Nonagenarian. Furthermore, strangely enough, this statement is not wrung from me as a reluctant admission, but is made as a boast—though I fear many of my confreres in that occupation may regard it as unjustified bragging.

But as I look back over the years, I find that, while I seem to have spread myself out over a number of fields—education, politics, social problems, even the fine arts and religion—my interest in these issues has been specifically an outgrowth and manifestation of my primary interest in philosophy.

It has been an outgrowth in two respects—one negative and one positive. On the negative side, the demands of philosophy upon various forms of technical skill—one might say professional academic skill—are so taxing that excursions into outside areas are inviting on the old familiar

[First published in *John Dewey at Ninety*, ed. Harry Wellington Laidler (New York: League for Industrial Democracy, 1950), from speech delivered at the Hotel Commodore, New York City, 20 October 1949; reprinted in *The Later Works*, Vol. 17.]

246

principle that the berries on the other side of the fence are more numerous and brighter and bigger. The other and positive reason is that
philosophy cannot flourish indefinitely nor vitally by ruminating on its own
cud. Philosophers need fresh and first-hand materials. Otherwise the
story of the ideas and beliefs of *past* philosophers will become an end-in-
itself instead of a resource in dealing with the problems that are urgent in
contemporary life.

It may well be that those engaged in the kind of inquiry that bears the
name *philosophy* have exaggerated what philosophers can do in the way of
solving problems. But there is a need that comes before that of solution.
That is the need for getting a reasonably clear sense and statement of
what the problems are that have to be met: what they arise from and
where they are located. Here is a matter in which it is possible for
philosophers to make good their claim that they go below the surface; go
behind the ways in which things appear to be. It is quite possible for
philosophers to become pretentious; but it is hardly possible to exaggerate the importance of obtaining a moderately clear and distinct idea of
what the problems are that underlie the difficulties and evils which we
experience *in fact;* that is to say, in *practical* life. Nor is it easily possible, I
believe, to exaggerate the intellectual alertness and even excitement that
could attend a systematic endeavor to convert our practical ills and troubles into intellectual terms, so that plans may be developed and subjected
to intelligent inquiry as a condition of remedial action. For in technological and the medical arts, we have learned that to plunge into action
before we have located what is the matter is the way to make things worse
than they were before. For apart from engaging systematically in search
for the source of evils, the only alternatives we can employ are acting
either mechanically on the basis of routine precedent and blind habit or
impulsively from fear.

At the present time, tradition and custom are pretty well broken down
as dependable resources in guiding our activity. Living as we now do in
what is almost a chronic state of crisis, there is danger that fear and the
sense of insecurity become the predominant motivation of our activities.

Of the various kindly and generous, often over-generous, things that
have been said about my activities on the occasion of my ninetieth birth-
day, there is one thing in particular I should be peculiarly happy to
believe. It is the statement of Alvin Johnson that I have helped to liberate
my fellow-human beings from fear. For more than anything else, the fear
that has no recognized and well-thought-out ground is what both holds
us back and conducts us into aimless and spasmodic ways of action,
personal and collective. When we allow ourselves to be fear-ridden and
permit it to dictate how we act, it is because we have lost faith in our

fellowmen—and that is the unforgivable sin against the spirit of democracy.

Many years ago I read something written by an astute politician. He said that majority rule is not the heart of democracy, but the processes by which a given group having a specific kind of policies in view becomes a majority. That saying has remained with me; in effect it embodies recognition that democracy is an educative process; that the act of voting is in a democratic regime a culmination of a continued process of open and public communication in which prejudices have the opportunity to erase each other; that continued interchange of facts and ideas exposes what is unsound and discloses what may make for human well-being.

This educational process is based upon faith in human good sense and human good will as it manifests itself in the long run when communication is progressively liberated from bondage to prejudice and ignorance. It constitutes a firm and continuous reminder that the process of living together, when it is emancipated from oppressions and suppressions, becomes one of increasing faith in the humaneness of human beings; so that it becomes a constant growth of that kind of understanding of our relations to one another that expels fear, suspicion, and distrust.

The friendliness that is radiated from this gathering is something to be sensed, not just talked about and hence, I take it, is a good omen for the causes I have had the privilege of sharing. For while it is, I am aware, the conventional thing to recognize such a tribute as one to cause, not to the person, I *know* in this case that such a manifestation of friendliness as I have experienced is a demonstration of sympathy for the things that make for the freedom and justice and for the kind of cooperative friendship that can flourish only where there is a freedom which we and untold multitudes possess in common: i.e., enjoy together.

I want to conclude with a reference to a letter from an old friend in Texas in which he said that while he should have liked to be here this evening, he does not regret his enforced absence so very greatly because the order of the day is not so much the commemoration of the past, as it is, "March Ahead into the future with resolution and courage."

I am happy to be able to believe that the significance of this celebration consists not in warming over of past years, even though they be fourscore and ten, but in dedication to the work that lies ahead. The order of the day is "Forward March."

The over-generous recognition that has been accorded me I take as a sign that faith in the will to realize the American dream through continued faith in democracy as a moral and human ideal remains firm and true even in a time when some people in their despair are tending to put their faith in force instead of in the cooperation that is the fruit of reciprocal good will and shared understanding:—and of nothing else.